The Long War for Freedom

The Arab Struggle for Democracy
in the Middle East

Barry Rubin

WILEY

John Wiley & Sons, Inc.

Published by John Wiley & Sons, Inc., Hoboken, New Jersey
Published simultaneously in Canada

For general information about our other products and services, please contact our Customer Care Department within the United States at (800) 762-2974, outside the United States at (317) 572-3993 or fax (317) 572-4002.

Wiley also publishes its books in a variety of electronic formats. Some content that appears in print may not be available in electronic books. For more information about Wiley products, visit our web site at www.wiley.com.

Library of Congress Cataloging-in-Publication Data:

Rubin, Barry M.
    The long war for freedom : the Arab struggle for democracy in the Middle East / Barry Rubin.
        p.   cm.
    Includes bibliographical references and index.
    ISBN-13 978-0-471-73901-2 (cloth)
    ISBN-10 0-471-73901-4 (cloth)
    1. Democracy—Middle East. 2. Democratization—Middle East. 3. Middle East—Foreign relations—United States. 4. United States—Foreign relations—Middle East. I. Title.
    JQ1758.A91R83   2006
    320.956—dc22

                                                                2005020231
Printed in the United States of America

10 9 8 7 6 5 4 3 2 1

For Judy, Gabriella, and Daniel

There is nothing worse than allowing what is attainable to slip from our grasp while we strive for the unattainable!

—Tarek Heggy, "Let's Assume It's a Conspiracy!"
Al-Ahram, January 26, 2002

Hatred prevents us from knowing reality as it is.

—Ali Salem, quoted in *Cairo Times,*
September 4, 1997

CONTENTS

INTRODUCTION

The most dramatic event at the January 1992 Cairo Book Fair was a debate between Muhammad al-Ghazali, a Muslim cleric who was also a leader of the radical Islamist group the Muslim Brotherhood, and Farag Fouda, an outspoken liberal. The discussion was over what Egypt's future course should be: a more secular democracy or an Islamist state. The audience was packed with Ghazali's supporters, whose chanting prevented Fouda from speaking. But Fouda outwitted his opponents. "If you really think I'm right," he shouted, "keep heckling me because you can't defeat my arguments! But if you have faith in your own views, be quiet and listen since you have nothing to fear from my contradicting them." Fouda's gambit worked. The audience fell silent and the debate continued.

Only five months later, though, the Islamists won the debate by other means. A radical Islamist fish seller shot Fouda dead with an AK-47. Under interrogation, the killer confessed that a declaration by a group of scholars from al-Azhar, the state-sponsored Islamic university, calling Fouda a heretic, convinced him that murdering Fouda was a religious duty. One of the defense witnesses was Ghazali, who testified that killing was the proper punishment for an apostate like Fouda. After being sentenced to execution, the defendant shouted, "Now I will die with a clear conscience!"

By such means as slander, harassment, threats, and violence has liberal reform long been kept at bay in the Arab world. Yet the battle is not merely between small numbers of liberals and large numbers of radical Islamists. The true winner has always been the rulers, the dictatorships of various kinds that have continuously ruled virtually every Arab country. It was the regime that simultaneously sponsored those who ordered

Fouda's killing and then executed his murderer. The Islamists hoped to seize power, but control remained in the hands of the Arab nationalist regimes.

The regimes held off the challenges of radical Islamists and liberals alike. In so doing, they ensured that relative stability prevailed, but so did near-absolute stagnation. The Arab world fell further behind almost every other region on the globe. Despite oil wealth, in virtually every aspect of social well-being, economic success, and political democracy, the Arab lands did very badly indeed. Given the existing situation, there was no reason to believe that things were going to get any better.

Without the open debate and thoroughgoing reform that the liberals demand, the Arab world is not going to solve its problems. Under the sway of the demagoguery that controls the defining of their difficulties—blaming them on the West and on Israel—and solutions—militant nationalism or radical Islamism—these countries remain virtually the only part of the globe incapable of articulating their real shortcomings and priorities. Only the liberals are offering workable solutions that can eventually free the Arab world from its malaise and allow it to join the rest of the planet in moving forward.

This is not merely a local, or even a regional, problem. Locked into dictatorial ideologies, methods of debate, and patterns of political behavior, the Arab world has generally rejected peace with Israel, a real encounter with the West, and the kinds of change needed for successful modernization. The rise of international Islamist terrorism—embodied most vividly in the September 11, 2001, attacks on the United States—has made the internal problems of the Arab countries a matter of immediate global concern.

Indeed, it is no exaggeration to say that the future of the world in this era rests in large part on what happens in this three-way battle between Arab nationalist regimes, Islamist revolutionaries, and liberal reformers. Yet while becoming so engaged on this issue, the West—and indeed most Arabs themselves—knows relatively little about the liberal forces in the Arab world and their ideas, their arguments, their strategies, and their prospects.

One problematic aspect of the situation lies in the relative weakness of the Arab liberals. Many in the West assume it is inevitable that the masses support the liberals' agenda and that it will ultimately triumph. This may prove true, but the appeal of Arab nationalist and Islamist ideologies as well as their powerful institutions should not be underestimated. It is likely that the Arab people want to choose their leaders, but those they would choose might well be antidemocratic and extremist ones. This is true even of women, who suffer much discrimination in the Arab world. In Kuwait, arguably the country where liberal ideas have most taken root, it is estimated that the majority of women, if granted the vote, would cast their ballots for Islamist parties that do not want to give it to them.

Regarding terrorism, a similar pattern emerges. The vast majority of Arabs oppose terrorist attacks in their own countries, yet the liberals, who argue that all terrorism is bad, are in the minority. Most Arab writers make a distinction between "good" terrorism, against Israel or the United States, and the "bad" terrorism at home. The same basic type of dichotomy applies to other issues as well.

Whatever help may be offered by the outside world, only the Arab reformers can win this battle and transform their own countries. They still stand a distant third in their competition with Islamists and nationalist regimes. Only the strength of their arguments, the cogency of their strategies, and the ingenuity of their methods can bring them ultimate victory, a process that will probably take an entire historical era.

This battle is both the most fascinating and most important struggle of ideas in our time. Even for those in the West, it can help clarify many burning questions in the lives of their own people: the best way to structure a democracy; the proper role of religion and the media in public life; the definition of human rights and civil liberties; the task of civil institutions in governance; the nature of modernity; and how different societies can preserve their own cultural traditions while participating in an increasingly global society.

This book's purpose is to examine the ideas and strategies of Arab reformers. The movement has become critically important in the early twenty-first century as a force for shaping the future of the Arab world, the Middle East as a whole, and even the entire planet.

No definition of liberal Arabs is perfect. This book defines them as people who support one or more of the following concepts: multiparty parliamentary democracy, human rights, women's rights, a more tolerant interpretation of Islam, rapprochement with the West, and peace with Israel. These ideas often come as a package, but when individuals do not accept all of them, this significant point is noted in the book.

The basic concepts of Arab liberals may also include additional ideas such as the diversification of the economy, a higher emphasis on toleration of other cultures, and opposition to terrorism in principle. Other concepts can also be added to this list.

The book does not include as Arab liberals those who merely give lip service to democracy or reform in order to maintain existing dictatorial systems. The existence of this phenomenon, however, is an important sign of the extent to which liberal ideas have influenced the Arab debate, and this is discussed in the book as well.

This book focuses on those who seek to function primarily within existing states. It does not include Palestinians or Kurdish, Lebanese Christian, and Berber nationalists who have their own sets of issues and problems.

It also focuses on those who function mainly within the Arab world, so it does not include those living in the West, with the exception of journalists whose main output is in Arab-language newspapers intended for readers there. While it can be argued that such people have influence on the Arab debate, these external sources are less influential. Moreover, to a large extent they reflect their local milieu rather than conditions in the Arab world itself.

U.S. policy after September 11, 2001, had an important role in this story by expressing support for democracy and reform in the Arab world. It should be stressed that this is not a book about U.S. policy and takes no position on the efficacy of the American strategy or the correctness of the 2003 Iraq war. The concern here is to consider how Arab liberals viewed these matters.

The same point applies to the Arab-Israeli conflict. This is not a book on that issue but merely on what Arab liberals think about it.

The reader should consider several other useful points in reading the material in this book. First, the reader should make a distinction between what appears in Arabic publications in the Arab world—whose readers are the intended audience for the political debate—and what is written for Western audiences in English or in English-language newspapers published in Arab countries. The tone of writers is different in these cases, with the latter being more explicit, open, and far-reaching.

In addition, it should be noted that liberals often go further in private than they do in public in breaking away from mainstream thinking and the extent of the change they advocate.

Moreover, the newspapers cited often have small audiences that come disproportionately from the elite. The effect of any given article is thus limited, but the point here is to use such materials as reflections of their authors' thoughts.

While each individual cited in the book represents the thinking of others as well, the very fact of focusing on liberals intrinsically overstates the extent of their proportional number in the Arab political debate. The reader is cautioned against overestimating the power of the liberals' viewpoint on this basis.

This book does not fully develop the arguments of the liberals' rivals and enemies, but their positions are presented to give a baseline for how the reformers deviate from the mainstream and try to persuade it. For a fuller view of the situation in the Arab world and the mainstream side of the equation, see my book *The Tragedy of the Middle East.*

Since the goal is to let the liberals and their opponents speak for themselves, I have deliberately used large numbers of direct quotations. As one activist wrote, "Many 'liberal' Arabs have a difficulty in coining the exact term to define their ideas: sometimes the term 'liberal' is used, sometimes 'democratic' movement, sometimes 'civil society movements,' and sometimes 'reformist' movements." I use the term *liberal* mainly to show its kinship to the history of the West and other world regions, though the other labels are also employed interchangeably in this book.

Translation is inevitably imperfect, but I think that the reader will get a good, if necessarily inexact, sense of what is being said. Whenever possible, I have used the work of professional translators rather than my own.

Regarding transliteration, this book uses many sources translated or written in English by Arab liberals and others in which the names of the writers—often with their approval—have been transliterated in inconsistent, and at times flatly wrong, ways. Imposing my own system of transliteration might have been more correct but it would have contradicted these sources and made trying to use them a nightmare for others. As a result, for purely practical purposes, except to maintain consistency in spelling within the book, I have left spellings as they appeared in the sources.

In terms of notes, I have preferred to give the authors' names—especially when they are liberal Arabs—and titles (which often reveal interesting elements in the authors' and editors' thinking) rather than merely the source and date of the source.

It is also worth stressing that while I am responsible, of course, for my analysis, the main purpose of this book is to present the ideas of liberal Arabs and their opponents rather than my own views.

Those who wish to misinterpret what I am saying through the usual tricks of distortion and taking details out of context will no doubt have their ambitions gratified. The purpose of this book, however, is to understand, without advocating a specific position, an extremely interesting and important phenomenon that affects not only the Arab people or the Middle East but also, as recent history has shown, the entire world.

1

Heartbreak and Hope

There is a battle raging within the Arab world whose outcome is of the utmost importance for the entire globe. This struggle between the forces of democracy and authoritarianism, modernity and stagnation, is not so different in kind from the titanic conflicts that have shaped the lives of many other lands. But the specific Middle Eastern version of such events is also quite distinct from what happened elsewhere.

What is going on in the Middle East today is part of the great, centuries-long transition wrought by secularism, industrialization, democratization, urbanization, globalization, and all the other historic changes that have shaped the modern world everywhere on the planet. Indeed, the struggle over the Middle East may be the last of these great battles over alternative futures. Within each country, the issue has been what kind of society and polity would prevail there. On every continent, the regional question to be resolved was whether a single country, leader, or ideology could dominate that vast landmass or even, using it as a base, the entire world.

For example, Europe's political, social, and ideological throes during the nineteenth and twentieth centuries gave rise to international tidal waves that carried violence to every corner of the planet. Three world wars, including the Cold War, as well as fascism and communism, arose in the strife of that great debate over how people should and would live their lives.

Compared to Europe's upheavals, such catastrophic events as September 11 and the three wars emanating from Iraq are mere ripples.[1] But the great battle over what system and worldview will dominate the Middle

East is happening now, and this struggle will probably be our era's central drama.

In the long term, the outcome may be inevitable for the Middle East, ending with the triumph of the same basic positive trends that prevailed in Europe and elsewhere. Getting there, however, is what history is about. How many decades this will take and how many thousands of people will die in the process still hang in the balance.

At present, though, Arab liberalism, purported to be the inevitable victor, remains enormously weak. Ammar Abdulhamid, a Syrian novelist who started the Tharwa Project, one of the main Internet sites for reformers, said the movement is caught between powerful regimes that hold tightly on to power and religious extremists who are increasingly popular. He said, "Arab liberals are indeed under siege, and that's putting it mildly. [They are] fighting to retain the last foothold that liberal values still have in the Arab world."[2]

One Arab liberal admits, "Are we a small minority? Certainly, for now. Still, this movement is not a movement of a few liberal professors living and preaching in the United States and Europe. It certainly has a 'popular' and 'militant' aspect which was missing in earlier movements."[3] Be that as it may, while they are becoming increasingly more active, there is still not a single liberal leader or movement anywhere in the Arab world able to mobilize large groups of people. Perhaps a "silent majority" of Arabs and Muslims do want democracy and modern society in the Western sense of those words, but it is also possible that such people are really only a "silent minority."

The liberals' agenda has found its strongest voice at a number of conferences that have produced ringing manifestos for reform. For example, a 2004 meeting in Cairo organized by the Egyptian Organization for Human Rights and the Cairo Institute for Human Rights Studies brought together one hundred participants from fifteen Arab states. In such venues liberals can speak their minds fully. The meeting's final communiqué declared that Western initiatives "can be the basis for a partnership." While many Arab people "doubt the true intentions and seriousness of the international initiatives for reforms," they also "realize their governments reject reforms." The Kuwaiti columnist Ahmed al-Rubei told the conference, "Reform is not a vice, it is a virtue. Without reforms, this area will explode and will blow up the whole world with it."[4]

In contrast, though, the liberals' nationalist and Islamist rivals control armies of followers and usually shape events in the region. Even if the success of these competing movements can be attributed to repression or manipulative propaganda, they are nonetheless very powerful forces not easily defeated. Decades of thought and education are required to make a liberal, while a few already familiar, widely espoused slogans—accepted by many as legitimate and authentic—suffice to produce followers for their enemies. Such attitudes seem entrenched among the younger generation, more of whom appear to be committed to an extreme Islamist view of the world than were their elders. Even a university education produces more Islamists than liberals.

What makes this situation so hard to accept is the combination of Western expectations and hopes to the contrary among the most articulate, courageous voices in the Middle East.[5] Yet there is a big gap between believing liberal democracy to be a better system and feeling certain of its ultimate triumph.

The really engaging question, then, is why has it been so hard to gain popular support for reform and moderation? A common claim by Arab liberals is that the masses really—but secretly—do support them. "Our numbers are small," said the Egyptian liberal Saad Eddin Ibrahim, "not so much for lack of fellow citizens yearning for liberal governance, but out of fear of publicly expressing those yearnings."[6] Opinion polls only partly bear out this view, and the problem deterring support is far more than just fear alone but also the persuasiveness of competing ideologies and the material or spiritual rewards they can offer their adherents.

One of the apparently strongest liberal arguments is to get people to focus on the seemingly undeniable failure of Arab systems, regimes, and ideologies to solve problems or make progress. This point is well expressed by Rami Khouri, an Arab journalist and columnist who grew up in the United States, who noted that the list of issues confronted by Arabs today is identical to those faced by their grandparents a century ago and are now being passed on to still another generation. The list includes:

> The quality of our sovereignty; the nature of our governance systems; the well-being of our economies; the provision and protection of the Arab individual's basic human rights; our relations with Western powers; the balance between religiosity and secularism; the nature of Arab citizenship;

the role and rights of women; coexistence or confrontation between Arabism and Zionism; the balance between the identity of the modern Arab state and older indigenous identities such as religion, tribalism, family, ethnicity, monarchy, and regionalism; the role of civil society in the face of state power; the individual and collective right to bear arms; and the role of the military and security services in society."[7]

Ibrahim put the onus for this inability to solve problems on the Arab regimes that retained power by mixing a doctrine of populism, national liberation, socialist economics, cultural authenticity, and repression. The possibility of democracy was postponed to a distant future when total victory could be attained on all other fronts. Over time, though, it became clear that this Arab nationalist system failed domestically and brought repeated warfare in the region. To make matters worse, the resulting desperate situation made people believe that only radical Islamist movements could provide a better alternative.[8]

Of course, it is easily forgotten how tiny and apparently weak at times have been the forces of progress, moderation, and reason during the past in every other corner of the world. Yet it is equally true that in the Arab world the reactionary forces maintaining the status quo are markedly powerful and persuasive. They have clear ideas and programs that may not work, but they have been sufficient to provide the bread and circuses needed to persuade and soothe the masses.

Consequently, while it might seem obvious to many in the West and to Arab liberals that the problems of Arab societies require a new type of solution, the existing system offers its own justifications for why little or nothing should be changed. First, it downplays or denies that these social, economic, and political problems exist. Second, it attributes them to external interference by imperialism and Zionism. The Arabs have not made mistakes, argue Arab nationalists; they have merely been defeated by evil forces. If real Arab unity and militancy were to come into being, all the ruling mechanisms and ideas would work very well. To give up on these ideas and goals would be nothing less than surrender, inducing a state of permanent slavery.

The Islamist view is merely a variation on this theme. The cause of failure, it argues, is external interference and the mistake of not adopting Islam as the main ideology and organizing principle for government and society. If only this were to be done, the foreigner would be quickly defeated and all internal problems solved.

Those opposed to reform also effectively use many of the tools that at other times and places were wielded by reformers. For example, nationalism and religion have often served the cause of progressive change elsewhere, but in the Middle East they have been monopolized by the armies of the status quo. Similarly, prodemocratic forces in the West invented the idea of mobilizing the masses, a strategy now used most effectively by Arab nationalists and Islamists. Religious revivals and sects identified with grassroots or ethnic groups in other regions have often advocated freedom against autocratic regimes, a tactic now most often wielded by extremists in the Arab world.

In the Middle East, generally, the antidemocratic side has shaped the ideals of nationalism and religious devotion to its own purposes. Nationalism is identified with radical Arab nationalists, while national liberation from Western imperialism has been that group's calling card. These weapons are pointed not, as in other places, at a reactionary monarchy or authoritarian dictatorship but are used by those very systems against the democratic West and Israel. Ayatollah Ruhollah Khomeini and Usama bin Laden took this rhetoric, put it into a modern Islamist framework, and proclaimed their movements as the Muslims' national liberation struggle. In this context, the liberals are portrayed as reactionary traitors who want to hold their countries back and enslave them to imperialists.

Both the nationalist and Islamist schools of thought have far more followers and a much deeper influence on the Arab world than do their liberal competitors, who often seem a virtual footnote in the ongoing Middle East discourse. Still, whether the liberal impulse in the Arab world is the wave of the future or a fragile endangered species, many aspects of this worldview reveal a great deal about the contemporary Middle East. And if liberalism is going to be the Middle East's wave of the future, it is all the more important to understand the thinkers and ideas shaping its infancy, the barriers to their progress, and the issues at stake.

While the roots of failure for liberalism and the interlinked stagnation of the Arab world have by no means been based on inevitable or immutable processes, they are the product of a clear historical progression.

Within living memory, from the 1920s and until the 1950s, the Arab world's future seemed open. The main challenge it faced was how to become independent, successful, and strong. In debates over the best solution, the liberal democratic perspective seemed to have an advantage. This was, after all, the route taken by the West, and many Arab intellectuals of the day would have agreed with the dictum of their Turkish counterpart, Kemal Ataturk: "There is only one civilization, Western civilization."[9]

Although on the religious front the situation seemed grimmer for liberal ideas, it was by no means hopeless. Aside from the secularists, there were many others who wanted to revive the old liberal strain of Islam from the Middle Ages. Centuries earlier there had been great Muslim philosophers and scientists but—unlike in the West—the reactionaries had won the battle to direct society. There had been no Reformation or Renaissance in the Arab world and, perhaps as a result, no rise of the modern nation-state, no scientific revolution, and limited industrialization.

On the ideological front, the medieval moderates had been defeated by hard-line religious thinkers who demanded a conservative reading of Islam. In the eleventh century, Ibn Salah al-din al-Shahrouzi issued a fatwa banning the study of logic as a "heresy delivering man into Satan's bosom." The advocates of such ideas favored the narrowest possible reading of Muslim texts, as opposed to thinkers who tried to analyze them using the tools of comparison and logic. The former, victorious, school preached, in the words of the Egyptian liberal thinker Tarek Heggy, "a dogmatic adherence to the letter rather than the spirit of religion [which slammed] the doors shut in the face of rationality."[10] The rulers of the day preferred the conservative approach, which stamped down on dissent and defended the status quo against liberals who raised subversive questions.

Consequently, the gates of *ijtihad*—allowing qualified scholars to debate the reinterpretation of religious texts to fit new times and situations—were closed. Creative thinking or critical inquiry regarding the meaning of the Qur'an and later religious texts was forbidden. Only rulings already made and narrowly adhered to would be acceptable.

The greatest irony is that it was Europeans who heeded the rationalist Islamic scholars of the Middle Ages in their revival of classical Greek thought. Thus, these Muslim scholars helped pave the way for Europe's great cultural and scientific progress while being forgotten by their own people. In the West, rationalists defeated dogmatists. The backward Middle Ages had given way to the Renaissance and the Reformation. Had the same side won in Europe as in the Middle East, Heggy noted, Europe today would be at a far lower stage of development and enlightenment.[11]

There was another chance for change beginning in the nineteenth century, however, as the political and social weakness of the Arab and Muslim worlds could no longer be hidden or ignored. European development was accelerating and, in the form of imperialism, gaining power over the Middle East. Many Arabs thought that this cultural, intellectual, and technological gap could be bridged only by copying some of the features that had made European superiority possible.

In 1799 Napoleon Bonaparte invaded Egypt with his army and an entourage of scientists and philosophers, heirs of the French Revolution. He easily defeated the rulers at the Battle of the Pyramids. Modernity in all its multiple forms, from military organization and technology to scientific inquiry, had come to the unavoidable notice of the Egyptians.

When the Egyptian military officer Muhammad Ali seized power and founded a new dynasty there in 1805, it was taken for granted that he would seek to imitate the Western model as a matter of both survival and progress. If Egyptians were being challenged to transform their society and jettison old ideas, this was no more than was being demanded of their counterparts all over the world and in Europe as well. Moreover, the definition of modernity was still in flux. It was a work in progress, and Egyptians could participate in the great enterprise, getting in close to the ground floor, so to speak.

And so Muhammad Ali called on European technicians and thinkers to help bring his people the benefits of modern civilization. Egyptians were sent to Europe to study and bring back these ideas and innovations. A small but influential Egyptian Westernized elite set about the task of transformation. Other Arabs paid attention. If Egypt could imitate the West, so could they. Clothes and music, the study of languages and modes of thought—all were seen as part of a package whose benefits would far exceed their cost.

These Egyptian and other advocates of change were not traitors or lackeys of imperialism. On the contrary, if they had succeeded in modernizing their countries, there never would have been any Western domination of the region. They rightly saw real progress—not loyalty to tradition—as the best way to maintain independence. Equally, they believed that a self-directed program of modernization, including borrowing a great deal from the West, would allow their people to remain Arabs and Muslims while enjoying the fruits of everything new and good in the world.

The kinds of things they were trying to do would arouse the utmost revulsion among Arab politicians, intellectuals, and even the masses in later years. But in retrospect one can also see how their more fortunate counterparts in places like Japan, Korea, India, and Turkey used the same strategies of borrowing, reform, and enlightened preservation of selected traditions to succeed.

What were the Western secrets that served so well people who accepted the liberal doctrine? Constitutions and parliaments, mass production and urbanization, encouragement for new inventions and a willingness to make social innovations, equality for women and of opportunity across ethnic and religious backgrounds, rationalism and pragmatism, and clothing that allowed more freedom of movement, hand in hand with the protection of individual liberties. All were interwoven.

The modernizers saw the key to success as mastering these skills and adapting these institutions to their own societies. Through many twists and turns of history, this concept would remain a guiding star in Latin America, Asia, and Africa, as well as in less-developed sections of Europe. The path was not smooth. Some fought passionately against change. There were wars and setbacks, humiliations and competing ideologies. Yet the fundamental idea remained that the basic mix of ingredients transforming Western Europe would work everywhere.

Did this approach fit the Arab world's needs? Was it doomed to failure? These are questions that cannot be definitively answered. Certainly, elsewhere in the world the road to modern liberal society underwent perils and setbacks from such elements as communism and fascism, religious reaction, dictatorship, and civil war.

In England, the pioneer in the transformation to modernity, the rise of democratic institutions was a six-hundred-year-long process; in France the development of stable, representative government, from the Revolution to the Third Republic, took almost a century, followed by several more bloody adjustments. Extremely serious crises developed in Germany, Italy, Spain, and other places in Europe where reactionary forces made a last stand under fascism, which came close to destroying the world. In Russia the Bolshevik revolution brought a seventy-year-long detour. Even the United States required a civil war to consolidate its democracy, while Japan needed eighty years of effort, punctuated by a disastrous defeat in war and a foreign occupation, to finish the process.

Between the 1920s and early 1950s, the Arab world seemed to be doing reasonably well in this effort. The liberal age of Arab politics included not only a more open intellectual debate but also the adoption of Western institutions, including elections and parliaments. In 1919 the liberal nationalists of Egypt's Wafd party staged a bloodless revolution amid their massive popularity. Three years later they won a big election victory and declared Egypt a modern, independent nation-state. The next year they promulgated a liberal constitution.

During this period, a number of great Arab intellectuals advocated major reforms through writing and participation in public life, especially in Egypt. They studied in the West and absorbed many elements of its best ideas, which they sought to blend with their own traditions. The main message they promoted was that Egypt and other states could advance, through education and development, along the same basic route the West had followed. Within a few decades, they would then become democratic, industrialized states with a strong middle class, high living standards, and a culture blending their own traditions—both Arab and Mediterranean—with those of European societies.

One such thinker was Qassem Amin, born in 1863, who studied law in Cairo, then spent several years in Paris before returning home to become a judge. Amin was worried lest modern life undermine Islam, but unlike the later Islamists, his solution was to adapt the actual practice of religion as well as society to new conditions. In 1899 he published *The Emancipation of Women*, which suggested that the way to save Islam and Egypt was to make women into frontline warriors in the war against ignorance. Only by being given education and equality could women teach their families the moral strength and social virtues needed both to advance society and preserve tradition. He insisted that Islam had advocated this concept but had been distorted by ideas brought in by converts from other religions.

Another great Egyptian liberal intellectual was Taha Hussein, born in 1889. A prolific author, professor, reformer, and editor, in 1950 he was appointed minister of education. He advocated free schooling for everyone and the use of reason. In his controversial book analyzing pre-Islamic poetry, he applied this method to the Qur'an. He suggested it was written by people, rather than God, by trying to show some verses had existed in earlier times. Warned to desist by clerics—a sign that there were boundaries logic would not be allowed to cross—he afterward avoided this topic.

Then there was Salama Moussa, born in 1887, who studied in Paris and London for many years, where he was influenced by democratic socialist thinking. Returning to Egypt, he was involved in many journalistic, political, and literary projects. One of his books, *Freedom of Thought*, published in 1927, was a history of courageous individuals who fought against dictators and ignorance. He founded the Egyptian Association of Scientific Culture and advocated Egypt's economic independence, using methods pioneered by the Indian nationalist leader Mahatma Gandhi.[12]

Among the last of this group of liberals would be Naguib Mahfouz. Born in Cairo in 1911, he became a civil servant and published his first novel in 1934. While continuing his government career until retiring in 1972, Mahfouz was a prolific writer. The appearance of the *Cairo Trilogy* in 1957, penned before Nasser took power, made him internationally famous. In 1988 he was awarded the Nobel Prize for Literature. But his books were considered blasphemous by the Islamists.

During the 1920s and 1930s, such thinkers and political figures—especially, but not exclusively, in Egypt—declared themselves rationalists, patriots of their own countries rather than pan-Arab nationalists, part of a Mediterranean people whose history was rooted in all those who had lived on that soil and not just the Arabs or Muslims among them. They dreamed of making Egypt a modern state along European lines while at the same time preserving its own traditions.[13] The view of one such man, Tawfiq al-Hakim, could well stand as a contemporary liberal credo: the highest priority was to understand past mistakes to avoid repeating them; the biggest task was to expose truth no matter who was offended or what established ideas were challenged.[14]

While liberal thought was flourishing, so were democratic norms. In many Arab countries during the liberal era, there were elections, political parties, a free press, and the other accoutrements of this type of government. True, democracy was subverted by British or French interference at times, dominated by the wealthy, challenged by extremist demagogues, and lacking widespread popular participation. Yet this system still offered hope for becoming stronger and more successful in the future.

Moreover, none of these problems were unknown in a Europe where in some countries totalitarian ideologies were riding high. Indeed, Egypt was an electoral democracy at a time when Spain, Germany, and Italy were ruled by fascism and the Soviet Union by communism, murderous systems that stopped at no crime. Nobody talked about Islam or the character of Arab society as preventing the rise of democracy in those days. The problems were considered to be poverty and lack of education, shortcomings that time and development would inevitably remedy.

Still, the fact remains that by the mid-twentieth century, ideas of democracy, representative government, free enterprise, and civil liberties—the entire package—would be as discredited in the Arab world as any political philosophy could be. A complex worldview and system had to compete against extremists wielding slogans offering fast, total solutions and who were ready to use violence. The idea of taking responsibility for the ills of one's own society lost out to the ease of blaming everything on evil foreigners. A moderate approach based on persuasion went up against militant doctrines quick to resort to violence and suppression of anyone who disagreed, labeling them as spies, traitors, and infidels.

Everywhere in Arab lands by the 1950s democracy became associated in people's minds with failure, corruption, and national weakness. But instead of turning to a more faithful manifestation of democracy—as had happened in Europe and North America—liberalism, pluralism, democracy, and free enterprise were rejected altogether.

Arab nationalism became the dominant ideology, and populist dictatorship was extolled as the way to achieve unity and progress. Ideologues and military officers were influenced by communism and fascism to various degrees. They also looked to nineteenth-century Prussian and Italian nationalisms that had succeeded in assembling a single country out of smaller, weaker states.

But theirs was a selective adaptation of Western nationalism that had usually replaced conservative monarchies with a liberal system. In the

Middle East, however, nationalism was a weapon used against liberal-oriented systems, a philosophy more akin to the radical transformations intended by Marxism or fascism. Moreover, rather than espousing loyalty to a particular nation-state with its own identity and interests, these nationalists were pan-Arabs seeking to coerce or subvert their neighbors into unification. As for democracy, prosperity, and social modernization, these were postponed to the far-off day when all Arabs were united and had triumphed over their foes.

Instead, too, the regimes and dominant ideologies borrowed the most illiberal ideas from the West. Many of the institutions identified with modernity were largely introduced to the Arab world, and especially to the common people, not through liberalism or democracy but through the interpretations of autocratic regimes and ideologies. Instead of free enterprise capitalism there were statist economies. Rather than citizens being organized from below by independent groups, they were regimented from above by state-mandated mass organizations.

As in communist countries or other radical Third World regimes, democracy came to mean the mobilization of the people in support of a charismatic dictator, uniting against local reactionaries and foreign imperialists, and sacrificing all for the cause of national strength and development. Thus, an election in which 99 percent of the people voted for the ruler was presented as a victory for "real" democracy. The main slogan of the Baath party, which ruled Syria and Iraq, was "Unity, freedom, and socialism." Unity was the prime virtue, which meant conformity, a rejection of political pluralism, and ultimately the fusing of all Arab states into one. "Freedom" was defined as the ability of Arab states to act as they pleased without foreign interference. And "socialism" meant the regime's control over the economy, and to a large extent, over all social institutions.

Indeed, it is quite reasonable to see radical Arab nationalism and Islamism as the Arab world's equivalents to what communism and fascism were for the West: oppressive systems posing as agents of revolutionary change but in fact arising from a reactionary rejection of modern liberal democratic society. New ruling classes and their dependents were created, and their vested interests built a high dam to protect the status quo. They declared war against largely phantom enemies, mobilizing society for unnecessary battles that, when lost, created even more resentment and hatred. At the same time, they rejected as subversive and evil the very ideas that—at least if properly filtered and adapted—were most needed to solve their societies' problems.

Defeat has always been a central part of such processes. Before their communist and fascist revolutions, both Russia and Germany had lost wars. The myriad defeats and humiliations at falling behind the West were central factors in the evolution of Asia, Africa, and Latin America. Arab states were repeatedly defeated by Israel on the battlefield, starting in 1948.[15] And the greatest defeat of all had been the frustration with a society that seemed incapable of advancing and impossible to change by any other means. Once addicted to a worldview based on hatred, enemies, paranoia, and the certainty of one version of the truth, people turned to new radical ideologies as old ones failed. When Arab nationalism was found wanting, Marxism and Islamism offered to replace it; when internal revolutionary Islamism was defeated, jihadist global Islamism claimed its place.

Beginning in the 1950s, Europe, Asia, and the Americas entered a phase of rapid advancement in the economic, scientific, and creative realms while the Arab world—except as a consumer of these products— played no role in this process. As one Arab writer explained, Arab leaders talked endlessly of battling foreigners and "liberating Palestine" but were only able to defeat their own people. The Arab world fell steadily further behind, rejecting innovations as threats and blaming their relative backwardness on Western, especially American, sabotage.[16]

At any rate, in the 1950s, anger at their own governments, humiliation by the West, defeat in Palestine, frustration at the slow pace of development, utopian dreams, and the belief that they had all the answers created a generation of pan-Arab nationalists. Their battle cries were that liberalism was a form of traitorous servility to the West and multiparty electoral democracy was a guarantee of backwardness. Such things blocked the Arabs from making the great leap needed to achieve rapid development and a renaissance of Arab power.

At the time, most Arabs thought themselves to be living amidst a bright dawn of freedom, unity, and socialism. In retrospect, it was a dismal period of endless squabbles and wasted opportunities. Yet in the twenty-first century such thinking still dominates the scene, and all indications are that it will not soon be displaced, either in words or in power.

Some called themselves Nasserists, others Baathists, and there were a range of other varieties. The need of the hour, they declared, was for a charismatic dictator, a militant doctrine, and total unity in order to mobilize the nation for struggle. They all had the same basic plan: a revolution, which usually took the form of a military coup, would produce a strong, disciplined state (modeled on the army), a nationalized economy (based on that of the Soviet Union), and the merging of all the little Arab countries into one big powerful empire that could restore their people to greatness, destroy all enemies, and march forward to utopia.

Arab nationalists seized power in Egypt, Syria, and Iraq in the 1950s, while challenging the regimes in every other country. Equally important, they dominated intellectual life, the media, and the entire Arab discourse. These revolutions and ideologies resembled more those of communism and fascism in Europe than of democratic life there. In short, the worst Western ideas were imported and had a regressive effect: they created even more barriers to social, economic, and political progress.

The remaining regimes were still traditional monarchies, but they had to be somewhat apologetic for not acting like their more revolutionary counterparts. To avoid being labeled primitive lackeys of the West, traditional regimes had to spend much of their time appeasing powerful radical neighbors and proving they were part of the community of right-thinking Arabs.

Just as the gates of religious *ijtihad* had been closed in the eleventh century, those of political *ijtihad* were sealed in the 1950s. And by the 1980s even *ijtihad* on intellectual and social matters was stopped by the Islamists. Other than the right to chant a set of permissible slogans, there was little freedom of thought or speech. As the system faltered, the sphere of liberty contracted further. By the late twentieth century, it was almost impossible to find support for the concepts of Islam's bolder thinkers from a millennium earlier or for what Arab liberals had said a half-century before.

The regimes' battle against the West and Israel, as well as the struggle for unity and mobilization, provided good excuses for silencing dissent. The only remaining debate was among different shades of radical Arab nationalism, with a growing variation of radical Islamism. Arab liberalism's fate seemed settled: the West was the enemy, its influence subversive, its institutions unsuited for the Arab world, and its local sympathizers or would-be imitators were traitors.

During the long interim between the collapse of the old liberalism in the 1950s and the almost half-century required just to start its revival, most of the remaining Arab liberals were either actual or internal exiles. They either kept quiet or emigrated, spiritually or physically, to the West. Their influence on society was even further reduced. Mahfouz was a rare exception, but he remained self-consciously apolitical, though even in his case, the works that made him famous were written before Nasser took power in Egypt.

Abd al-Rahman Badawi was an example of the few remaining, and aging, holdouts. Born in 1917 into a wealthy village family in Egypt, he studied at a European-type school, became multilingual, and earned a doctorate at Cairo University writing on French existentialism. He also produced books on Friedrich Nietzsche and the heritage of the Greeks. But following Nasser's 1952 revolution in Egypt, Badawi spent almost all his time in Paris and rarely mixed with other Arabs. In 1954 he produced a volume of readings from independent-minded and secular-oriented Arabs in the Middle Ages titled *Atheism and Islam.* The book was quickly suppressed and forgotten. When he left Egypt again in 1967 to return to the Sorbonne, he described this move as escaping "the big jail."[17]

When Badawi did venture back to the Arab world, he was reminded of why he felt that way. In April 1973 Libyan dictator Mu'ammar al-Qadhafi visited the university in Benghazi where Badawi was teaching. When some of Badawi's students told Qadhafi they wanted more rights and freedom, the angry dictator had the professor arrested. But Badawi's friends in Paris and one of his devoted readers, the Egyptian president Anwar al-Sadat, urged that he be let go. After seventeen days, Badawi was released from prison and returned to Paris for good.

Badawi viewed much of the Arab problem as starting with Islam, or at least with the interpretation of it that had prevailed. As long as Arab civilization was based on the concept of God's sovereignty and man's submission, he believed, there could be no relying on logic or human creativity. Badawi rightly expected that there would be no progressive change in his lifetime.

The generation following Badawi's largely rejected liberalism. From the 1950s on, Arab intellectuals, journalists, and teachers devoted themselves instead to pan-Arab nationalism or Marxism. They struggled to uphold the line of dictatorial regimes or revolutionary movements whose enemy was a West based on liberal thought. Advocating liberalism required a reckless, even suicidal, courage. And when a few brave souls revived the old ideas after radical Arab nationalism's bankruptcy should have been apparent to all—written as it was in the Arabs' myriad defeats and failures of the 1950s, 1960s, 1970s, and 1980s—their fate did not inspire the fainthearted to follow in their path. Islamism, not liberalism, filled the vacuum.

Consider the story of one not so intimidated. Farag Fouda was born in an Egyptian village in 1945. He studied agriculture and received his degree from Ayn Shams University in June 1967, that fateful moment of Egyptian defeat in a war that Nasser had provoked with Israel. Fouda earned a doctorate in agricultural economy in 1981. He founded a consulting firm, but his passions were reserved for politics and intellectual life.[18]

Fouda wanted to re-create the pre-Nasser liberal movement and thought the best means to do so was by using its old political vehicle, the Wafd party. But after joining that group in 1978, he saw, to his horror, the party's leadership ally with the Muslim Brotherhood for the 1984 elections. How could the liberals join forces with the militant Islamists—Fouda called them "thinkers of darkness"—the greatest threat to any effort toward modernization, civil liberties, and democracy in Egypt?

For its part, the Wafd, which had originally welcomed Fouda, now saw his opposition to its opportunistic policy as an unwelcome irritant. He resigned in 1984 and formed his own party, al-Mustaqbal (the future), but it was stillborn. Instead, Fouda poured his considerable energies into writing eight books, all critical of political Islam. Fouda's concern was understandable. The Islamists' numbers and their boldness were rising in Egypt, leading them to the 1981 assassination of President Anwar al-Sadat and continuing on a path toward a full-scale insurgency throughout the 1990s.[19]

Fouda's keen sense of how to puncture the Islamists' pretensions made them furious. In one article, he ridiculed a prominent Islamist's claim that the Americans had used demons to invent their highly advanced warplanes. Why, he asked, did genies act only against Arabs and help their enemies? By attributing American success to magic, Fouda sought to show, Islamists were refusing to confront the social and intellectual, as well as technological, changes that had brought Western superiority. By the same token, they were rejecting the very steps necessary to achieve progress for Muslim people. Angry at Fouda's article, some Islamists charged he was a heretic, a crime punishable by death.[20]

But Fouda was not intimidated. In his writings he pointed to the ironies of Islamist claims easily shown to be contradictory or false. Why, he asked, should the Arab model for social and political success be the seventh-century rule of Islam's first four caliphs? After all, that was a time of incredible strife, three of those leaders were murdered as a result of conflicts, and the whole system fell apart within twenty-nine years. Why should anyone expect that such a problem-ridden arrangement offered answers to today's very different society? Again, Islamists were enraged, in no small part because they were so vulnerable to such simple arguments.

Long before the rise of Usama bin Laden, Fouda was warning of the dangers of radical Islamists spreading hate and justifying violence against other religions. As Egyptian Islamists attacked Christian citizens, Fouda condemned a professor of the prestigious al-Azhar mosque university, later that institution's president, for urging Muslims not to be friendly or cooperate with non-Muslims.[21]

To call Fouda fearless would be a pale understatement. His greatest moment may have come in January 1992 when he publicly debated Muhammad al-Ghazali and Maamoun Hodeibi, two important Muslim Brotherhood spokesmen, at the annual Cairo Book Fair. The audience was packed by his opponents' supporters, whose chanting prevented him from speaking. Fouda announced that if they believed he was right they should continue heckling him since they could not defeat his arguments. Only if they had faith in their own ideas should they be quiet and listen. His gambit worked, and the debate was able to continue.

But the Islamists won the debate by other means. Five months later, a fish seller belonging to a revolutionary Islamist group shot Fouda dead with an AK-47. He later confessed that a declaration by a group of al-Azhar scholars calling Fouda anti-Islamic convinced him that the murder was a religious duty.[22] Indeed, at his trial, some leading clerics from al-Azhar were brought in as defense witnesses to suggest that the killing was legal under Islamic law.[23] Al-Ghazali, who had been unable to defeat Fouda in debate, testified that the killing was the proper punishment for an apostate, at which point the defendant shouted, "Now I will die with a clear conscience!"[24] Two years later, in 1994, Naguib Mahfouz, Egypt's greatest literary figure and the first Arab to win the Nobel Prize in Literature, barely escaped a similar fate when he was stabbed by a radical Islamist.

Yet while Islamists and Arab nationalist regimes silenced liberal critics by a variety of means, they could not prevent some debate during the 1990s. The reality of the crisis facing the Arab world could be ignored largely but not totally. During decades of nationalist rule, Arab regimes had failed at home and abroad. The Arabs had not united into a single country or indeed even cooperated very much. The Iraqi invasion of Kuwait in 1990 was one more unmistakable sign of the fact that pan-Arab nationalism had increased tensions among states. In direct contradiction of Arab nationalist doctrine, Arab regimes had to turn to the West to save them from Saddam.

The same situation applied regarding the Arab inability to destroy Israel. As military defeats followed one after another in an unbroken chain, Arab states abandoned the fight while keeping up the militant rhetoric. Egypt signed a peace treaty with Israel in 1979, the Palestine Liberation Organization made the Oslo agreement in 1993, and Jordan accepted a full peace treaty thereafter. By the 1980s it was clear that the United States was becoming the sole superpower, while the USSR, the Arab nationalists' old ally—and to some extent their role model—was tottering into the dustbin of history.

As the list of the Arab nationalists' international humiliations and domestic failures grew longer, it should have been apparent that the Islamists offered no better alternative. Not a single regime had been overturned by them in the years since Iran's revolution. The bloodshed and antagonism they inspired actually pulled the Arab world backward as well as engendering even more bloodshed. The Islamists' alternative was merely to promise they would do battle, wielding Islam as a weapon superior to nationalism. Bin Laden's ideas were no departure from the basic concepts that had long dominated the region, which was why his analysis—whatever people thought of his tactics—was so widely accepted after September 11, 2001.

Finally, the masses were not completely under their rulers' spell. Perhaps they would be open to a different explanation for their problems and a different prescription for solving them? The Egyptian writer Hani Shukrallah scoffed that people understood that the truth was often the exact opposite of the regime's claims. "When an official pronounces

Egypt free of mad cow disease, Egyptians immediately start stocking their freezers with poultry."[25]

No one could deny that the Arab world was in bad shape. But the reasons for this situation were hotly contested. Against the liberals' demand for major reforms, the prevalent view remained the old Arab nationalist/Islamist excuse that the Arab world was a victim of outside forces. Continued stagnation was due to imperialism and Zionism, which subverted and oppressed the Arabs. If local regimes were to blame, it was only because they were the agents of these forces or did not fight bravely enough against them.

In contrast, the liberal view was more unfamiliar and complex, requiring a painful reexamination of cherished beliefs and sacred matters. It blamed the Arab world's sad state on internal forces and backward ideas that blocked progress. Without change, including democracy, the Arab world would not be able to join the modern world and enjoy its benefits.

But these arguments were made mostly by Arabs who had already immigrated to the West or were writing in English. The situation was grim, wrote the Arab American professor Fawaz Gerges, because "authoritarianism and patriarchy are highly consolidated on every level of society, from the public sphere to the dinner table. These shortcomings, not U.S. foreign policies, are largely responsible for the lack of Arab development and progress."[26] Rami Khouri, at the time editor of the *Jordan Times*, added that the main reason for the poor performance of Arab society was the unlimited power held by the state. This problem had long existed but up to now had "been camouflaged" by the decades of the Cold War, early state-building, the oil boom, and the Arab-Israeli conflict.[27]

Or, in the words of Hazem Saghiya, a journalist living in London, the Arabs were stuck in the past while the rest of the world was quickly advancing. No one spoke about solving economic problems, raising the level of education, freedom, the status of women, or the other real issues that had to be addressed. As a result, the Arabs had constantly missed opportunities. The priority was put on confrontation with Israel while postponing progress. To justify this stance, calls for reform and moderation were portrayed as attempts "to plunder our treasures." As a result, he concludes, dictatorship, and not progress, was spreading. Only among Arabs did one-party states still thrive, while Russia, South Korea, Mexico, and Taiwan had embraced democracy. Even the Nicaraguan dictator Daniel Ortega had accepted the results of free elections removing him from office, something unthinkable in any Arab state.[28]

Nevertheless, while the best, most courageous Arab intellectuals have complained about this dreadful situation, they are few in number and face determined opposition from regimes that continue to control the media and other institutions. Some of them left to the West out of frustration, though even there they remained minorities in the field of Middle Eastern studies, which often seemed largely devoted to rationalizing the dominant Arab viewpoint.[29] Such people as Fouad Ajami and Kenan Makiya, brilliant exiled scholars from, respectively, Lebanon and Iraq who lived in the United States, were vilified and even threatened by colleagues.

Thus, the 1990s did not change anything either. Liberal forces remained very weak, the Syrian and Palestinian leaderships rejected peace with Israel, and the Islamist movement tried switching from a domestic revolutionary to an international jihad strategy. September 11, 2001, heralded a new paradigm that threatened to plunge the region into another half-century of catastrophe, violence, and intolerant ideology.

"Where," asks the American diplomat Hume Horan, "are the politically engaged intellectuals who can help a young Arab make coherent, responsible sense of a troubling modern world? . . . The few that even try are threatened, jailed, forced into exile—or worse." Who, then, could young Arabs turn to for guidance in understanding the world other than Islamist, nationalist, or Marxist extremists?[30]

This sad state of affairs led the liberal Egyptian journalist Ridha Hilal in 2001 to write an obituary for the brief, faint hopes of real change: "The calls for democracy and economic prosperity disappeared in favor of the slogan: 'No voice should rise above the voice of battle.'" It felt as though "we are forever doomed to wallow in the mud of violence, dictatorship and poverty."[31] Within two years of writing these words, Hilal had disappeared in Cairo, presumably kidnapped and murdered by radical Islamists.

There was, however, a definite liberal revival as well, and there were reasons for prodemocratic forces to believe that something might change.

Had not the extremist doctrines' claims become so obviously false and their costs too excruciatingly high? Had not the emperors flaunted their nakedness to an unmistakable degree? Clearly, in the twenty-first century's opening years there was a revival of the argument that liberalism, democracy, reform, moderation, and good relations with the West were the real elements needed to solve the Arabs' problems and improve their lives.

Still, given these factors, the upsurge in liberal criticism was far less than one might have thought. Many in the West expected a new liberal age and magnified the significance of any changes, turning every promising green shoot into a forest of moderation. Under President George W. Bush, the entire U.S. foreign policy strategy came to revolve around promoting democracy in the Arab world, and in 2003 a war was fought with Iraq in large part over that goal. This happened because many American leaders reached the conclusion that the region's problems, which had become the world's problem due to international terrorism, could be managed only by challenging the ruling system of dictatorship and antidemocratic ideology.

Yet even if one believes the Arab liberals' eventual triumph to be inevitable, that process could take decades. The liberals' first task is to insist that their success is indeed possible. They have been especially sensitive to any hint that Arabs or Muslims are incapable of achieving democracy. They defended the idea that democracy is by no means an alien concept for the Arab world by citing the pre-1950s era when, in Heggy's words, "true democracy prevailed." Liberals were just starting to make progress when the experiment was throttled in its cradle.[32] Instead of viewing this history through the radical nationalist paradigm—a corrupt incompetent regime being overthrown by courageous patriots— liberals blame the extremists for wrecking a march toward modernization that would otherwise have been successful.

Heggy also rejects the notion that lower levels of education and living standards make democracy impossible. Didn't England become democratic under even worse conditions centuries ago? Aren't Egyptians capable of making intelligent choices? Didn't the highly educated and cultured Germans elect Adolf Hitler? Why should Arabs, then, be deprived of democracy, "the finest achievement of humanity?"[33]

But this was not the only possible interpretation of this history, even among liberals. The more skeptical Tunisian intellectual al-Afif al-Akhdar, who himself lived in Paris, pointed out that even most well-educated, middle-class Arabs had opposed the liberals, who "were more represen- tative of their Parisian teachers" than of their fellow citizens. And even most of the liberals recanted their beliefs by the 1950s to back the new Arab nationalist dictatorships or even become Islamists.[34]

Indeed, says Akhdar, the Arab world has retreated so far as to be less open than at almost any time in its history. "The best Arab poets and thinkers of the early centuries of Islam would not be able to exist in the present-day Arab world." They were too free-spirited and secular, or else they favored religious ideas that would be considered heretical. At the same time, aspects of democracy left behind by the British and French, such as freedom of the press, a multiparty system, or the right to strike have been abolished by the Arab nationalist regimes.[35]

Even taking for granted now that Arabs could establish democracies, it is going to be a long and difficult road to get there. Structural change is unlikely to come from above. Regimes may promise reform, especially after the U.S. overthrow of Saddam Hussein in 2003 made democracy the region's catchword of the moment, but much of this talk is for show.

A humiliating example of this situation was what happened in Syria, nominally a radical republic, when power passed from Hafiz al-Assad to his son Bashar. What better symbol of the nature of dictatorship could there be? After a few months of vain hopes for reform, the new regime settled down into the pattern set by its predecessor. Discussion groups were closed down; journalists were warned not to go too far. As a sole exception, the regime permitted publication of the satirical magazine *Addomari* (The Lamplighter), by the cartoonist Ali Farzat. So hungry were Syrians for something to read that didn't follow the party line that the first issue sold out within hours.[36]

Farzat had already been involved in another small victory of that type. In 1988 an exhibition at the Institut du Monde Arabe in Paris had featured one of his cartoons showing a general doling out medals from a stewpot to a man in rags. Implicitly this criticized one of the Arab regimes' main ways of retaining power: by stirring up war and conflict as a substitute for material achievements. Officials of Iraq, then at the end of a long bloody war with Iran, accused Farzat of making fun of their country, ironically confirming his observation by this act of recognizing it. The Iraqi government threatened to withdraw funding for the exhibit and, although the show was on free French soil, Farzat's cartoon was removed, an example of how the regimes' repression is so often accepted and even reinforced in the West. But the other cartoonists rebelled, adding their own names to the offending picture and threatening to remove their work. For once, Iraq backed off.[37]

Yet such victories were small, rare, and short-lived. When it comes to Arab regimes, a mild poking of fun is permitted at certain marginal phenomena far removed from the leader himself: rising prices, pay hikes for officials, low-level corruption. But that is about the limit. It took only a couple of months for the Syrian authorities to decide that even one free publication was too much. Cartoons in Farzat's magazine were censored as critical of the prime minister. The magazine's print run was cut, its distribution sabotaged, and several issues canceled. Sadiq al-Azm, who seemed to be Syria's sole officially sanctioned dissident (and who paid his dues by supporting the regime at key junctures), explained that the magazine's mere existence proved the old guard "realized that the country cannot be run in the same way anymore."[38] But wasn't Syria still being run in 99.9 percent the same way?

Perhaps only in Kuwait was there a real liberal movement by the early twenty-first century. Press censorship ended after the liberation from Iraq in 1991, and there were regular elections for parliament. Newspapers are now privately owned, and the State Security Court was abolished in 1994. There is an independent and reasonably fair judiciary. And if Islamists are even stronger, the more open system lets liberals and Islamists fight their battle with words in parliament and the press. As one Kuwaiti liberal notes, "This is much healthier than having no public debate in an atmosphere that might encourage terrorism."[39]

At the same time, though, one should not exaggerate the state of democracy even there. Since it is almost impossible for even longtime residents to get Kuwaiti citizenship, only about 10 percent of the country's population—all of them men—are allowed to vote. The cabinet, appointed by the emir, rarely includes more than one elected representative, while all the appointed (unelected) ministers also sit in parliament. The liberals succeeded in electing only sixteen members of the fifty-member parliament at the peak of their success in 1999 against a larger number of Islamists. Even this was temporary. In the 2003 elections, the

Islamists took twenty-one of fifty seats and the number of liberals fell to three seats, plus several supportive independents.[40]

There are two liberal groups in Kuwait. The National Democratic Movement (NDM) and the smaller Kuwait Democratic Forum. The NDM is led by Ahmad Bishara, a professor of chemical engineering at Kuwait University. Ironically, the party arose from the radical Arab nationalists who had demanded more secularism and opposed the ruling monarchy because they wanted to make Kuwait more like Iraq. After Kuwait's experience with Saddam Hussein, however, that was not a very attractive position, and so liberalism was born on this shaky foundation.[41]

The general rule about extreme liberal weakness prevailed throughout the Arab world, both politically and in the public debate. Even the merest acknowledgment of reality could come to seem as a miracle of freedom, a festival of truth-telling. Such was the impact of the Arab World Competitiveness and UN-sponsored Arab Human Development reports of 2002 and 2003.[42] They pointed out that Arab economic growth, despite its huge oil and gas income, was stagnating, lagging behind the rest of the world in education, technology, and freedom. Unless drastic action was taken, the gap would grow wider. And there were no signs of the kinds of reforms needed to meet the challenge.

Education systems were poor, illiteracy high, research limited, and access to the Internet rare. An astounding 51 percent of young people said they would like to live elsewhere. There was little real growth during the 1970s, 1980s, or 1990s. The amount of cultivated land declined, as did productivity, jobs, savings, and non-oil exports. The states did nothing effective beyond maintaining their military might and working to ensure their continued monopoly on political and economic power.

The Arab Human Development Report of 2002, produced for the UN Development Program (UNDP) by a group of Arab intellectuals with strong establishment credentials, painted a devastating portrait of the situation. It warned that the lack of progress in the Arab world was due to such internal barriers as the lack of political freedom, the absence of civil liberties, and the low status of women. In almost every category—political rights, a free media, literacy education, Internet use, maternal mortality, or agricultural productivity—the Arab Middle East lagged behind every other region except sub-Saharan Africa. In many respects, things were getting worse, not better.[43]

Such failures were said by the reports to be the true cause of Arab discontent. Rima Khalaf, the UNDP assistant administrator, warned that unless these deficits were addressed, "the Arabs will not be able to make it."[44] So devastating was the picture that the Kuwaiti daily *al-Watan* described the report as saying, "the Arabs live in the dark ages."[45]

Yet who was actually going to convert this assessment into a political philosophy, a set of arguments, and a program for action? One of the most prominent people trying to do so was Shafiq Ghabra, a Kuwaiti political science professor who held degrees from Georgetown, Purdue, and the University of Texas. Ghabra served as his country's information attaché in Washington from 1998 to 2002 and then returned home to become president of the new American University of Kuwait.[46]

As with many other liberals, it was contact with the West—and especially the United States—that influenced Ghabra's thinking. When as an eighteen-year-old student he came to study in Lincoln, Illinois, Ghabra was a radical leftist highly critical of the United States. Yet he was very impressed that people in that conservative Republican area were tolerant of his views even while disagreeing with them. Those he met, including the first Jews he had ever encountered, went out of their way to treat him well and judge him as a person and a student aside from his ethnic background and political stance. Thus, he learned the value of tolerance—which he described as not stereotyping people merely on the basis of their views—and the value of "dialogue and decency."[47]

The real "clash of civilizations," Ghabra explained, is not between Islam and the West but within Arab and Islamic civilization. Governments blocked change by "repression and the clever distribution of privilege," while the Islamist opposition had no solutions either. Who was going to do something about such massive problems as "exploding population, smothering poverty, vanishing water supply, collapsing social welfare systems, rigid governments?" Ghabra asserted that the vast majority of Arabs wanted neither a radical nationalist nor an Islamist solution. But the educated classes were too silent and passive, failing to take the lead in changing things because they lacked hope.[48]

It was easy to see why. Aside from the privileges to be gained by going along with the system were the penalties suffered for refusing to do so. Fouda was one case in point. Another Egyptian example is Nasr Abu Zaid, who, as a lecturer in Islamic Studies at Cairo University, wrote a book published in 1990 that suggested the Qur'an be analyzed in terms of textual evidence and the context of its time.

Such questioning of what was officially regarded as God's timeless word, however, was a very dangerous thing to do. Islamists threatened Abu Zaid with death but then thought up a more innovative punishment. In 1995 they sued and had him officially branded as an apostate by Egypt's highest court. His marriage was ordered dissolved, since under Egyptian law a Muslim cannot be married to a non-Muslim. Abu Zaid and his wife, who supported his position and did not want a divorce, fled to Holland.

Also suffering serious harassment was the best-known Arab liberal of all, Saad Eddin Ibrahim, head of the Ibn Khaldun Center in Cairo and an internationally respected sociologist. Back in the 1960s, Ibrahim recalled, "We were idealistic. We thought we could change the world. Forty years later, some of us are naive, and a few of us still think we can change the world."[49] In his scholarly work, Ibrahim criticized undemocratic practices and discrimination against Christians. The Egyptian government accused him of treason, and a state security court sentenced him to seven years' imprisonment at hard labor. One charge against him was that he had accepted research grants from the European Union. Few Egyptian intellectuals openly defended him. Only after a couple of years of legal struggle did he succeed in regaining his freedom from jail.

Why was the situation so bad in terms of the prospects for democracy? Ghabra cited a number of reasons, in contrast to the usual claim that all Arab problems were due to Western and Israeli hostility. One was the fear of an Islamist takeover. Many who might otherwise advocate reform preferred to support their local dictator and to maintain the status quo lest too much freedom lead to having an even worse Islamist dictatorship. Equally, many feared there would be chaos if class, ethnic, religious, and other differences were played out in public. Then, too, was the dictators' own repression, propaganda, and intimidation. Finally, a failed Arab-Israeli peace process crushed hopes of a new era for the Arab world.[50]

Faced by terrible problems and denied moderate outlets, liberals argue, Arabs were pushed toward embracing extremist Islamist creeds. This was especially true because religion is, in Ghabra's words, the "only uncensored public expression in most Arab countries."[51] The Arab regimes stopped radical Islamist movements that were using terror from seizing power at home, but since they changed none of the conditions creating the problem, the movement and its violence were merely exported. The result was September 11. Thus, the whole world has a stake in the victory of Arab moderates over extremists.

But Ghabra, always candid, admits the battle will be steeply uphill, with many advantages going to the extremist enemies. Unlike their opponents, who have no compunctions, the moderates are always ready to compromise and do not want to use violence. Similarly, the individualistic advocates of freedom and pluralism cannot easily compete with the extremists' disciplined organization and unity. They lack the militants' certainty and sense of righteousness, fanaticism, and single-mindedness, and also do not have an equivalent big base of popular and financial support. The prodemocratic forces consist mainly of small groups of intellectuals and professionals. Even if, as Ghabra claims, they are supported by "many members of the silent majority,"[52] the problem is that these people are so silent.

Despite the odds against them, however, there is no choice. The radical nationalists have led the Arabs into a quagmire; the Islamists would make things even worse. Nothing else has worked for the Arabs, and only reform and democracy remain as the way to save Arab society.

Ghabra, Ibrahim, Heggy, and others courageously took a path of difficult struggle with small forces against overwhelming odds. Yet there came to the fore an unexpected and most unlikely ally. For suddenly the most powerful country in the world embraced their vision. America's post–September 11 battle, President George W. Bush decreed, would be fought on two fronts: a war against terrorism and a battle for democracy. Beginning in 2002, Bush and his colleagues articulated a worldview that seemed scripted by the Arab liberals. For example, in a May 2003 graduation speech at the University of South Carolina, he articulated a virtual manifesto for reform and democracy in the Arab world as the highest priority for U.S. foreign policy.

Bush explained that the situation in the Arab world was intolerable: all Arab countries combined have less economic productivity than Spain and less access to the Internet than the people of sub-Saharan Africa.[53]

The effort to change all this, Bush said, was one to which massive U.S. resources and even the country's lifeblood should be devoted:

> In an age of global terror and weapons of mass destruction what happens in the Middle East greatly matters to America. The bitterness of that region can bring violence and suffering to our own cities. The advance of freedom and peace in the Middle East would drain this bitterness and increase our own security. . . . We will use our influence and idealism to replace old hatreds with new hopes across the Middle East. . . . We have reached a moment of tremendous promise, and the United States will seize this moment for the sake of peace.

The United States would do this, he continued, by supporting the advance of freedom in the Middle East out of both principle and national interest. Oppressive regimes have nurtured and protected terrorism, but in free nations "the appeal of extremism withers away" in the face of tolerance and enterprise. "Free governments," Bush explained, "do not build weapons of mass destruction for the purpose of mass terror."[54] Thus, democracy in the Middle East was necessary for America's well-being because it would end the threat against the United States. More liberty for Arabs means more security for the United States.

Not only did Bush insist that democracy in the Arab world was possible, he asserted that it was inevitable. People in the Muslim world also wanted freedom to improve their lives. As in many other countries, the dissidents and political prisoners of today would become the national leaders of tomorrow. By this means, as elsewhere, states that had once been enemies would become "loyal friends of the United States."

But Bush also had to strain himself to find "hopeful signs of change." He claimed that many Muslims already lived under democracy by including non-Arab societies like India, Turkey, and Indonesia, and he boasted about the holding of some not-so-free or -fair elections in Bahrain, Morocco, and Jordan.[55] By using simplistic analogies to such former dictatorships-turned-democracies as Germany and Japan, he ignored differences with the Arab situation such as the power of nationalism or religion to be mobilized against democracy there, the weakness of internal democratic forces, and the way that liberal ideas are discredited as tools of imperialist infidels.

Another major problem for a prodemocratic U.S. policy was how to deal with the regimes themselves. "America is working with governments and reformers throughout the Middle East," Bush explained. Yet this was a contradiction. He flattered Egypt as the Arab world's leading country that might be at the vanguard for reform and suggested the Saudi monarchy was moving toward greater openness. But the fact that the United States had to cooperate with regional governments on many other issues made it hard for Washington to press them on democracy and human rights. For example, the United States needed a good relationship with Pakistan for its effort in Afghanistan, despite the fact that this government was a dictatorship and a sponsor of terrorism and had helped radical Arab states obtain weapons of mass destruction.

The regimes would hardly help Bush subvert themselves. How could Bush simultaneously ensure that the regimes were not frightened or angered into wielding terrorism and anti-Americanism at the prospect of such U.S. prodemocratic subversion, and appeal over the rulers' heads to masses who had far more in common with them than with him? What would the United States actually do if the regimes ignored its demands? These contradictions could not easily be resolved. In Iraq the regimes would take their revenge and seek to sabotage his campaign, some by sponsoring anti-American violence, others by cheering it on.

In general, too, Middle Eastern public opinion polls did not agree with Bush's assessment. True, surveys showed a high regard for democracy as a system, but on the specifics of all outstanding issues they continued to show a strong support for the local status quo in practice. And even producing a resolution of the Arab-Israeli conflict—supposedly the magical solution to all such contradictions—would not alter at all the political realities of the Arab world. In fact, the regimes and radicals had worked hard to block peace precisely because it might undermine their power. This kind of situation had doomed Bush's predecessor's peace process and stymied his own attempts to encourage a more moderate Palestinian leadership.

Finally, there was the vital problem of an Islam dominated politically in this era by militant voices and interpretations. "When terrorists and tyrants resist and attack freedom," Bush said, "they are resisting and attacking the hopes of Muslims everywhere. When terrorists go on missions of suicide and murder, they defile the high ethical teachings of Islam itself."[56] But even if these steps truly deviate from Islam as generally practiced over the centuries, what if many or most Muslims do not think so? And how can this situation be altered? Despite the respect he paid to Islam's moderate and humanitarian aspects, Bush was backing one interpretation against another in a battle within that religion. His opinion, or that of the West in general, will have little effect in that struggle nor will the side it prefers necessarily win.

The dictators' and extremist ideologies' effort to sabotage democracy, the inherent difficulty of building such a system, the radical interpretation of Islam's political role, and local people's doubts about reform's benefits have been blowing up Americans in post-Saddam Iraq. Whatever the United States says or does, most of the region's regimes, the Islamists, and the intelligentsia will tell their people that America is an enemy brutalizing Arabs, hostile to Islam, eager to steal oil and to turn Arabs into slaves of its empire.

For all these reasons, the task before the Arab liberals—and the United States, if it is going to help them—is a monumental one, consisting of many discrete problems, any one of which is daunting in and of itself:

- Building a mass movement out of a few dozen scattered intellectuals who face determined adversaries with millions of supporters
- Overcoming radical ideologies that have already convinced the Arab majority of their correctness and virtues
- Outcompeting a powerful, violent, well-financed Islamist opposition deeply rooted in the people's lives and capable of winning free elections
- Defeating the forces of repression belonging to governments willing to do anything to stay in power
- Outtalking a mainstream intelligentsia that benefits from its servility to the state and identifies itself as the bearer of the dominant antidemocratic ideology
- Transforming almost every government in the Arab world
- Avoiding a descent into anarchy if they ever do actually gain power
- Reconciling massively conflicting interests in terms of ideologies, factions, regions within countries, and ethnic groups
- Preventing other dictatorial regimes from subverting democracy in neighboring countries, as Iran and Syria do by encouraging insurgency and terrorism in post-Saddam Iraq

- Building new democratic structures despite a lack of experience in managing such a system
- Demonstrating they could deliver higher living standards, wealthier economies, stability, and other tasks hard to fulfill in developing societies even under the best conditions
- Doing all these things in far less time than was required to accomplish such achievements elsewhere in the world

That is not to say these tasks cannot be accomplished, but it will be truly remarkable if they are achieved. And, worst of all, as Heggy points out, the longer it takes to institute thoroughgoing change, the harder it will be.[57]

2

"Better Saddam's Hell Than America's Paradise"

In contrast to the history of Western thought during the eighteenth and nineteenth centuries, there has been no great manifesto of secularism, reason, or democratic reform in the Arab world. There is no Arab equivalent of John Locke, David Hume, Jean-Jacques Rousseau, Thomas Jefferson, John Stuart Mill, John Dewey, William James, and the many other political philosophers who developed Western liberal thought.

Of course, Arab liberals can use these already existing works rather than having to re-create them, but this, too, is a problem because these Western-born ideas did not originate in Arab experience, historical references, or conditions. Thus, they and the institutions based on them arrive as cultural imports, viewed suspiciously and easily discredited by the many who wish to do so.

For example, even prodemocracy efforts by Western foundations can be portrayed as imperialism. The Cairo University political science professor Mustafa Kamel al-Sayid pointed out in the country's most important newspaper that by making support for reform, democracy, international cooperation, civil society, and gender equality a major element in determining their grants, such institutions as the Ford Foundation and the World Bank can be said to control the Arab world's research agenda. Because local funds for those promoting alternative views are not available, research centers that serve the Western priorities become richer and more powerful.[1]

The author did not mention, however, the fact that regime support—and sometimes Islamist money—remains by far the most powerful source of financial aid and means for success in promoting ideas in the Arab world. Nor did he note how the government put the most successful liberal think-tank director, Saad Eddin Ibrahim, in prison precisely because his success at raising foreign funds gave him a degree of independence from government control. It is also, of course, a delicious irony, and one noted by its Islamist enemies, that the Egyptian government accepts $2 billion in U.S. aid every year while branding civil society activists who accept small American grants as traitors.

In addition, despite the relatively tiny efforts of Western foundations and governments to support democratic and liberal thinking, only a narrow circle of people in the Arab world have even a limited familiarity with such concepts in the first place, because historical and philosophical works focusing on that tradition are not widely available in Arabic. Access to them requires a good knowledge of Western languages and a sophisticated understanding of those countries' cultures and history, both in short supply. In contrast, messages advancing a simple, emotionally appealing nationalist or Islamist doctrine are readily accessible to Arabs at all levels of society.

At least those Arabs who have studied or lived in the West might be expected to have more comprehension and sympathy for its institutions. Some of the most energetic liberals do fit this pattern. In many other cases, however, exposure to the West has pushed people toward antagonistic doctrines, like the wealthy Arab students in Europe who were recruited as September 11 hijackers. And much of the educated, articulate elite, the kind of people who usually became advocates of democracy elsewhere—intellectuals, teachers, journalists, union officials—are instead entrenched as servants of dictatorial regimes or of antidemocratic doctrines.

Furthermore, even when Western political concepts were integrated into Arab thought, some of its other products—Marxism and fascism—had far more influence than did liberalism. The Arab nationalist Baath party, which long ruled Syria and Iraq as well as being influential elsewhere, was shaped by both. Aside from communist parties and radical leftist revolutionary sects,[2] Arab nationalist regimes also borrowed a great deal from Marxist concepts, as with the Nasser government's "Arab Socialist" policies and Saddam Hussein's modeling himself on Stalin.

Even radical Islamism appropriated Marxist-derived notions of imperialism and class struggle, revising them for its own needs. Equally significant is the fact that Islamist ideas and movements have usurped the role liberals could have played as the existing system's main opposition.

An example of the problems that arise from such a situation can be seen with the liberals' struggle to define freedom in their countries. In the Arab nationalist conception, freedom is something for the nation as a whole—freedom from external control or interference—and not for the individual. By freedom, Islamists mean the right to practice "proper" Islam and to impose that duty on everyone else in society. For example, bin Laden claimed that Bush lied when he said that radical Islamists hated freedom, explaining that real freedom meant freedom for "our nation," that is, Islam as a state-community rather than as a right for individuals.[3]

Thus, in Saudi Arabia, the official definition of freedom is to be able to live under Islam's proper laws, a slavery (*Islam* means submission) to the will of God. By local definition, Iraq under Saddam Hussein, Afghanistan under the Taliban, Islamist Iran, and Wahhabi Saudi Arabia were countries enjoying freedom.

For almost every other place on earth, however, freedom is defined as a set of individual rights: freedom of speech, freedom to practice or not practice religion, and so on. In the Western world even nationalism has often appealed to people as a way of achieving a state where they will have more individual freedom, with the American Revolution a perfect case in point. The liberal Arab definition is the same as the Western one. It may be what many other Arabs want, as well, but it has not yet been defined publicly as the main goal of society in their countries.

The space left for liberalism to make its case has thus been contracted to a minimum, with its appeal based on three relatively weak arguments, each of which its enemies have found easy to counter.

First, the liberals insist, other doctrines' failures have shown that change is a necessity. The establishment response, however, is that its defeats can be attributed to foreign subversion, the faulty application of nationalist ideology, or the need to take an Islamist approach instead. At any rate, the "lesson" from these setbacks is that Arabs and Muslims must fight harder for their cause.

Second, liberalism is the system that has worked elsewhere in the world. Again, the nationalist establishment and Islamist opposition respond that such an alternative is incompatible with Arab and Islamic needs, innately hostile to their interests, and has actually produced a bad, immoral society in the West rather than one worth emulating.

Finally, liberals claim their approach is most logical and best fits reality. But their audience's lives prepared them for a different worldview and set of premises.

At any rate, the liberals' voices remained faint, drowned out by their enemies' demagogic arguments and the masses' predisposition to interpret ideas and events in the context of what they had long been taught. Consequently, events have not measured up to the hopeful expectations of Arab liberals and their supporters. Even Arab liberal thought itself remains fragmented, advocated by largely isolated individuals and with little systematic expression. There is no powerful liberal media or organization transcending countries or even within any one country. A relatively high proportion of its advocates live outside the Arab world, and even those inside are able to express their ideas fully only through English-language Arab newspapers.[4]

Despite being constantly accused of acting as Western agents in gigantic, all-powerful conspiracies, the liberals have far less funding than do their opponents. They have little influence in universities, and even less in secondary schools. Television and radio are largely, though not completely, closed to them. The most common form of liberal expression is the newspaper column or opinion article. Even here, their arguments must be diluted to avoid censorship or punishment and adjusted to be even faintly acceptable to a suspicious, hostile audience. On top of this, every word they write or say is drowned out by a tidal wave of opposing utterances through every conceivable channel of communication.

True, the Internet extends the liberals' potential influence, especially by providing Arabs with much greater access to Western materials, albeit in foreign languages. But, again, there has been no great liberal Arab enterprise in that sphere either. Islamists have made far more effective use of the Internet than have liberals, owning many sites that generate a steady stream of material both religious-political (fatwas, theological works) and political-religious (Islamist analyses of events and conditions, advocacy for specific groups).

As a result, the liberal case is heard by only a tiny portion of Arabs, its small space hedged about with the thorns of its enemies. Liberal advocates are also deprived of many specific tools. For example, nationalism has been monopolized by those who define it in authoritarian terms domestically and in radical, confrontational terms externally. Thus, one key option for nineteenth-century European and American liberalism—a populist-oriented liberal nationalism—is now foreclosed.

Ironically, another lost opportunity for recruiting liberals came with the decline of the Marxian left, which proved to be a transitional stage for many who would later become liberals, like Kanan Makiya, Afif Akhdar, Saad Eddin Ibrahim, and Hazem Saghiya. Marxism and communism were Westernizing influences for Arab intellectuals, new ideas that distanced them from both tradition and Islam. The left's demand was for fast, thorough change toward a Western model, albeit the Soviet one. As a result, leftists were the Arab world's most avid modernizers. Today, though, the "left" has been reduced merely to the most rabid Arab nationalist extremists, eliminating the only alternative to the Arab nationalists and Islamists to win young people's loyalty and shape their thinking.

Finally, liberals face constant harassment and slander. Their opponents' main argument is that the reforms and institutions liberals want are foreign imports unsuited to their societies or downright harmful to them. The liberals are said to be traitors and saboteurs, heretics and atheists who have sold out for money or who have been seduced by an egoistic desire for Western praise.

These liberal ideas, they argue, would actually prevent Arabs from achieving their proper goals (defeating the West, destroying Israel, uniting themselves, maintaining their identity, and revitalizing Islam). On a social level, they would bring about a total breakdown by subverting Islam and promoting political and ethnic strife. In political terms, a weakened government would collapse into chaos or a radical Islamist takeover.

A good example of this type of vituperation came from Faisal al-Qassim, host of an Al-Jazeera television show, who complained that Arab liberals "stand to the right of Fascism and Zionism," are close to those

American leaders "who are destroying the world," and are enemies of Islam and Arabism who despise their own countries and mistakenly absolve foreign enemies "from being responsible for the backwardness of the Arab world." On top of all that, they are the ones who are truly intolerant, more "fundamentalist and radical than Usama bin Ladin." In summary, they are nothing "more than a fifth column," seeking to destroy the Arabs."[5]

Thus, Arab liberals face the tough task of converting a hostile group of people far larger than their own adherents while being constantly denounced and harassed. How can they best respond to this situation? Reformists have developed two groups of arguments. The direct argument openly sets out the advantages of major reforms in terms similar to the way they have been presented elsewhere in the world and in Western history. This has the advantage of clarity but the problem of being more easily refuted by Arab nationalists and opposition Islamists, as well as more incomprehensible or unpalatable to the masses whose most cherished ideas are being challenged.

More often, liberals use indirect arguments that they try to fit into existing doctrines. Those less consistent (or more opportunist) among them insist that reforms will strengthen the regimes and ensure that Arab nationalism succeeds by beating the Zionists, Americans, and Islamists. Thus, they try to persuade the rulers that democratization is in their interests and so they should support it. This strategy may be more acceptable to the regimes and their supporters, but it also makes the liberals more vulnerable to being manipulated or co-opted by the regimes. By appearing to support the very ideas and goals that maintain the status quo, reformists risk reinforcing the status quo and adding more bricks to the walls blocking real change in the Arab world.

Another technique used by both liberal approaches has been to try to turn their enemies' arguments against these adversaries by insisting that liberals are the true patriots while their rivals are responsible for the Arab world's sad and weak situation. Only by moderating and adapting can Islam remain strong in the people's hearts. Only through reform can the Arabs keep up with the rest of the world and avoid being even more victimized. To circumvent the accusation that liberal ideas are foreign importations, reformers claim that the seemingly Western notions they favor were originally Arab-Muslim concepts, truly universal, or at least could be adapted without sacrificing Arab identity and Muslim values.

Their enemies ridicule this argument, however. For them, pragmatism is a sin, and abandoning ideology and tradition for purely expedient reasons is a dishonorable surrender. Besides, their opponents continue, imitating the West is a trap and an illusion. The West is against the Arabs and wants you to be disloyal. Liberalism is the problem, not the solution, a Western-Zionist plot of seduction. Why should one care what the West thinks? Since it is the enemy, everything it favors is bad; all that it opposes, good. To accept its standards is to betray one's own people.

The regimes' supporters also insist that reform means instability and instability threatens chaos. This was a very real fear for the masses already, and the post-Saddam anarchy reinforced that concern. It was understandable that non-Iraqi people wondered whether Saddam's tyranny was preferable to the instability following the U.S. invasion in 2003. Democracy and freedom were nice slogans, but wouldn't they be painful in practice? Look at the USSR and Yugoslavia, which rejected functioning systems only to be plunged into national weakness and devastating civil strife. Leaders who allowed political reform ended up being overthrown or killed.

Widening the scope of free expression, much less free elections, could subvert not only the existing regime but society itself, say the status quo's defenders. What if radical Islamists took advantage of this opening to increase their influence or even to seize power? What if ethnic or religious groups tore the country apart in a civil war? Wouldn't free speech bring licentiousness and destroy morality and religion? Just look at what the Western world is like! Economic change could mean collapse in that sector as well because the existing backwardness makes it hard to compete with foreigners. Might not foreign investment also bring hostile outside political and social influences? The wealthy and powerful could easily see such changes as challenging their privileges; those just barely surviving may fear that reforms will make their situation worse.

Even if the liberals are 100 percent right, this does not mean their arguments overcome these considerable objections. Even if their reforms may benefit the country as a whole, they will damage the interests of those most able to implement these changes. Despite their attempts to soften the message, the truth is that the liberal perspective threatens the Arab world's rulers, the economically privileged, and the intellectual establishment.

After all, the main changes the reformers advocate involve abandoning the ruling doctrine and ending the regime's educational-cultural monopoly (which validates the existing intellectual elite); reducing high military spending (which keeps the armed forces happy); breaking up the statist economy (which enriches the regime and its followers); putting corrupt civil servants and human rights violators in jail while firing the incompetent (thus threatening the government bureaucracy); and holding fair elections (which will throw the current rulers and political elite out of power).

If the Arab world requires, in Rami Khouri's words, a more responsive and efficient state, wider participation in decision making, decentralization, accountability, and competition, this is the death knell for the entire existing system and all who benefit most from it.[6] As for such liberal ideas as building positive relations with the West, making peace with Israel, and modernizing or moderating Islam, would not such measures threaten the most cherished ideas dominating their societies?

In short, the liberals may pose as reformers, but the Arab nationalists and Islamists, the rulers and their opposition, as well as conservatives and traditionalists, know very well that the implications of their program are revolutionary, indeed far more revolutionary than what took place in Egypt when the Arab nationalists came to power in 1952 or in Iran when the Islamists seized control in 1979.

Knowing the stakes to be so high, the radical nationalists and Islamists have not restricted their arguments to the merits of the issues involved. One of their main weapons, and a central pillar of the system, is to use conspiracy theories. If Western and Zionist conspiracies explain all the Arabs' problems, there is no need to examine the political, economic, and social shortcomings that the liberals insist must be fixed.

Thus, their powerful opponents constantly charge that the liberals are a key part of the subversive efforts of the Arabs' and Muslims' foreign enemies. Tarek Heggy was not exaggerating when he pointed out that any critic of the system or advocate of democracy is immediately accused of treason, being called "an imperialist agent, an infidel, or a heretic."

Liberals must battle against this conspiracy thinking not only to defend themselves but also to break the control of doctrines whose appeal is based on xenophobia, paranoia, and irrationality. Abd al-Mun'im Sa'id, head of the Al-Ahram Center for Political and Strategic Studies in Cairo, has warned that conspiracy theories like the widespread attribution of an unsolved EgyptAir plane crash—most likely caused by a politically suicidal or psychologically unstable copilot—to a U.S. or Israeli plot "keep us not only from the truth but also from confronting our faults and problems." Blaming problems on external elements blocks any hope for creating a rational response to solve them.[7]

The constantly cultivated sense of being victimized by the West coupled with a belief in endless conspiracies and strict government control poisons public discussion and makes many thoughts impermissible. Wrote Hazem Saghiya, a London-based former leftist now in the liberal camp, "When the facts do not reach [the public], rumors, exaggerations, fantasies, and fears develop. History is not debated. . . . The main issues are not subject to [serious] discussion."[8]

People are taught to ignore what is right in front of their noses on a daily basis—that is, the shortcomings of their governments and societies—and attribute what happens to shadowy behind-the-scenes forces. If the evils come from outside, the "victims" bear no responsibility for the problems and are not expected to solve them. On the contrary, criticizing or altering the existing system weakens its ability to protect the people from the demonic forces that want to destroy them completely.

This belief runs across the political spectrum. Islamists view the central issue as a conflict between Islam and the Judeo-Christian world, a combination of the Crusades and Jewish attempts to seize world domination. Arab nationalists and Marxists see the struggle as between imperialism and the oppressed nations. Ordinary citizens receive such indoctrination from every direction, including schools and mosques, media and gossip, government and opposition.

Heggy concludes: "Even the most outlandish statement, if repeated often enough, can . . . be accepted as true . . . in a society in which half the population is illiterate and the other half displays only a very modest standard of education and culture." This situation provides "a fertile breeding ground for the most untenable, demagogical and unfounded assertions to take root and flourish."[9]

Conspiracy thinking disables more than it mobilizes, however, leaving as alternatives only passivity or futile defiance. Consequently, Arab failures do not require a reexamination of methods or premises but merely louder complaints against untouchable outside forces. Because the enemy is so powerful, invisible, and clever, the victim can only accept that defeat and humiliation are inevitable.[10] In this context, Arab societies can justify believing they are in a permanent state of war for which terrorism is a reasonable defensive measure. But terrorism merely amounts to a form of vandalism, minor sabotage or ineffectual graffiti on the mighty machine.

This type of paralysis, or at least the lack of any constructive response, is reinforced by the fact that, as Ibrahim says, "the message of rejection and suspicion of everything new that Arab intellectuals, religious leaders and politicians convey makes the Arabs as a people suspicious of all innovations."[11] Instead of effective action, politicians merely provide emotionally powerful but illogical slogans that hypnotize the people, fueling hatred and leading to even more destructive impulses.[12]

As the real reasons for defeat—such as paranoia, confrontation, and militancy—are ignored, the misguided policies that lead to failure are glorified, justified, and reinforced. Anyone challenging this worldview by advocating moderation, compromise, or reform is merely added to the list of those participating in the conspiracy.

Such warnings—often accompanied by threats—cannot be lightly disregarded and must shape the way liberals present their message. For example, Shafiq Ghabra, a Kuwait University professor, became the center of a major controversy in 2002 when he was head of his country's information office in Washington. Ghabra had almost finished a three-year term in this job when he participated in a Davos World Economic Forum seminar in New York. Israelis happened to be speaking on the same panel.[13] Islamists and radical nationalists in Kuwait launched a campaign vilifying Ghabra as a traitor and demanding his firing.

Ghabra's ability to launch a public countercampaign defending his actions was considered a sign of progress. Although he did resign, the government kept him on to finish his term, making it possible to judge this a small victory for the liberal cause. But of the four basic strategies Ghabra used to defend himself, two used mainstream, arguably anti-liberal, arguments against his accusers: he was defending the Arab cause and following the regime's policy. His other two points—attacking his accusers' methods and defending free speech—reflected more explicitly liberal goals.

Initially Ghabra employed traditional Arab nationalist arguments to justify his participation. The Arabs would be foolish to pass up an opportunity to present their case, he explained. The Palestinian struggle was going through a particularly difficult period, requiring "a redoubling of effort to represent the conflict in an honest and sensitive way." He had thus served the Arab and Muslim cause by championing its position to an important American audience.

Such actions were especially important after September 11, Ghabra warned, because the just Arab and Palestinian causes were being distorted by Israeli efforts to identify them with terrorism. Moreover, speaking on the same panel as Israelis does not imply any normalization of relations with Israel. After all, he added, "Egypt had even exchanged ambassadors with Israel without really normalizing relations." He concluded, "To defend truth, I say we should debate even with the devil."[14]

To this point Ghabra had followed a very orthodox Arab line. In fact, his strategy was to suggest that anyone opposing his strategy was really trying to sabotage Arab efforts. Ghabra did not suggest that he went to the seminar in order to hear what others think, to understand Israelis' views better, to move his country closer to Western views, or to encourage peaceful dialogue and conciliation. Rather, he explained his goal only as trying to convince influential Americans that the Arabs were right and Israel was wrong. This is one alternative position for liberals: to insist that they are achieving the usual Arab goals better than their rivals.

A second conservative argument used by Ghabra was to insist that he was more loyal to the regime than his critics. He was defending the status quo; his enemies were the real rebels. Kuwait's ruler, Ghabra pointed out, opposed normal relations with Israel but allowed his country to participate in conferences that included Israel during the 1990s peace process. Moreover, the hard-liners were the ones who took a "stubborn and haughty stand against the wishes of His Highness" in opposing his proposal to give women the vote. In this conception, liberalism is made to seem the defender, rather than challenger, of the status quo.[15]

At the same time, however, Ghabra also used some explicitly liberal arguments. He said he was a defender of free speech, always ready to listen to Arabs even if he disagreed with them. In his view, his totalitarian, antidemocratic critics who brand anyone who disagrees with them as an enemy deserving to be killed are the ones leading the Arab world into backwardness, isolation, and even destruction.[16]

One cannot be critical of Ghabra, a consistently courageous and creative liberal thinker, for protecting himself by claiming to adhere to the orthodox approach. After all, his life and that of his family, as well as his career, were at stake. But this incident reveals the limits on liberal criticism, the continuing strength of taboos, and the difficult decisions individuals must make every time they speak out on any controversial issue.

The irony, suggests Heggy, is that those who boast of their militancy and loyalty do the most to sabotage legitimate Arab interests. By rejecting reforms, radical nationalists and Islamists ensure Arab weakness. No country can have any international importance, he explains, unless it is internally strong and stable. Those who make big demands, reject compromise, and alienate the West are the ones who really make Arab failure a certainty. The hard-liners can explain this contradiction away by passing "themselves off as warriors battling against impossible odds," but they are just "false prophets drawing the gullible into a net of false hopes and dreams."[17]

This is the basis for the sometimes frantic frustration of the liberals. Why is it so hard to persuade their own people to adopt a position that, in Heggy's words, is "based on reason, common sense and a realistic assessment of the situation?" Why is it so difficult to show the futility of a worldview whose record is so abysmal?[18]

In contrast to these tough realities, many Western journalists, politicians, and intellectuals tend to underestimate the problems and act as if the liberals' victory will be quick and inevitable. Referring to Kuwait, for example, one U.S. newspaper article discussed how "liberals are on the offensive," engaging in "a dramatic battle of ideas between the forces of modernity and . . . fundamentalism" there.[19]

True, Kuwait might be the place where liberalism most flourished in the Arab world, the only place truly without press censorship and with liberal parliamentarians and political parties. One such politician, Muhammad Jassem al-Saqer, chair of the national assembly's foreign affairs committee, expressed confidence that because "all over the world democracy rules . . . the same will happen in the Middle East, especially the Gulf states. Kuwait is the model. This is the way of the future."[20]

But the future might be a long way off. The Kuwaiti liberal forces, at their peak in 1999, comprised only about a dozen out of fifty legislators, far outnumbered by Islamists, and declined sharply thereafter. The fate of the reform movement in Syria showed even more graphically that history was not necessarily heading in the liberals' direction, at least with any assurance or speed.

After the early realization that President Bashar al-Assad would not be more flexible than his father, many in the Syrian reform movement sought to prove their loyalty to the regime. After the government largely ignored two earlier, more ambitious, reform manifestos in September 2000 and January 2001, almost three hundred Syrian intellectuals, professionals, lawyers, and political activists tried a new tack in a May 2003 letter to the president.

How did they hope to change his mind? By using traditional arguments and invoking the regimes' own goals. Reform is needed, they stress, because Israel's occupation of the West Bank and Gaza, along with the U.S. occupation of Iraq, threatens the homeland, which is caught between two strong enemies. Only reform would make Syria strong enough to handle this threat.[21] In this way liberals hoped in vain to strengthen their case and reduce the risk of repression. Yet this more cautious and seemingly clever strategy also reinforced the very ideas that ensured the dictatorship's continuity and the radical Islamist opposition's strength.

Thus, the May 2003 letter argued that national survival requires reform. Arab governments are impotent or collapsing and Syria is surrounded by enemies, especially the "aggressive, racist, egotistical, and evil policies" of the United States and Israel. The only way for Syria to save itself and stop the United States from taking over the region is by a sweeping program of reforms that include the release of political prisoners, allowing all democratic freedoms, and reducing the security forces' power.[22] Unsurprisingly, Assad was not persuaded.

Yet trying to turn traditional arguments against the establishment by purporting to be on its side has been a favorite liberal tactic despite its lack of success. For example, a number of Arab writers, like the Lebanese editor Ghassan al-Tueni, proposed in early 2003 that Saddam Hussein must resign or initiate real reform in order to protect Iraq and the Arab world from a U.S. invasion.[23] Other writers suggested that democracy would best ensure that Saddam and his regime stayed in power.[24] This was a back-door way to advocate democracy and pluralism, demanding that Saddam put Arab nationalist sovereignty above his own personal selfish interests.

Ghabra, too, tried to transform U.S. pressure for democracy into an acceptable Arab nationalist argument for reform. We must, he wrote, "conduct these reforms ourselves" precisely to avoid the need or likelihood—more establishment Arabs might use the word "excuse"—for U.S. intervention.[25]

These arguments might seem more compelling than the explicitly liberal ones that reform should be adopted mainly because it would benefit Arab societies and peoples by getting rid of the dictators. It was certainly easier to tell governments that following liberal advice would ensure they remained in power and to promise the masses that such reforms would more surely defeat the United States and Israel. Yet this approach did not seem to be any more effective in bringing reform from the top.

Moreover, governments and radical Islamist oppositions correctly see that such steps would change Arab aims as well as weakening themselves. After all, if the Arab world wants the benefits of modernization and peace, it will have to negotiate a compromise agreement with Israel, discard anti-Americanism and anti-Westernism as a tool, privatize an economy designed to benefit government officials and their supporters, dismantle the repressive apparatus that keeps them in power, and rethink currently dominant interpretations of Islam.

All these problems are underlined by one of the most ingenious liberal critiques of the status quo, a fictitious interview with an Arab leader by Naji Sadeq Sharrab, a Palestinian political science lecturer at Al-Azhar University in Gaza City.[26] The ruler explains that his family runs the country by hereditary right, a system that applies both to monarchies—Morocco, Jordan, and the Gulf states—and to so-called republics like Syria, Iraq, and perhaps Egypt. The leader then explains that he must rule forever because if he steps down, "the result will be anarchy, violence, instability, and a political vacuum."

Q: Aren't you afraid that the people will revolt, protest, and rebel?

[Ruler]: What are the security apparatuses and police for? Why do we equip the army and buy weapons?

Q: How do you choose your ministers and deputies?

[Ruler]: According to the principle of their loyalty, from among my relatives and from among those who listen but do not see.

Q: What is your opinion of democracy?

[Ruler]: We have our own democracy that is based on obedience and loyalty to the ruler, and thus the people work and produce in order to support the regime, and enslave themselves so as to protect it. . . .

Q: How do you see the future of your people?

[Ruler]: Their future is linked to my future and to my remaining in power. . . . We have no opposition. . . . But we will not let them harm the regime. . . .

Q: Have you advice for your [fellow] rulers?

[Ruler]: May Allah help you against your people.[27]

While this was satire, reality rather closely mirrored it, as shown by an actual interview with Muhammad Moussa, a member of Egypt's ruling National Democratic Party and a leading figure in parliament. He explained that Egypt needed no reform because it is already fully democratic. "What is it we are lacking that we are asked to implement such reform?" Everyone was "perfectly free to vote" and could express themselves on every issue. The courts ensured the honesty of elections, and there was a multiparty system, along with "one of the best" constitutions in the world, the envy of other states.[28] Everything was just perfect, thank you very much.

At their May 2004 summit meeting in Tunis, Arab governments were supposedly producing a document outlining their own reform program to prove that Western interference to encourage democratization was unnecessary. In fact, only two of the twenty-one paragraphs of their statement dealt with this issue. One merely gave a general endorsement to human rights; the other said the regimes would continue their efforts to consolidate democratic practice, broaden participation in political life, and strengthen civil society. Liberal Arabs hardly found this sufficient, seeing it rather as another example of how the rulers have tried to stall and discourage real change.[29]

Another instance of a regime suggesting that progress required no change was a 1990s Syrian slogan advocating "development without change." No one denounced this concept's absurdity.[30] A Bahraini writer, Muhammad Jaber al-Ansari, explains that even if some Arab leaders wanted to implement reforms, they would be blocked by the majority of their colleagues, who have held power so long that they have "gone rotten in their thoughts and conduct."[31] Thus, appeals to leaders to reform themselves are unlikely to produce results.

Another skeptical analysis comes from Hossam Itani, a Lebanese writer who, in June 2003, explained that all the talk by governments about democracy is intended to "avoid U.S. pressures without depriving the regime of any of its powers." *Democracy* has just become a cover word for regimes doing as they please and simply calling it their own version of that system.[32]

The regimes might take into account public opinion, he continued, but without giving the masses any real "share in power." This in-between status is a breeding ground for extremism. The people have no means to peacefully express their opinions. The gap is dangerous, with satellite television stations stirring up people whose needs their economies and political systems cannot meet.[33]

This is especially so because people know how bad things are even if they don't agree on why. Mustafa al-Feki wrote in a United Arab Emirates newspaper that Arabs are in "a state of humiliation and disintegration." Yet Feki shows how easy it is to straddle the line by contradictory statements, first demanding change, then depriving it of all meaning: thorough reform is required, but it should not threaten the existing systems and prevailing ideas. Reform must be gradual but any delay would be disastrous; rulers should not fear reform, but it will doom them.[34]

Similarly, Sheikh Yousef al-Qaradhawi, one of the most influential Islamist thinkers, combines demands for reform with a hard-line position. He blasts "oppressors and tyrants" who so badly mistreat the people, yet he then holds out hope they might learn a lesson from what happened in Iraq, and transform themselves.[35]

But being under so much pressure, Arab liberals also understandably engage in wishful thinking in the hope that the regimes will take up their cause. A good example of the reform-is-in-the-regimes'-interest approach comes from an Iraqi journalist, Ghassan al-Atiyya. "Under wise leadership," he explains, "crises become opportunities to effect reform and change." For Saudi Arabia, "the current state of drift" is more dangerous than the bitter pill of reform. Unless changes are made, both dynasty and state might collapse. In contrast, if the Saudis reform, they will have more influence in the Arab world. He praises the late King Faisal, a notorious reactionary, as a modernizer and cites his oil embargo during the 1973 Arab-Israeli war, the height of the kingdom's anti-Western activity, as a great success.[36]

Atiyya seems to overestimate the regime's need for liberal reform in order to survive and to underestimate how much conservatives would rebel and jeopardize the regime's survival if it did embark on reform. In trying to make his case that the rulers might really want to become liberals, he incredibly—but not untypically—blames the United States for the rulers' preference to appease the Islamists instead of doing what liberals want.[37]

Appealing to incumbent rulers to make such alliances is a liberal tactic to avoid repression, get government support, and pose as the system's savior from Islamists. Yet the distance between Arab nationalist rulers and Islamists is in many ways narrower than the gap that divides them both from the liberals. The radical Islamist opposition does not criticize the system as such but only complains that the regime is too timid and mistakenly fights for nationalism rather than Islam. It does not reject the rulers' goals or institutions but just wants to give them a different flavor. Caught between these twin authoritarian forces, the tiny democratic opposition is constantly faced with having to choose the incumbent government as the lesser of two evils.

Much of the general population is in the same situation. In contrast to the large numbers of people who adhere either to the regime—whether from fear of change or genuine belief—or the Islamist opposition, few see the liberal democratic alternative as legitimate or preferable. Even many pious Muslims think the radical Islamists hold heretical ideas and prefer the existing Arab nationalist dictatorship to risking such a revolution.[38]

Understandably, whether rightly or wrongly, fearing that a major reform effort may bring more chaos and violence, many people are not ready to support such a change. That, perhaps, is the biggest victory of the rulers and Islamists in their battle against the liberals.

3

The Courage of Their Convictions

A rab liberals represent relatively small minorities who advocate a
range of reforms, including a more open economy, greater democracy, free speech, better relations with the United States, peace with
Israel, and other ideas. They do this out of a genuine concern for their
countries, their societies, and their people. Examining ideas and events
elsewhere in the world and looking at recent history with a critical eye,
they have concluded that the terrible problems the Arabs face and have
failed to address are the result of poor choices that can be corrected.
While the number of such social critics and activists is small, other similarly sized groups have succeeded in making dramatic changes in other
parts of the world, notably Communist Eastern Europe.

Dictatorships in the Arab world, however, handle liberals and reformists more easily than have the governments in other regions facing such
situations. The state-controlled media attack reformers as imperialist
and Zionist agents preaching an alien doctrine; clerics denounce them as
un-Islamic. Their countries' constant state of crisis—a situation often
whipped up by their leaders precisely for this purpose—has been said to
make reforms too dangerous, an unaffordable, even fatal, luxury.

It takes a strong individual to stand up to such constant vilification,
in which even friends and colleagues angrily dispute what seem to liberals to be the most obvious realities. Such accusations can be followed by
everything from death threats to the destruction of one's livelihood and
reputation. Even in Jordan and Egypt, public dissent can mean being
barred from working and expulsion from professional organizations.

At the same time, everyone knows that voicing the official line can ensure fame, fortune, success, and an easy life.

Tarek Heggy gives a good sense of what it feels like to be on the receiving end of such vicious attacks. He knows that whenever he speaks up, "the self-appointed knights in shining armour riding on their steeds of big words and empty slogans will rush to fire their arrows of insults against my . . . integrity." Their main weapon is personal defamation and intimidation, and the only way to avoid being so targeted is to suspend one's critical facilities and "tell people what they want to hear." But to do this would guarantee that things will never get any better.[1]

One of the rare humorous moments of such harassment came when Heggy won a lawsuit against a publication that had accused him of being an agent of U.S. imperialism. Asking to address the court, Heggy explained that it was not only the slander that bothered him but the sloppiness and stupidity of it. After all, he explained, because he had worked so many years for the British-owned Shell Oil Company, if he was going to be accused of being a foreign lackey it should be of British, not U.S., imperialism.

It took a lot of courage for liberals to take on such powerful and ruthless forces. But it was even tougher knowing they could not depend on much support from others. Often, liberals had to act as individuals or along with a few colleagues. The social groups that elsewhere in the world form the main prodemocratic constituency—professionals, intellectuals, journalists, students, and teachers—are in the Arab world dominated by regime loyalists (or sometimes Islamists) who shout down democratic dissenters. The working class is weak and independent trade unions virtually nonexistent. Businesspeople are often dependent on regime patronage or linked to ruling circles by family or partnership. Coherent ideologies, both religious and secular, tie the common people to the rulers in a much stronger way than in dictatorships elsewhere.

Sharply in contrast with experiences in Africa, Asia, Eastern Europe, or Latin America, liberals are hardly ever able to build a mass base of supporters. Trying to make the case that the people did want change, Saad Eddin Ibrahim, writing in an American newspaper, claimed as proof the many political prisoners held in Arab regimes' jails and a Saudi women's demonstration demanding the right to drive cars. Yet most of those prisoners are in fact radical Islamists or extreme leftists who do not favor democracy, while the small, never-repeated Saudi women's protest had taken place fourteen years earlier. More persuasively, Ibrahim can point to a growing group of intellectual advocates of reform, such as the authors of the Arab World Development report and the Alexandria Declaration, which enumerated the attributes of "genuine democracy."[2]

This is not to deny that liberals have impressive arguments, but simply that they rarely persuade their intended audience, especially given the blizzard of counterclaims and built-in resistance from many years of indoctrination. It is true, for example, as liberals assert, that the governments' failure to combat Islamist extremism let radicals become a bigger threat. In Egypt Sadat used Islamist groups to combat the left in the 1970s and then was assassinated by them in 1981. The same basic case can be made for Saudi strategy. It may not matter how many terrorist cells are arrested by the government "if the royal family fails to win the hearts and minds of ordinary Saudis," wrote one Saudi liberal.[3]

Liberals do not mention, however, that Syria, Iraq, Algeria, and Egypt all destroyed Islamist insurgencies in the 1980s and 1990s without making any reforms whatsoever, while liberals in those countries were forced to side with the local dictators against that more frightening menace. Moreover, regimes must take into account the reality that permitting liberal reform would anger conservative forces, which might then join Islamist revolutionary groups trying to overthrow the government.

In addition, the Islamist factor can actually strengthen regimes because both agree on opposing liberal democracy and keeping the system's current goals intact. The more the Islamists scare people away from supporting reform or toward backing the existing regime as a better alternative, the more it suits the incumbent rulers. Posing as both champions of tradition and defenders of society against Islamist revolution, even the dictatorial regimes may know that opposing liberals and blaming the West and Israel for all their problems will not solve their nations' real shortcomings, but rulers understandably consider this a more effective strategy for regime preservation.

Sometimes liberals perceive and even proclaim that the true, albeit tacit, alliance is not between Arab nationalist rulers and liberals but between those in power and the Islamists. Thus argues Ahmad Bishara, leader of a Kuwaiti liberal party, in pointing out that governments let radicals raise money for terrorist groups abroad. Some of this goodwill money to bad-will people is also used to finance Islamist parliamentary candidates and media at home.[4]

Governments will certainly repress radical Islamists and oppose radical incitement when these forces seem to threaten them, but they have no motivation to embrace the liberal view. For example, when Saudi Arabia became a direct target of Islamist terrorist attacks in 2003, it arrested or fired from their jobs some extremist preachers but did the same thing to liberal journalists and teachers. Even at the height of the Islamist threat, the regime felt it needed to prove even more that it was still conservative enough to avoid antagonizing those who opposed change and might otherwise support Islamist revolution. Repeatedly, regimes concluded that avoiding reform would be more likely to cool tensions and reduce recruitment by revolutionary Islamist groups than stepping up the speed of change or loosening the government's hold on society.

At any rate, as Hazem Saghiya wrote, "The state continues to be the boss, as it always has been." "From where," he asked, after a half-century of this system, "would a free man appear?"[5] When free men did appear, however, they often did not remain free for very long. The regimes were quite willing to use repression to stop such criticisms. Murder was rare, with intimidation being the more usual tactic. The liberals, more an irritant than an immediate threat, were also not deemed as tough as the revolutionary Islamists, and so torture was not really necessary to discourage them.

Far from being mindlessly heavy-handed, though, regimes used repression cleverly and selectively, often acting in ways designed to manipulate and fool the West. Fathi Eljahmi, a Libyan oppositionist held in prison for two years, was released in March 2004 when high-ranking U.S. and European officials were coming to Libya to praise that country for divesting itself of weapons of mass destruction projects. Three weeks later, he was arrested and thrown back into prison.[6]

In every Arab country, albeit with much variation, there is an intense atmosphere of intimidation, a bizarre juxtaposition of rigid official doctrine and tendrils of freedom perhaps best described by Saghiya:

> Egypt's Islamists range between two poles: [assassinating] people on the one hand, and controlling the cultural and even social [public] space, on the other hand. Egypt's intellectuals swing between Emanuel Kant on the one hand, and Saladin on the back of a horse in the battle of Hittin [against the Crusaders], on the other. The popular desire is war [against Israel], but Egypt was the first Arab country to accept peace. An overwhelming majority of Egyptians prefer the severing of relations with the

United States, but American aid to Egypt has reached $50 billion since Camp David in 1979.[7]

It is, indeed, in Egypt, a relatively more open country, where these contradictions are most sharply visible. Periodic confrontations in which specific intellectuals are accused of political or religious heresy keep up the pressure for conformity and self-censorship. The novelist Salman Rushdie, condemned to death by Iran allegedly for libeling Islam's founder—but more likely for ridiculing Ayatollah Ruhollah Khomeini—is internationally the best-known case, but there have been many others. When a fifteen-year-old novel by the Syrian author Haider Haider was suddenly declared defamatory of Islam after being reprinted, Egypt's Ministry of Culture ordered that it be quickly withdrawn, but student protest riots against the book took place in Cairo anyway.[8]

Few paid attention when Haider complained that his words were taken out of context or when the Egyptian Organization for Human Rights condemned "cultural violence" and "campaigns that label writers and artists as apostates." Their voices were drowned out by Islamists intent on forcing the government to be more repressive and by the regime itself, happy to have an opportunity to flaunt its piety.

The best-known instance of persecution involved Saad Eddin Ibrahim and twenty-seven colleagues in Egypt. Ibrahim, one of the Arab world's preeminent social scientists, heads Cairo's Ibn Khaldun Center, a think tank he founded in 1988. It has examined such issues as the fairness of Egypt's elections and the treatment of the Coptic Christian minority. He also helped establish the Center for the Study of Arab Unity in Beirut, the Arab Think-Tank Club in Amman, the Arab Organization for Human Rights, the Egyptian Organization for Human Rights, which he also headed, and a committee to monitor the 1995 Egyptian elections. In short, Ibrahim is a one-man reform movement.

Ibrahim was one of seven children born to a landowning family in a Nile Delta village. When he was just sixteen years old, he met President Nasser to receive an award for an essay about the dictator's autobiography, which laid down the main principles of Arab nationalist ideology. According to Ibrahim, he bravely told Nasser, "I am worried that our revolution will turn to eat its people as every revolution in this world did before." The remark was prompted by the arrest and torture of one of his friends, who Ibrahim said had been falsely accused of being a radical Islamist.[9]

After graduating from Cairo University in 1960, Ibrahim went on to get his doctorate from the University of Washington, married an American woman, obtained U.S. citizenship, and taught at several universities. In 1975 he returned to Egypt, where he became a professor. Ibrahim did not lack good establishment contacts. President Anwar Sadat took him off the Nasser-era list of undesirables who should not be let into the country. Later, he was given special access to interview imprisoned Islamist terrorists to find out what made them tick, an experience Ibrahim would say made him hopeful, because these people were willing to sacrifice their lives for change. His students included Suzanne Mubarak, the wife of Egypt's president, with whom he maintained good relations.

One of Ibrahim's most formative experiences was what he learned from Anwar Sadat. When Egypt's president made peace with Israel in 1979, Ibrahim, then a radical, opposed him. According to Ibrahim's account of the argument, he told Sadat that the Egyptian street was against peace. Sadat disagreed. When Ibrahim took a public opinion survey, he found out that Sadat was right: 71 percent of the Egyptian public backed the peace treaty.[10] From this discovery, Ibrahim seemed to conclude that it was the radical intelligentsia that was out of touch. If anything was going to be accomplished in Egypt, the people should be trusted and their opinion solicited.

At the same time, though, no issue was too controversial for Ibrahim to examine. One taboo subject in Egypt is serious discussion over the Coptic Christian minority, which is thought to comprise 10 percent of the population. The Egyptian government seeks to conceal evidence of discrimination and bigoted violence against them. In 1994, Ibrahim organized a conference on minorities in the Arab world. Conflicts between ethnic groups, Ibrahim estimated, had resulted in ten times more casualties than all other Arab wars. The government refused to deal with the problems of Christians, partly to assuage Islamist militants. But, Ibrahim stated, the radicals did not need any excuse to carry out antigovernment violence and should not be allowed to set the national agenda.

Another of Ibrahim's activities that provoked the government's anger was to make a film with the dramatist Ali Salem urging Egyptians to vote. In the film, masked men are shown stuffing the ballot box in front of a sleeping guard and an election observer. A woman announcer explains that the people should be allowed to choose the government that rules them: "Participate in the elections and elect a person you believe in, be it a Muslim or a Christian, a man or a woman . . . and then demand accountability."[11] But this film also illustrated a contradiction liberals could not really confront, for if Egypt's elections were rigged, how could they ever produce a democratic result? Ultimately, the problem was not getting out the vote but changing the regime whose policies ensured that elections did not matter.

In 1999 Ibrahim's center issued a critical report about the Egyptian school curriculum's shortcomings in teaching tolerance. The response was a four-month media hate campaign in which almost every article charged the report was part of a Western-Zionist conspiracy, while editors refused to print the center's defensive rebuttals. Preachers in mosques claimed the center was anti-Islam.[12]

The following year, Ibrahim criticized how Syrian president Hafiz al-Assad had passed on power to his son. Ibrahim coined the word *gomolokiya* for such a system, combining the Arabic words for republic and monarchy. Because Mubarak was reportedly considering possibly making his own son the successor, he apparently took offense. "It was," Ibrahim remarked, "the straw that broke the camel's patience."[13]

One evening in June 2000, Ibrahim's house was surrounded by dozens of secret police. He and his staff were arrested, the center was closed, and its staff was charged with embezzlement, receiving foreign funds illegally, defaming Egypt's reputation, and bribery. In May 2001 Cairo's Supreme State Security Court found them all guilty, gave twenty-two defendants suspended sentences, but ordered Ibrahim to serve seven years at hard labor for "harming society's interests, values and laws." Media coverage in Egypt applauded the verdict, though six human rights groups there called it a repressive act intended to silence independent institutions.[14]

Some Arab intellectuals rallied to Ibrahim's side—an important historical first. In an appeal published ironically—but symbolically, too—in a pro-Saddam, anti-Egypt London-based newspaper, they urged Mubarak to free him.[15] The appeal tried to persuade Mubarak through flattery—ingenuously suggesting that the government had done a great deal to increase freedom previously—and claiming that Ibrahim was serving the regime's true interests. Releasing, even honoring, Ibrahim would enhance Egypt's international image, the signers insisted, while intimidating civil society activists would make it more likely that radical Islamists could seize power.[16]

While these arguments were understandable attempts to make the case that more liberty strengthened the regime, they might have had the reverse effect on their intended audience. After all, the regime did not want more democracy, as this jeopardized its own power. Instead, the rulers felt their interest was served by intimidating civil society activists because they posed a threat to the reigning dictatorship while not being much of an asset in combating the Islamists. Indeed, the government thought that cracking down on liberals would keep traditionalists content enough not to rebel and appease radicals enough to keep them from causing trouble. Arresting Ibrahim was not a mix-up on the government's part, it was a conscious effort to reduce the liberal threat, make the regime seem patriotically Arab, and show it to be battling those who allegedly sought to reduce Islam's role in the country.

As for foreign criticism regarding the Ibrahim case, this was an absolute bonus for the regime in domestic terms. Xenophobia has always been one of the Arab regimes' most valuable tools, with the anti-America and anti-Israel cards as the aces in their hands. In the Arab world, patriotism is the first refuge of scoundrels, who defend their privileges by denouncing reformers as traitors. Mahfuz al-Ansari, chief editor of the Egyptian government's Middle East News Agency, alleged regarding the Ibrahim case that the United States complained about human rights violations only in Egypt but not Israel, sarcastically claiming, "The quickest reaction to the verdict came from Jewish and Zionist circles."[17]

The editor of a progovernment weekly proposed that "those who ally themselves with foreign quarters to harm Egypt's national security . . . should be executed in a public square."[18] Continuing in this vein, he sneered that Ibrahim's supporters thought defending his "crime" was more important "than defending Iraq and Palestine." Instead, they were supporting "the murderers Bush and Sharon," in order to back the "Zionist death camps." The real issue was the damage to their homeland done by Egyptians living in London, Paris, and Beverly Hills. Advocating a civil society and human rights in Egypt showed they were Western lackeys. They were even the real enemies of democracy because they dared ask Mubarak to act like a dictator and reverse a court decision!

Consequently, such people were really the ones who threatened to lead Egypt into an "age of darkness."[19]

Such intimidation was effective, at least for a while. A number of groups shifted their attention from domestic human rights to safer issues such as supporting the Palestinian intifada and condemning sanctions against Iraq.[20] In other words, groups that might otherwise criticize the governance of their own country and demand change were co-opted into being allies of the regime, furthering its trump issues and foreign policy agenda.

The government thus gained from persecuting Ibrahim even though in the end it lost its case. After two years of struggle and eight months in jail, Ibrahim and his codefendants were cleared by Egypt's highest court in May 2002. When the staff returned to their offices, the entire place was ransacked and empty, all its files, books, and computers kept by the government. Still, in celebrating his release, Ibrahim said the case should be a lesson encouraging intellectuals to fulfill their proper role in opposing tyranny.[21]

Yet, understandably, his unpleasant experience did not seem to inspire imitators, though the prodemocratic campaign in Egypt continued. On November 18, 2002, Egypt's five major opposition parties and ten civil society organizations formed the Committee for Defense of Democracy (CDD) and drafted an elaborate but gradual plan for constitutional and political reform. In 2003 and 2004 the CDD organized four rallies in Cairo that tried to present a petition to Mubarak calling for democracy and free elections, though no official would meet with them. On March 3, 2004, even the new Supreme Guide of the Muslim Brotherhood endorsed the demands contained in the CDD manifesto, though this statement was more likely to frighten the government than persuade it that reform was a good idea.[22]

In 2005, the regime announced—amid international congratulations— that opposition candidates would be allowed to run against Mubarak in the elections, and a license for the Tomorrow party was issued after a three-year struggle and four court cases. But Ayman Nour, a member of parliament and the party's leader, was quickly arrested and thrown into prison on trumped-up charges that he faked petition signatures. Posters appeared around the party's headquarters accusing the party of being an American agent.[23]

In fact, in the case of Ibrahim, Haider, Nour, and many others, the regime could be satisfied with its success in using trump issues—Islamism, anti-Zionism, anti-Americanism, and xenophobia—to impede anything more than the minimal openness routine in all but the most totalitarian societies. Groups and institutions that elsewhere would have demanded freedom—like students, professors, universities, and the press—instead endorsed repression. Even the masses seemed to be persuaded by demagoguery into applauding the restriction of their own rights and material welfare. Dissent would be channeled into safe, permissible areas—supporting the Palestinians, attacking Israel, criticizing the United States, upholding Islam—that did not threaten the system. The government then showed that it sided with these grievances, indeed was their true champion.

Thus, liberals and reformers have faced tremendous and effective intimidation from both governments and Islamists. Not only does this discourage them directly, but their opponents' passion drowns out their rational arguments and frightens others from joining them. For example, when the Moroccan writer al-Saleh Bu-Walid merely proposed on Al Jazeera television in July 2001 that Arabs should renew negotiations with Israel in order to achieve their goals, many callers threatened his life. One proclaimed that Bu-Walid was an enemy of Allah and that it was a religious duty to intimidate him. A second added that such scum were holding back the masses and should be sent to hell. A third remarked, "I think that he is actually a Jew." No caller supported Bu-Walid's position.[24]

More traditional methods were also used. The liberal Egyptian editor Ridha Hilal was kidnapped and presumably murdered in 2001. In November 2004 Tarek Halim Qandil, the well-known fifty-seven-year-old editor of the left-wing newspaper *Al-Arabi al-Nassiri*, was kidnapped after writing many articles opposing the succession of Mubarak's son as the next president. He was tortured and then thrown out completely naked from a speeding car into a Cairo street. Meanwhile the son of Mubarak, whose agents were probably behind this assault, portrayed himself as a champion of reform.

Any serious efforts to challenge the system have usually been blocked by the power of the society's taboos, constantly enforced and reinforced by governments, journalists, and intellectuals, while always backed up by the threat, or application, of repression. When one sees how effective a verbal assault can be mounted by just a single fearless liberal writer, though, it is easy to understand why such strong defenses are needed.

One such man is Ali Salem, a bald, powerfully built Egyptian playwright born in 1936. After apprenticing at a half-dozen trades, including running a puppet theater, he found his way to the regular stage, producing his first play in 1965. Among his two dozen plays and fifteen books were many with liberal themes, advocating humane reform and denouncing demagogues who promise quick solutions. In *School of the Troublemakers*, a 1971 comedy, a kind female teacher reforms a class of riotous teenagers. Another play is about a city that crowns as its king a man claiming to have slain a menacing monster only to discover that he was lying when the beast returns stronger than ever.[25] The plot parallels the way Arab rulers justify their reign by falsely insisting they have defeated the United States and Israel.

On May 24, 2001, the Union of Egyptian Writers expelled Salem because he supported normalization of relations with Israel, despite the fact that this had nominally been Egypt's policy for more than twenty years. Salem denounced the association as an instrument of the regime and not the servant of its own members. Nevertheless, he could no longer have his plays produced in Egypt. Salem's literary counterattack was a book on his 1994 trip to Israel that became a best-seller in Egypt, and he also cofounded the Cairo Peace Movement. After he wrote the screenplay with Ibrahim for a short film on elections, he was briefly arrested. Salem did not give up, but his effectiveness was severely limited.[26]

However bad the situation may have been in Egypt, in Syria it was far worse. While the movement in Egypt faced intimidation, its counterpart in Syria was crushed outright. Coming after such high hopes for change, this outcome was all the more demoralizing. Syria had briefly seemed ripe for a transition from dictatorship to a more open society. The regime of Hafiz al-Assad had literally wrecked the country. As happened elsewhere, liberals argued that reform was the only way out of the dilemma.[27]

The crisis manifested itself on every front. For example, Syria's Soviet-style economic structure led to stagnation. Such men as Nabil Sukkar, an economist who headed a Damascus consulting firm, and Rateb Shallah, president of the Federation of Syrian Chambers of Commerce and

Industry, warned that rapid reform was a necessity.[28] They posited just two alternatives: either Syria's rulers would reduce government control, unleash the country's able commercial sector, and attract investments by opting for peace and stability, or it would head straight into a huge crisis that could bring about the regime's collapse.

Saghiya even wrote a speech for Bashar in which the new leader could opt for reform on his own terms, promising democracy and freedom in these words:

> The arduous times that Syria went through necessitated a regime that is no longer needed. The world has changed and so have we, or at least we should, so as to find the time to [deal with] our real problems and compensate for the long years we were busy handling problems that withheld our progress.
>
> The Cold War has ended and sooner or later so will its Middle Eastern parallel. The [continuation of the conflict] is more harmful to us than it is to Israel, which is building a thriving technological economy while neutralizing its [internal] conflicts by the democratic means it has developed over decades.[29]

According to this scenario, Bashar would tell his people that Syrians must "live as a normal state in a normal region." He would then announce free elections, a multiparty system, the rule of law, the release of political prisoners, the end of emergency laws, the reduction of security controls, an anticorruption campaign, major economic reforms, and a reduced budget for the military which has not performed well in wars. He would pledge to withdraw from Lebanon. Once Syria took such stances, the world would support its position and Israel would be ready to make an acceptable deal.[30]

But Assad never made such a speech, largely because the reform option was not so attractive for him and his supporters as the liberals claimed. They viewed the economy's function in a different way from foreign observers and local businessmen. For them, the goal was not to provide higher living standards or more successful development but rather to enrich the elite and to ensure that the maximum possible resources were in its own hands and not those of potential rivals.

Regarding economic liberalization, Syria also has a unique problem. The Alawites—a relatively less-developed, non-Muslim minority group, but the government's main supporters—greatly benefit from regime patronage. The private businesses and entrepreneurial skills overwhelmingly belong, however, to the Sunni Muslim majority, which generally dislikes the regime. Thus, privatization and deregulation would weaken the regime's support base while giving more power and assets to those who would like to see it fall.

If prosperity required opening up the society to foreign influences and domestic freedom, this road—and not the route of continued militancy and dictatorship—seemed to the rulers to be the real highway to disaster. A Syrian merchant, expressing the frustration of his fellows, complained that the economic system was run so badly as to seem like a deliberate attempt to destroy the country's industry.[31] Yet this evaluation was not quite right. The government does not want to kill the goose that lays the golden eggs, but wants simply to ensure that it keeps most of the eggs for itself, even if that reduces overall egg production.

Consequently, the government's plan was quite different from the one recommended by the West and by Syria's domestic critics. The response, to change as little as possible, worked well enough to keep the regime going. For example, on the economic front, Syria's radical policies brought in money in some very nontraditional ways. Syrian domination of its neighbor, Lebanon, ensured lots of jobs for Syrian workers there at double the pay they received at home, and enriched Syria's elite through smuggling, counterfeiting, and drug production. Iran paid Damascus for helping Tehran's client in Lebanon, Hezbollah, so it could attack Israel from Lebanese soil. Profits were also made by helping Iraq circumvent international sanctions through state-sponsored smuggling. A steep rise in international oil prices in 2000 provided even more much-needed cash by increasing the value of Syria's exports.

As for political reform, the regime would ignore such ideas by making only the most microscopic, cosmetic changes. This intransigence discouraged dissent but also provided a safety valve for the disgruntled, maintained hope among its citizens, and fooled foreigners. The highest possible military budget would keep the generals happy and loyal. Inflaming the Arab-Israeli conflict continued to serve Syria's government in mobilizing mass support, silencing dissent, and providing an ideal excuse for keeping everything the same.

President Bashar al-Assad ridiculed the idea that there was a need to do anything differently from the way his father had done during his three-decade-long rule. He pronounced himself amazed, for example, that anyone could propose that the media might have any independent role in Syria. That was a Western notion, Assad explained, that did not work in a country where the leader shared power with no one.[32] In a statement full of unintentional irony, Bashar explained that Syria really did have freedom of speech and only the most dangerous dissidents were punished. After all, he told a Western interviewer, the regime did not have enough prisons to find space for all those who criticized it.[33]

This was the man who was supposedly going to break Syria's cycle of dictatorship. When his father, Hafiz, died in June 2000, the thirty-four-year-old Bashar was immediately elevated to the office. Syria's constitution, which required the president be at least forty years old, was quickly amended. Bashar then received 97.2 percent of the vote in an uncontested election. It was a very strange situation: a radical regime that had always rejected hereditary monarchy as the height of reactionary backwardness now openly treated Syria as a family fiefdom.

The idea that Bashar was a Western-educated reformer rested on very thin ice. He had spent only two years in Britain, studying medicine, when he was called home after his older brother Basil, the family's crown prince, fatally drove himself into a bridge abutment in 1994. As on-the-job training, Bashar's father put him in charge of Lebanon and made him a colonel in the elite Republican Guard. Many foreign observers portrayed Bashar as a moderate, modern guy because he was chairman of the Syrian Computer Society. In fact, however, the position had previously been held by his brutal playboy brother Basil, who no one thought of as any improvement over their father.

Ridiculing the idea that Bashar might bring reform, Muhammad al-Hasnawi, a Syrian dissident writer living in London, thought about the mother of a political prisoner jailed in Syria who wept when she heard of Bashar's succession. She understood that this meant nothing would change. Why did an illiterate woman have no illusions about the situation, Hasnawi wrote, while Syrian liberals who thought themselves fit to lead the country understood nothing?[34]

In his inaugural speech, Bashar was happy to let such people go on fooling themselves, though he also made clear his real intentions. True, he explained, the ruler needed constructive criticism and should examine different viewpoints. But there were limits to this process, and any solution must be in Syrian style because "we cannot apply the democracy of others to ourselves."[35]

Bashar did make some small changes. More than six hundred political prisoners, mostly Islamists held for twenty years, were released. One prison notorious for ill treatment and the military courts for trying civilians were closed. Bashar suggested that there be fewer pictures of himself or banners praising him in public places. Newspapers ran a few articles supporting reform, but only if the government decided what the reforms should be. Bashar met with several reformers and told them they could criticize the state on economic matters, but only if the state-run Syrian press was willing to print their complaints. Small parties allied with the regime were offered the possibility of opening their own newspapers but only under censorship and on the condition that they reflect the government line.[36]

Those interested in change, however, wanted more. In September 2000 a manifesto was published abroad signed by ninety-nine Syrian cultural and intellectual figures. It urged the regime to end the state of emergency and martial law in effect since 1963; pardon all political detainees and exiled dissidents; recognize freedom of assembly, speech, and press; and stop spying on the public.[37] Their goal was to establish a multiparty democracy and strong civil society. Only through political reform, they argued, could Syria deal with its problems. The state-run media refused even to mention the declaration, and the regime briefly imposed a ban on foreign newspapers that printed it. But no action was taken against the signatories themselves.

Encouraged by the apparent initiation of a new government-tolerated reform movement, more than a thousand Syrians, inside the country and abroad, signed a second manifesto in January 2001 that went even further than the first one. It directly urged the end of single-party rule and called for democratic elections under the supervision of an independent judiciary. Even the Muslim Brotherhood supported it.[38] Seventy Syrian lawyers signed another petition calling for the government to conduct political reforms, revoke emergency laws, and permit independent parties.[39]

Activists founded the National Dialogue Club, which held meetings at the home of Riyadh al-Seif, one of the few independent-minded members of parliament, to hear lectures on democracy and civil society. At a January 2001 gathering, the lecturer, Shibli al-Shami, an engineer, spoke words that would have been—almost literally—unthinkable a few months earlier: "Since 1958," he said, "the Syrian regime has been a dictatorship. The main problem is oppression. The oppression is from the inside." Defending the Western model, al-Shami stated, "The West is not bad." He personally had benefited from a good education in a British university. Rather, the evil in Syria stems from internal oppressors and repressors. He also stressed, though, that reformers should be patient and give the new leadership a chance to develop its programs.[40]

Bashar's planning minister could not even speak to the Syrian Society for Economic Science without Seif popping up from the audience, amid cheers from the crowd, to complain, "We have no transparency, no exact monetary figures, and no accountability. We don't have any development. We don't have dialogue. We don't have strong institutions. We have no anti-corruption campaign."[41]

Seif applied for permission to form a new party, to be called the Civil Peace Movement. At an organizational meeting of 350 people he criticized the one-party state, which used pan-Arab rhetoric to censure everyone else's ideas and to carry out failed radical socialist policies that damaged the economy. Five professors who were members of the ruling Baath party stood up to accuse him of collaborating with foreign elements.[42]

The regime's first line of defense was to let people know they had better stop this nonsense about civil society or face serious consequences. Bashar also made his view clear: whatever the reformers' intentions, the fact that their ideas would produce disaster meant they were guilty of the most dangerous crimes against the fatherland.[43] Turki Saqr, editor of the ruling party's newspaper, said the reformers merely represented one more wave in the imperialist assault on Syria, trying to force their anti-Arab ideas on the people.[44] The Arab Writers' Association, in Syria as in Egypt a Stalinist-style government front group, published an article claiming that Syria's four-thousand-year-old [sic] Arab culture already had enough civil society.[45]

From the regime's standpoint, the reform movement was not a group of people trying to make Syria better, stronger, and more prosperous but a malignant movement threatening national survival. To some extent, its fears were genuine. In a meeting of regime loyalists at Damascus University, Vice President Abd al-Halim Khaddam insisted that no citizen has a right to destroy the very foundations of his own society. He warned that reforms would push Syria toward a breakdown like that occurring in Algeria, which faced a bloody uprising after the regime blocked Islamists from winning an election, or Yugoslavia, which was torn apart by ethnic strife when the heavy hand of dictatorship was removed.[46] These two examples embodied the regime's fear that greater freedom would lead either to an Islamist takeover or to a communal civil war.

Seif's call for a pluralist democracy taking into account the needs of the country's different religions and ethnic groups especially horrified the regime, which worried that the Sunni majority would overthrow the Alawite-dominated system and perhaps even massacre their community. Leading government and Baath party officials warned that such talk would destroy the country's stability and lead to catastrophe.[47]

According to Khaddam, himself a Sunni, pluralism was a Western plot to shatter countries by demanding self-determination for their ethnic groups. Any such step would set off a civil war within the country.[48] While the regime's intention was to maintain a ruling minority group's privileged status, there were good reasons for concern, as the post-Saddam violence among Iraqi communities would show, though Iraq might also demonstrate how democratic pluralism could solve these problems.

As always, manipulating the Arab-Israeli conflict was one of the regime's main ways to stifle dissent. Knowing this, the reformers carefully avoided mentioning that issue and put the focus on domestic affairs. it was too dangerous to suggest that peace with Israel would be beneficial for Syria. But the reformers' desire to avoid discussing the issue was nevertheless used against them to hint that they were Zionist agents.[49] Ali Diyab, head of the Baath party's Foreign Affairs Bureau, scolded that no issue in Syria could be discussed without reference to the conflict. Anything that strengthened Syria's ability to fight was good; anything that created internal divisions or detracted from the primacy of this battle merely served the enemy.[50]

So when even Baath party members asked Khaddam at a public meeting why the regime did not do more to solve the problems of corruption, incompetence, and the slow pace of reform, his answer was that the Arab-Israeli conflict permitted no changes at home. "This country is in a state of war as long as the occupation continues," agreed Information Minister Adnan Omran. "You have threats coming against Syria every day, and the capital is only sixty miles from the front line."[51]

The irony of this argument, however, was that the regime itself now had the power to end the conflict whenever it wanted to do so. In exchange for peace, in 2000 Syria had been offered by Israel the return of every square inch of the Golan Heights. Was the issue preventing a diplomatic resolution Syria's demand for twelve square miles of additional land on Israel's side of the international border, or was the endless state of war really the government's insurance policy against domestic problems?

Instead of dealing with Syria's real issues, the rulers seized every opportunity to parade their own patriotic demagoguery and steadfastness. Bashar roared, "An inch of land is like a kilometer and that in turn is like a thousand kilometers. A country that concedes even a tiny part of its territory is bound to concede a much bigger part in the future. . . . Land is an issue of honor not meters." He added that this was his inheritance: "President Hafiz al-Assad did not give in," boasted Bashar, "and neither shall we; neither today nor in the future."[52]

Nor would he give up to the demands for reform. In January 2001, Information Minister Omran proclaimed that, like ethnic pluralism, *civil society* was an "American term." Noting that Ibrahim was then on trial in Egypt for being a subversive agent in the pay of foreign governments, Omran explained that "neocolonialism no longer relies on armies." The implication was that Syrian reformers were traitors and might soon find themselves in the courtroom on trial. The very next day, one of the civil society committees' main organizers, the novelist Nabil Sulayman, was attacked by two assailants and badly beaten.[53]

The government reminded the public that martial law made it illegal for more than five people to gather for a political meeting without a permit. To obtain a permit, security agencies must be given two weeks' notice of any gathering, the speaker's name, a copy of the speech, and a complete list of attendees. Bashar explained that any change would take a very long time, concluding, "The development of civil society institutions is not one of my priorities."[54]

The serious and immediate reform challenge was basically ended for some years. As'ad Naim, an exiled Syrian scholar, thought that many reformers, being insiders who had benefited from the regime in the past, would go back to supporting the government, and he bitterly predicted that his countrymen might soon return to the same kind of lives they had endured for thirty years.[55] This is precisely what seemed to be happening. A critical opportunity for progress had been thrown away. Syria seemed set to keep following all the ideas, policies, and leaders that had served it so badly for so long.

By March 2002 the regime felt secure enough to sentence both Seif and Ma'moun al-Homsi, a dissident member of parliament, to five years' imprisonment. As Seif was taken away to serve his sentence he shouted, "This is a badge of honor to me and others like me. Long live the people!"[56] Like Seif, who owned the Syrian franchise of Adidas sportswear, Homsi was no naive academic but a successful self-made businessman, a living example of the prodemocratic role that might be played by a bourgeoisie disgusted by waste, incompetence, corruption, and bureaucratic mismanagement. Homsi was charged with trying to change the constitution by illegal means, with the evidence being a manifesto he wrote urging the authorities to rein in the security services and end high-level corruption.[57]

The former head of Damascus University's economics department, Aref Dahla, was sentenced to ten years in prison for dissident activity. New crimes were invented to keep up with technological advances. Thus, a state security court in Damascus sentenced three people to prison terms ranging from two to four years after they sent material on Syria to a Gulf Internet publication. They were accused of "transmitting to a foreign country information which should have stayed secret," of "writing articles banned by the government and damaging to Syria and its ties with a foreign state," and "publishing false information."[58]

There was still a little reform activity and a great deal of grumbling, expressed in private and in the foreign Arab press. In March 2004 twenty Syrians held a demonstration outside parliament and organized an Internet petition drive, with several thousand people signing, calling for the abolition of military law; an end to arbitrary arrest; the release of political prisoners; and the right to establish political parties and civil associations.[59]

In Saudi Arabia, liberals are effectively managed in keeping with that society's own distinctive style. One day in the spring of 2003, the religious police pulled in a reporter from *Al-Watan*, a newspaper in the southern city of Abha. Sent to their central office in Riyadh, he was questioned by Inspector Abu Abd al-Aziz, who complained that the reporter's long hair made him look like a homosexual and must be cut immediately. When the reporter refused, the police forced him to watch the beating of another prisoner. The journalist gave in and, to complete his humiliation, had to pay for the haircut. He was then threatened with a charge of "lusting after girls by the school gates" but was told that he could save himself by informing against fellow reporters. He was urged to accuse them of engaging in dangerous secular activities and the "intermingling of male and female employees."[60]

Why all this trouble over a reporter for a provincial newspaper? Because *Al-Watan* was an island of liberalism in a royal sea of centralized control. Shortly after the reporter's harassment, in May 2003, the Information Ministry ordered the firing of the newspaper's editor, Jamal Khashoggi, who had held the post for only three months. Under Saudi law, the government approves the hiring and firing of all editors, a symbol of its tight control over the media.[61] Khashoggi, a tall man with a trim beard and a pale, moon-shaped face, was a veteran journalist who had covered the Afghan insurgency against the Soviets, where he had become friendly with bin Laden, though he rejected his turn toward international terror.[62]

It should not be thought, however, that *Al-Watan* had been so bold as to criticize the regime. Far from being the organ of liberal rebels, the newspaper was owned by the Saudi prince then serving as provincial governor. Crown Prince Abdallah had laid the cornerstone of its office building, and its board of directors was headed by Prince Bandar bin Khaled al-Faisal. Aside from publishing articles supporting such basic rights for women as letting them drive automobiles, the newspaper had merely warned about the dangers of religious extremism. It ran an article by Khashoggi criticizing ibn Taymiya,[63] the extremists' favorite medieval theologian, and published caricatures linking Islamists with terrorism.[64]

"It's time," warned Khashoggi, "we treated the affliction and held those who strayed accountable."[65] Like other liberals, he claimed that such actions were needed to defend the regime from the Islamist radicals who were the real threats to the country's stability, a point made especially clear by the May 12, 2003, bombings that killed thirty-four people in Riyadh.

Aside from the religious police, Khashoggi's main detractors had been pro–bin Laden Web sites. Bin Laden's supporters had gone so far as to parody *Al-Watan*'s (The homeland) logo as *Al-Wathan* (The pagan idol).[66] While the newspaper had displeased the regime, the official campaign against it was intended to appease hard-line Islamists to keep them from joining an antiregime rebellion. In other words, the monarchy rejected the liberals' offer of alliance against bin Laden's followers, preferring to propitiate the most conservative elements in society, the ones who were closer to supporting bin Laden. At best, Khashoggi's firing was a way to balance the dismissal of some extremist clerics from official positions following the bombings.[67]

Turki al-Hamad, a Saudi political scientist and newspaper columnist who was receiving death threats and accusations of blasphemy after writing a novel that hard-liners found offensive, suggested that Islamist terrorists would consider Khashoggi's firing as a victory for themselves. "It's like an invitation for more attacks."[68] While people like Hamad could still write for the Saudi-owned, London-based *Al-Sharq al-Awsat*, which had emerged as a liberal voice after September 11, other Saudi liberals lost their columns in newspapers published within the country. Khashoggi himself went to London to work there for a more moderately minded Saudi prince.

Like its Arab nationalist counterparts in Syria and Egypt, the Saudi regime had its own set of antiliberal arguments, often paralleling the others but depending more on religious justifications. For example, Dr. Fadhel Alha, of the University of Riyadh's Department of Islamic Preaching and Communications, explained that the liberal notion of freedom is an illusion. According to Islam, he said, God liberated man from the arbitrary laws of other humans by enslaving him to divine law.[69] This proper form of enslavement was what Saudi Arabia represented, and such God-given regulations neither could, nor should, be altered. Such remains the Saudi kingdom's ideological foundation.

This did not mean, however, that the regime and its supporters had any intention of surrendering to the revolutionary Islamists, who claimed that their own interpretation of divine commandments was superior to that of the rulers. When radical Islamists began a war of terrorism in Saudi Arabia in 2003, it forced the regime to move against the extremists threatening it. Some clerics favoring the rebels were fired or pressured into recanting. Crown Prince Abdallah appeared on Saudi television following a major terrorist attack and called those responsible "devoid of all Islamic and humane principles."[70] But the rulers believed that a combination of repression and the proper religious line—not reform—would bring them victory. Such a strategy seems workable, despite the criticism by Western observers and Saudi reformers.

True, there was talk from the regime about legal reform, elections, and equal treatment for the Shia minority. In 2005 Saudi Arabia, though not for the first time, held elections for half the seats in local councils—the other half were appointed—in a men-only balloting. Each statement was hailed in the international media with predictions of more to come, because that is what Westerners considered the natural and inescapable direction of history. In their view there was no way the Saudi people would not see democracy as a better system; undoubtedly reform would defuse extremism—certainly it was the inevitable wave of the future. In this vein, the Western media have frequently reported that many Saudis clearly see the need for democratic reform if the regime is to survive. Vague pledges to make changes were seized upon as proof that this was happening.[71]

Consequently, it was easy to exaggerate the amount of reform being undertaken and the number of people supporting liberal change. For example, according to an April 30, 2003, *New York Times* article, "Political reform is now judged by many princes, merchants, tribal leaders and Saudi military officials as essential to the survival of the government. . . . Many members of the royal household understand that . . . a restive population of young Saudis for whom there is little work, little wealth and no political participation is pressing relentlessly for change."[72]

But is it really true that so many Saudis see things this way or believe that liberal reforms would strengthen the kingdom? That is doubtful, and in fact remarkably little change has taken place. The regime's claim that reform would be destabilizing, creating a demand for more concessions or bringing a dangerous violent reaction from conservatives, was apparently accepted by many. Equally, promises of even minor reforms from Saudi officials have been repeatedly made and not kept.

It is often forgotten that in Egypt Nasser had promised more democracy in 1968 and Sadat had made similar statements in 1974 without anything ever changing. Maintaining the status quo, at least for a long time, continues to be a viable option for the Saudi, Egyptian, Syrian, and other Arab regimes, with minor cosmetic changes being allowed mainly to hide that reality.

Nor is any element of even the limited progress that does occur necessarily irreversible. For example, Crown Prince Khalid bin Saqr al-Qassimi, the UAE's deputy ruler and for many years heir to the throne in its Ras al-Khaimah emirate, was removed from these posts by his brothers in June 2003 at least partly because he was deemed too sympathetic to reform. He had been the first UAE leader to call for free elections with an equal role for women, and his own wife, Fawqai al-Qassimi, was a playwright and women's rights activist.[73]

Violence was always a last resort. In December 2003 a letter bomb was sent to Ahmad al-Jarallah, the editor and owner of Kuwait's *Al-Siyassa* newspaper, injuring his secretary. This was the fourth assassination attempt against him. He termed the attack "a response to what I have been writing against terrorists and extremists in the Arab world." He had been a supporter of the U.S.-led war in Iraq and a strong critic of Islamists and Syria's government which, he warned, would meet the same fate as Iraq's overthrown regime if it did not mend its ways.[74]

This is not to say that there have been no reform accomplishments in the Arab world, but they have been remarkably rare and highly concentrated in the Persian Gulf monarchies, mainly Kuwait, Bahrain, and Qatar. It is ironic that these most politically reactionary of Arab states have now become the most progressive. Yet this is probably due to the fact that they never achieved a form of calcified modernization as Arab nationalist dictatorships. The conservative monarchies proved to be more flexible than the ideologically set, Soviet-style mobilization states unwilling to share power with anyone.

That Qatar did so much was especially interesting, since it shared the conservative form of Wahhabi Islam with its Saudi neighbors, a demonstration that a society of believers in that branch of Islam was not innately reactionary. In April 2003 Qatari citizens voted on a constitution that gave legislative powers to a forty-five-member parliament, two-thirds of which would be elected. The emir's veto power would be like that of a U.S. president. Qatar had already given women the right to vote and run for office in 1999. A week after the constitution was accepted, the emir appointed the first female minister in any Gulf state. Qatar's other activities have included hosting the U.S. Central Command headquarters and sponsoring the radical nationalist, anti-American Al-Jazeera television station.[75]

In Bahrain, too, there were fair, multiparty elections in October 2002, despite a history of unrest from the majority Shia Muslims against the minority Sunni-controlled government.[76] The opposition was legalized and security forces curbed. Kuwait also had periodic free and fair elections following its liberation from Iraqi rule, with Islamists doing well but not gaining control of parliament.

The system there allowed more openness while setting strict limits. After the human rights activist Almezel Abdul Hadi al-Khawaja criticized the prime minister in a public lecture in October 2004, he was arrested, tried, and sentenced to one year in prison for "inciting hatred of the regime by publicly calling it corrupt." His Bahrain Center for Human Rights was disbanded. Within hours of the sentencing, however, he was pardoned by the country's monarch. Khawaja then stated that he would continue his efforts on behalf of human rights. An undertone to the affair was that Khawaja, who had recently returned to the country after twenty-two years living in Europe, was a member of the Shia Muslim majority in a country ruled by a Sunni Muslim dynasty. Thus, either repressing him or allowing him to speak freely became immediately entangled in potentially explosive sectarian issues.[77]

These are exceptions, however, and limited ones at that. In contrast, consider Jordan, rightly seen as one of the most moderately ruled Arab states. In an article for a Western newspaper, Foreign Minister Marwan Muasher explained that the Arab world must "take the initiative" in becoming more democratic. This cannot happen overnight, of course, he insisted and forcing the pace could lead to radicalization. Pressure from the United States to do so is "alienating Arabs and jeopardizing the efforts of genuine reformers, who now cannot advocate democracy without being accused of doing America's bidding." But the Arab world is ready to manage this transition itself. How do we know? Because, Muasher explains, Jordan's king and queen have endorsed the UN Arab Human Development Report![78]

But was this sufficient? Jordanians elected a new parliament in 2003, choosing mostly progovernment representatives. The elections were honest but unfair. After the prime minister had dissolved the previous parliament two years earlier, he had decreed dozens of "temporary laws" that limited free speech, tightened press controls, and gerrymandered districts to ensure the regime's victory. Amman, with a higher proportion of oppositionists, had about one parliament member for every 52,000 voters compared to one for every 6,000 people in Kerak, a regime stronghold. The number of seats was expanded from 80 to 110, giving more power to progovernment areas. As a result, Islamists received only 17 out of 110 seats, far fewer than they might have won in a fair system.[79] But if Islamists were to win, the result would be hardly conducive to stability or holding any future elections, much less the changes required to raise living standards and expand civic rights.

The main concern of Jordan's government seemed to be to appease the Islamists without giving them any real power, while making empty promises of more consultation and partnership.[80] At the same time, though, Jordanians do enjoy more freedom than most other Arabs. It is probable that this greater openness provides an escape valve reducing the level of Islamist violence in Jordan.

Jordan, then, is more of a democracy in appearance than in practice since its elections are not fair reflections of the population's views. In theory, parliament can dismiss the prime minister and cabinet; in practice, the opposite is more likely to happen. All the Senate's members are appointed by the king. The legislature is dominated by opponents of reform, either because they are instruments of the regime or radical Islamists.

Thus, the barriers raised against reform are extremely high in the Arab world. A close examination shows that less change was taking place than it might appear and that the liberals' arguments are not easily accepted by either rulers or the masses. When the Soviet bloc collapsed and it seemed that Arab regimes had no alternative but to conclude that such dictatorial, statist systems failed, the respected Egyptian thinker Fuad Zakaria sighed, "Do not be optimistic. In our country, no one ever learns lessons."[81]

4

What's Wrong with Arab Society?

The Arab liberals' most impressive achievement has been to provide a thoroughgoing critique of what is wrong with Arab society. This is such a persuasive indictment that one must remember it is also a relatively rarely heard one in an Arab world flooded by a sea of official statements, self-congratulatory proclamations, calls to militancy, and claims of victimization by outside villains. As a result, many Arab liberals show a profound frustration at their inability to convince others of what to them seems so obvious.

One of the most compelling such analyses is that by the Paris-based al-Afif al-Akhdar, a Tunisian intellectual. It is no accident that this essay appeared only on a liberal Web site—albeit the most important one, Middle East Transparent. Akhdar, formerly a columnist for *Al-Hayat*, had been fired by its owner, Saudi Prince Sultan bin Abd al-Aziz, after an October 2002 television interview in which he called the Saudi regime barbaric for amputating criminals' limbs—a punishment sanctioned by Islamic law—and its treatment of women.[1]

Born into a family of poor peasants in 1934, Akhdar studied law in Tunisia and then went to Paris in 1961, becoming an adviser to Algeria's left-wing government. Forced to leave Algeria after a coup against his employers, he lived in Amman and Beirut, where he wrote a number of books focusing on a critique of Islam. During the 1960s and 1970s he was close to Palestinian Marxist groups. When Lebanon's civil war began in the mid-1970s, he returned to Paris.

Everyone in the world, Akhdar complained, seemed to be advancing toward modernity, knowledge, and globalization while the Arabs were racing in the opposite direction. Whereas Eastern Europe rejected communist dictatorship in exchange for peaceful, rapid progress toward democracy and economic development, in the Arab world one blood-thirsty dictatorship succeeds another. While other peoples progress, the Arab regimes move from "backwardness into sub-backwardness and from poverty into sub-poverty" in a sort of antiprogress.[2]

The causes of this sad fate are multiple to say the least. "Why is it," he asked, that the Arab world is so wealthy in natural resources and so poor in human resources? Why does human knowledge elsewhere steadily grow while in the Arab world what spreads instead

> is illiteracy, ideological fear, and mental paralysis? Why do expressions of tolerance, moderation, rationalism, compromise, and negotiation horrify us, but [when we hear] fervent cries for vengeance, we all dance the war dance? Why have the people of the world managed to mourn their pasts and move on, while we have . . . our gloomy bereavement over a past that does not pass? Why do other people love life, while we love death and violence, slaughter and suicide, and call it heroism and martyrdom?[3]

Akhdar's answer, in brief, is the contradiction so central to the Arab self-image and worldview. On one hand, Arabs suffer from an inferiority complex, a sense of failure, self-hatred, and "national humiliation whose shame can be purged only by blood, vengeance, and fire." On the other hand, there is a sense of superiority at believing they are designated by God to lead humanity. Why would they want to borrow anything from the rest of the world which is both their oppressor and inferior?[4]

The Qur'an called Arabs the "best nation" among humanity. Yet history has contradicted this self-image, from Napoleon's easy conquest of Egypt in 1799 to the Arabs' repeated defeats by Israel two centuries later. Wounds from these events joined with a "deep-rooted culture of tribal vengefulness" to create "a fixated, brooding, vengeful mentality" driving out "far-sighted thought and self-criticism." The Arabs have failed to understand, as Japan did after its disastrous defeat in World War II, the "vital necessity to emulate the enemy . . . becoming like him in modern knowledge, thought and politics, so as to reshape the traditional personality and adapt it to the requirements of the time."[5]

By rejecting the West in general, Akhdar continues, Arab politics lost the chance to adapt such positive Western innovations as pragmatism in setting goals, strategy, and tactics; analyzing the balance of power in a detached manner; managing crises through negotiated compromises;

and building a rational decision-making process. Instead, public discussion is dismissed and negotiation is rejected both in domestic and foreign issues.[6]

That dead-end approach feeds the Arab world's obsession, what Akhdar calls "this insane obsession with vengeance" against the West and Israel, which has made reasonable thought impossible. Rather than learning from experience, people have curled "up within themselves like frightened snails, to brood about their dark thoughts" of revenge. They tried to lash back at others by adopting suicidal policies that injured themselves, blundering "from one destructive war into the next, much fiercer war." The Arab world became virtually the sole place on the globe incapable of identifying its real problems and priorities. Akhdar warns, "This is your last chance, O masters of the missed opportunity."[7]

This deliberate closing off from the world, rejecting ideas as threatening precisely because they came from elsewhere, was called self-imposed ghettoism by the Lebanese professor Radwan al-Sayyed.[8] Among its elements, explains an Arab diplomat writing under a pseudonym, is a mentality that "concentrates on the past, lives in it, and longs to return to it." Justifying positions on public issues by claiming one has divine authority inevitably brings intolerance and violent struggle. In contrast, the Western approach to religious matters is flexible, focusing on spirit rather than narrow adherence to texts. There, religion is a personal matter, and no one is supposed to harass others in its name.[9]

"A society that lives in a state of internal fear," he concludes, "avoids investigating its causes" or learning from different cultures. A society that blames all its problems on others "cannot escape from being encased in its shell." Successful societies are neither ashamed nor harmed by exposing their problems and making changes. On the contrary, such behavior allows them to improve themselves.[10]

A parallel analysis comes from Tarek Heggy. Born in Port Said, Egypt, in 1950, he studied law and management at Ain Shams in Cairo and Geneva University. Becoming an expert on international petroleum, Heggy taught at several Arab and U.S. universities. He also enjoyed a successful business career at the Shell Oil Company, where he rose to become director of Middle East operations in 1988. Eight years later he resigned to manage his own petroleum company and dedicate himself to the cause of reform, writing many books and articles on almost every aspect of the subject.

This background gives Heggy a useful combination of characteristics for such a mission. From business, he learned pragmatic decision making and management techniques, holding no illusions about the viability of the state socialism propounded with such poor results by Arab nationalist regimes. While secular, he is a serious student of Islam. He is wealthy enough to be independent-minded and well connected enough with the regime to be able to speak his mind. The problem, of course, as with many Arab liberals, is that these are not characteristics shared by most of his intellectual counterparts, much less his broader audience.

Heggy clearly states the dilemma of the Arab world's future: Is Arab society refusing reform, development, and modernization only because it perceives them as being imposed by foreign interference or does it reject them in principle?[11] A key element blocking the Arab world from taking such steps by itself, Heggy says, is the lack of a concept of compromise, an idea for which there is no equivalent word in Arabic and one generally associated with humiliation rather than as a clever way to maximize the advantages for both sides in a dispute. Arab history, Heggy recounts, largely consists of defeats that could have been avoided "had we not persistently rejected the notion of compromise as tantamount to submission, retreat, surrender, capitulation and . . . bondage to the will of others."[12]

"This all-or-nothing mentality is self-defeating," Heggy adds, because it means conflicts continue, often with the Arabs in a losing position, consuming resources and blocking progress on other fronts. It is often impossible to get everything you want, especially if you are the weaker side in a dispute. Nothing good can come from the "rigid refusal to consider the merits of anyone else's opinion and to insist on obtaining all one's demands."[13]

That kind of approach led to defeat in Palestine, where the Arab leadership first rejected a 1937 British proposal to give the Arabs 80 percent of the land and then a 1947 UN resolution granting them 45 percent. A similar suicidal policy drove Yasir Arafat's rejection of a negotiated solution a half-century later that threw away the chance for a Palestinian state and launched a new war leading to a worsening of the Palestinians' situation. Thus, too, Syria rejected an Israeli offer in 2000 to exchange all the Syrian land it captured in 1967 for full peace. Similarly, instead of becoming a prosperous country, Iraq turned into one of the world's most repressive states, wasting huge amounts of wealth on unneeded wars, even using chemical weapons against its own citizens.[14] In Heggy's view, this pattern epitomizes the wrong turn taken by Arab thought.

To the Westerner, in contrast, compromise is an acceptable alternative in any dispute. Such philosophers as Jeremy Bentham, William James, and John Dewey argued that systems, laws, institutions, and ideas should be judged based on how well they work and must be changed if they do not meet this test. That idea, Heggy notes, has spread throughout the world. The Western approach does contain many dangers. It can be used to justify a general assault on tradition, high standards, and all the good things of the past. Without this basic tool, however, everything bad about the status quo can be justified and make progress impossible.

Heggy decries Arab thinking as based not on present-day realities but obsolete clichés and slogans that are regarded as ultimate truths not challengeable by reason, science, or any test of success.[15] One proof of Arab thought's inadequacy, according to Heggy, is its rejection by the rest of the world. This argument is the exact opposite of the mainstream Arab intellectuals' assertion that the outside world's opposition proves the correctness of their thinking. In this view, the West should be ignored because it is a hostile force seeking to subvert the Arab nation and Islam. And if any Arab or Muslim agrees with the West, that only proves him to be a foreign lackey who should be ignored or punished.

Heggy, however, pulls no punches:

> We have dug ourselves into a cave, cut off from the rest of humanity thanks to a static mind-set that ignores the realities of our time and the new balances of power. . . . We remain locked in a fantasy world of our own making . . . a world in which anachronistic slogans are still widely regarded as sacrosanct, immutable constants. This has resulted not only in our growing isolation from the outside world and in alienating our former allies, but in a disastrous internal situation marked by a pattern of lost opportunities and a climate inimical to democracy and development.

The solution requires a very different kind of society, encouraging citizen participation and open debate, allowing those best equipped to lead the way toward progress. Equality for women is absolutely essential, since otherwise the contribution of half the citizens is lost.[16]

But who is going to lead in creating such a new society? Elsewhere in the world, groups composed of students, intellectuals, businesspeople, professionals, and members of the working class have been the motive power driving democratic change. In the Arab world, though, the proletariat has remained insignificant. Businesspeople are largely dependent on the government for patronage and are often partners in the regimes' corrupt practices. Intellectuals are servants of the rulers, wedded to ideologies that justify the regimes' policies. Professionals—lawyers, engineers, and doctors—fit all these categories and are frequently Islamists as well.

Much of the intelligentsia became public employees, part of the dictatorial regimes rather than independent thinkers or a true opposition. In Heggy's words, they are "almost completely subservient [bearers of] outdated slogans that have been discredited in every part of the world." Few intellectuals are thoroughly familiar with the great Western works, or even the classics of Arab philosophy, for that matter. Inasmuch as they have absorbed foreign social science, it is mainly its most doctrinaire aspects—Marxism, anticapitalism, cultural cynicism, the radical critique of democracy, postmodernism—which are used as one more tool to shore up their Arab nationalist or Islamist views. Instead of promoting "a cultural climate and system of values in keeping with the requirements of the age," writes Heggy, they have instead created "an intellectually barren and culturally stagnant landscape which has moved Egypt further away from its dream of catching up with the developed world than it was at the beginning of the twentieth century."[17]

Democracy is the key missing idea whose absence has brought this tragic outcome, explains Shafiq Ghabra. It is not the people who block progress, but the rulers who rely on power rather than reason, on slogans rather than action, on tribal solidarity rather than law, and on the enforcement of conformity rather than diversity.[18]

The Egyptian Usama al-Ghazali Harb, a professor and editor of *Al-Siyassa al-Dawliya*, agrees. Ordinary people, who speak in "timid whispers," know the status quo is very wrong. The intellectuals have become the enemy of freedom, exhorting everyone else to swallow the official line. Internal decay, not foreign threats, is the Arab world's fundamental problem. The best way for Arabs to defend themselves is by establishing democratic societies and legitimate systems of government. Despotism weakens a nation's ability to resist outside challenges rather than the other way around. But no one ever shouted out these truths until the West "came to knock on our doors and break into our homes demanding that we institute democracy."[19]

Up to that point, with fading prospects for a more open society, most Arab intellectuals hoped instead that a more militant regime or ideology would solve all their problems. In fact, though, Arab rulers and their repressive regimes have made things even worse. Hardly anyone considered going in the opposite direction, completely rejecting the premises they have long accepted and in turn taught others.

How could people know better since there was no country in the Arab world to serve as a model? Amal Dunqal, an Egyptian poet, was sitting in Cairo's Café Rish one day in the 1970s talking to a young journalist who was leaving Egypt to work in Baghdad. The journalist explained that he was leaving because there was no freedom in Cairo. Suddenly Dunqal shouted at him, "My brother, you sit here and curse Sadat and you think that in Baghdad you will be permitted to curse even the deputy manager of a post office?"[20]

How have Arab regimes and their vocal supporters remained in power and dominated the debate with so little dissent, at least of the democratic variety, for so many decades? The key factor has been their ability to deflect blame outward, to use the claim of victimization by the West and Israel as a way to mobilize everyone behind the dictator to battle these dreadful foes. Any other issue or concern becomes secondary, even harmful, as a distraction from that life-and-death battle. At any rate, no one need examine Arab shortcomings regarding religion, society, economy, or governance, because the real problem is imperialism.

This formula was well summarized by Abd al-Mun'im Sa'id, director of the Al-Ahram Center for Political and Strategic Studies: "Building is a long and arduous process; blaming others has always been easy and costs nothing. Denial is easy, whereas assuming responsibility is extremely difficult. After all, who wants to look at themselves in the mirror and see the truth?"[21]

In a remarkable column sarcastically titled "Long Live Dictatorship," published in a UAE newspaper, the journalist Abdallah Rashid fearlessly looked into the mirror and pointed out the considerable mass support for the existing system. The world simply cannot understand the Arabs, he explains, who act as if they come from another planet. Do the Arabs really want freedom, he asks, or do they prefer to live in "the dungeon of repression, pleased and satisfied with handcuffs on their wrists, bonds of steel on their ankles, and prisoner's collars about their necks?"[22]

It appears, he continues, as if the Arabs have become addicted to living under dictatorships. Their intellectuals curse the United States continuously for trying to establish democracy in Iraq but don't care that the Iraqi people want that system. Democracy is portrayed as a greater horror than dictatorship. In conclusion, Rashid asks, "Has the worship of a dictator and of oppression become the foundation of Arab thought and culture?"[23] The reader is left in little doubt that the answer is yes.

Still the question remains: why have the Arabs been so incapable of achieving democracy? A weak educational system is one factor Arab liberals often identify as a cause of this situation. Instead of schooling that encourages creativity and tolerance, Arab education is seen as merely indoctrination for supporting the existing system and extremist ideologies; it fails to prepare young people with skills needed for progress. As Anton al-Maqdasi, a Syrian political philosopher, complained, the apparent goal is to make citizens as identical as possible in their ideas and views, "as if they were cast in the same mold."[24]

Yet, liberals warn, instead of ensuring that everyone loves the dictator, radical ideas purveyed in the schools—anti-American, anti-Western, anti-Zionist, rejecting compromise, glorifying violence, offering extremist interpretations of Islam—push students toward revolutionary activity. Ironically, the system intended to control young people's minds has turned them against the very regime that educates them. Thus, liberals argue, rulers should support reform as a way of ensuring that young people do not rebel but instead become more productive in economic and scientific terms.

But while some governments have made limited modifications in the way Islam is taught in order to reduce the likelihood that students follow bin Laden, they reject any thoroughgoing changes toward modernization and away from indoctrination.[25] The Kuwaiti journalist Hamid al-Hamoud complained that rather than see the September 11 attacks as a wake-up call for reexamining the education system, Arab leaders have gone into a defensive mode. They reject the idea that the way students were taught pushed them toward "fanaticism and hatred" rather than acceptance of democracy, moderate Islam, or "modern human culture."[26]

The underlying problem is that the rulers know that any change undermines them. The regimes are eager to stop their subjects from criticizing, much less attacking, themselves, but hope to deflect their anger onto foreigners and even against domestic liberals. A free press means criticism of a system vulnerable to complaint; an anticorruption effort undermines the elite's income and attacks its mechanism for bribing key social groups to ensure their support. As a Syrian dissident asked, How can one monitor corruption without seeing that it involves the entire regime and all its officials, no matter what their rank?[27]

For example, in June 2002, Syria's Zeyzoun Dam collapsed just five years after being built. Five villages were destroyed, and dozens of people were killed. For forty years, wrote a dissident on an opposition Web site, the government has abrogated freedoms, imposed emergency laws, and killed tens of thousands of its own citizens on the pretext of leading a battle against foreign enemies. Yet it cannot solve the simplest domestic problems. Even the armed forces, on which so much money is spent, are effective only in killing Syria's own citizens. The real dam that must fall down is the regime itself, because as long as it stands, the Syrian people will never obtain either liberty or honor.[28]

As the Syrian writer notes, the struggle against imperialism and Zionism is the rationale used to uphold the status quo and to reject change. Yet it is in the waging of these largely fictitious struggles that the conflict is both sustained and lost. Xenophobic demagoguery has been very effective for Arab rulers and the intellectuals who do their ideological work. They merely have to say "Palestine," "Iraq," "Israel," "the United States," or slogans invoking these emotionally loaded terms, to quash discussion of any other subject.

For shock value, a very few bold liberals are ready to challenge this worldview directly, even citing Israel as a model for the Arab world. The Egyptian playwright Ali Salem, in a book on his visit to Israel that became a big seller in his own country, describes seeing an Israeli boy handing out bumper stickers calling for Israel to stay in the Golan Heights. For

Salem, the fascinating detail was that the boy didn't scream at drivers who disagreed with him that they must be enemy agents.[29]

Arabs should teach their own children, Salem observes, that people have the right to hold differing views as long as they don't act violently: "Let ideas do combat with each other, theory against theory, for the benefit of the nation." In the current Arab reality, though, only a single party and ideology are permitted, justifying its monopoly by claiming to be noble and pure. As a result, people die and kill one another for no reason except the stupid ideas inculcated by the system. He writes, tongue in cheek, that the regimes got rid of human rights but brought the benefit of making several hundred thousand people dead, wounded, or refugees. They enriched the Arab world by creating widows, bereaved parents, and orphans, as well as "relieving the Arab nation of the burden of governing a great deal of real estate."[30]

How can this dreadful situation be changed? Akhdar, like Heggy, says the Arabs need a pragmatic, rather than a nationalist or Islamist, worldview. Otherwise they will continue to make fatal miscalculations that include: "the inability to read rationally the balance of powers before entering any given struggle . . . the deluded belief that divine intervention in history will produce results contrary to the laws of the balance of powers. Finally [there is] the suicidal madness of the Jihad and of sacrifice on the altar of faith as a magical religious solution to the deficiency in the balance of power."[31]

One could imagine having a rational, efficient dictatorship, but even that modest goal eludes Arab regimes, whose decisions remain arbitrary and unrealistic. Such leaders as Arafat or Saddam Hussein merely acted out of whim or wishful thinking instead of consulting institutions and advisers in a serious decision-making process. Instead, their lieutenants "quake in their boots," afraid to tell the leader any unpleasant truths.[32]

As examples, Akhdar cites stories about Arab leaders making monumental decisions on the basis of mystical thinking. He recalls how the Iraqi dictator Abd al-Salam Aref awoke from a Ramadan nap in the 1960s in which he dreamed of having broken his fast. The presidential dream interpreter told him this meant he would receive good news. Aref claimed that a few hours later he received word of a cease-fire in his civil conflict with the Kurds. Akhdar adds similar stories about Iran's Ayatollah Khomeini, who said he learned in a dream that an Islamist revolution would take place in Iraq—so why should he end his war with Baghdad?—and Saddam, who told his staff that God had told him in a dream to invade Kuwait, justifying starting a war with that neighbor.[33] The Hamas spiritual leader Sheikh Ahmad Yassin in 1999 said that he read between the lines in the Qur'an that Israel would collapse in 2027 and that Palestinians would take over the whole country. This claim has inspired the organization's members to fight on indefinitely.[34]

A state governed by such hocus-pocus, Akhdar remarks, will surely fail. When divine intervention or magic is the main basis for decision making, it is not surprising that people expect jihad and martyrdom to conquer all. While postwar Japan responded to the challenge of a powerful West by learning its ways in order to surpass it, Arabs have closed themselves off and rejected Western ideas or methods, thus ensuring defeat.[35]

In critiquing their own society, Arab liberals raise arguments that would scare off a Western writer as not sufficiently "politically correct." For example, Abdullah al-Jasmi, a Kuwait University philosophy professor, wrote that the Arab mentality mistakenly focuses on results rather than causes, emotions over rationality, and generalizations rather than learning from specific events. In his view, the cause of failure and backwardness is a whole way of thinking in which the main missing feature "is the brain."[36]

How can this brain be exercised rather than exorcised? Radwan al-Sayyed, a professor of Islamic philosophy in Lebanon, said that the thing most needed in the Arab world "is self-criticism and self-evaluation."[37] In offering such answers, liberals have logic on their side but not the power of passion, simplistic rhetoric, and backing from a powerful political system or deep religious conviction. To narrow this gap, they have often tried to operate based on the assumption that the Arab world was indeed a victim of foreign aggression while insisting that this made reform all the more necessary. If it was true that the Arabs were facing a successful assault from the West, Sayyed asserted, it was their own weakness that made them so vulnerable. Only liberal reform could save them.[38]

Another approach to this problem came from Urfan Nizamuddin, a veteran journalist and former editor of *Al-Sharq al-Awsat*. Iraq and Palestine might be the most important issues facing the Arab world, but that didn't mean that other things, like education, should be neglected. Given the struggle of nations for power, an Arab failure on this front would ensure they would be the losers in every respect.[39]

The Bahraini intellectual Muhammad al-Ansari also tried to use the thought of foreign intervention as a spur toward liberal reform. The Arabs could win only by creating the equivalent of a liberation front to free themselves from backwardness. It was impossible to wage wars against their enemies with a 70 percent illiteracy rate, high unemployment, and systematic violations of human rights and women's rights. How can this war be won when ruling elites and their people are so divided and everyone is so desperate that they are driven to embrace fantasies as their only hope?[40]

The problem is that those forces of fantasy are quite powerful and continue to hold the loyalty of many—perhaps most—Arabs. On an Al-Jazeera television debate, Ghabra made the obvious point that bin Laden was not offering some great project for progress—like achieving democracy, improving conditions for women, or fixing the educational system—but merely proposing to turn the whole Arab world into one big Taliban-style regime. The program's host, Montaha al-Ramhi, then sprang into action, angrily interrupting him by shouting that someone had to stop the United States from taking over the Arab world.[41]

It was the standard exchange. To criticize extremists, explore a social or economic problem seriously, or call for real change sets off a patriotic-religious hysteria that begins by accusing the dissident of treason and soon results in death threats. The problem is not that so many people are ready to fight for bin Laden's basic ideas but rather that this same basic worldview is accepted and reinforced by so many intellectuals, journalists, and clerics. By doing so, they vicariously share in his revolutionary cult of martyrdom while not so courageously protecting their careers by thundering an officially approved defiance against the West. They pretend to be heroes while not daring to criticize their own rulers.

In frustration, many liberals complain that it is difficult to conduct a rational discussion with people who act this way, especially since they incite the emotions of people who are already suffering from so much frustration about their lives and the great difficulty to improve them.[42] How much harder it becomes since that stance coincides with the dominant political culture! In Ansari's words, the idea of a great hero who will rescue the Arabs is well grounded in history, from Saladin through Nasser and down to Saddam and bin Laden. He explains, "It doesn't matter whether the hero is a liar, adventurer, tyrant, or terrorist, because the Arab mentality will ascribe to him a sanctity that covers his sins."[43]

Indeed, the intellectuals even rewrite the heroes' ideas and goals as needed to fit their needs. Thus, despite the fact that bin Laden and al-Qa'ida virtually never mentioned the Palestine issue in their voluminous literature before September 11, fighting that battle is now portrayed as the motive for his actions.[44] Arab nationalist intellectuals have no interest in highlighting bin Laden's purely Islamist goals, while the existing regimes' supporters do not want to confess that he is a revolutionary whose main goal is to overthrow them. By portraying bin Laden as someone wreaking vengeance on the West and the Jews, they fit him into their own ideology, which extols external struggle while ignoring the need for internal change.

As Ansari notes, such is the long-established pattern. The regimes claim that the masses demand militancy, when in fact they use the state-controlled, regime-serving media "to mobilize and incite" them. The central idea purveyed in all Arab societies' "propaganda apparatus . . . education, culture, intellectual life, politics, and religion rests on the theory that outsiders are conspiring to divide, subvert, and hold back the Arabs."[45] In this context, many or most Arabs conclude that whether or not bin Laden's methods were right, his motive was anger at evil Western deeds and at least he was striking against a true enemy. In this context, the September 11, 2001, attacks were a completely, or at least partly, legitimate battle in a just war.

For liberals, in contrast, September 11 was supposed to have been a great political opportunity born in tragedy. It was the ultimate proof that their rivals had no constructive program but could only dishonor Arabs and Muslims in the face of the world, inspiring international intervention against them. If the main apparent Arab reaction to September 11 had been sincere—condemning the attacks, despite blaming them in part on U.S. policy—the liberal cause should have prospered. After all, Arab leaders would have wanted to crush extremist Islamists who not only committed an act they claimed to regard as a vile crime but also threatened their own lives. Might not this threat prompt rulers to ally with the liberals in order to save themselves?

This is not what happened. By and large, the rulers saw the new Jihadist movement as a problem for the West and a chance to strengthen themselves. This was in the tradition of deflecting blame outward. By abandoning the previous radical Islamist strategy that had put a priority on revolution at home, the global Jihad movement relieved pressure on the Arab governments. These Jihadists focused the energies of violent Arabs and the anger of the far more numerous passive ones on the West, not on their local rulers.

When Jihadists put the emphasis on blaming the United States and Israel for the Muslims' problems and urged Arabs to fight them, this was a propaganda theme that rulers—and the intellectuals, media, and clerics who backed them—could wholeheartedly endorse. Much of the Arab media even denied there was any Arab or Muslim involvement in the attack, attributing it to Zionists or to the United States itself. Thus, they considered the Western reaction to September 11 as merely one more event in the long history of unprovoked aggression against the Arab world and Islam, and still another reason for the Arabs to unite around their leaders battling this threat.

There was even a hybrid new liberal-reactionary argument: why wasn't reform possible? Because the United States demanded tougher laws to fight terrorism, it—not local regimes—was the cause of repression in the Arab world. But if the United States was responsible for the conflict between itself and the Arab world, terrorism, and September 11, why should anyone want or need to change anything in Arab society? The true solution was to unite more completely and fight with more determination against foreign interference.

These were some of the points critiqued by Abd al-Mun'im Sa'id in one of the most comprehensive looks at this issue by any Arab writer. The Arab knee-jerk response to September 11, he wrote, "was to deny that the perpetrators were Arab and that the event had any connection with Arab society and culture." The media and Arab public opinion spread wild conspiracy theories claiming bin Laden was innocent even after he claimed responsibility. The reason for this denial was clear: to confront the implications of September 11 honestly would require examining the real problems, especially Islamism, "which Arab societies have been so assiduously avoiding."[46]

The more Middle Eastern terrorism spread globally, "the greater was the rush to look the other way." Bin Laden was simultaneously treated as a hero and a U.S. creation (for use against the Soviets in Afghanistan), ignoring among other points the fact that Arab governments had supported him. While Arabs criticize Samuel Huntington's "conflict of civilizations" concept, they conveniently forget that this is precisely their own view of the world: that Arab-Muslim civilization faces an all-out attack from its Western counterpart.[47]

A similar approach was taken by Muhammad Ahmad al-Hassani, a Saudi columnist, who asks, where did these terrorists get their ideas? They were neither poor nor uneducated. Indeed, the problem was the way they were educated—by mainstream religious teachers who convinced them they must fight a battle of "good versus evil, truth versus falsehood."[48] But any discussion of Islam's role in society or as a doctrine promoting extremism invariably gets liberals in trouble.

Aside from such issues as governance, psychology, culture, religion, the role of women, the Arab world's economic problems are also tightly bound up with the dictatorial system's shortcomings. The Arab world is in a terrible economic situation. The statistics are devastating. Per capita income grew at only an annual rate of 0.5 percent over twenty-five years, less than half the global average. Even with massive oil income, the average Arab standard of living declined compared to the rest of the world. The combined gross domestic product of all Arab countries was less than that of Spain alone.[49]

To address these problems without making any real changes, many government officials and supporters advocate what they call a Chinese-type reform, modernizing the economy while leaving the political system untouched. Yet the economy's weakness is a product of the existing political system and its lack of democracy. This shortcoming, plus the resulting violence and instability it provokes, discourages foreign investment, at least outside of the oil and gas sector. International corporate disinterest is increased by bureaucratic problems and such factors as low productivity, public sector monopolies, and problems in the state-controlled banking sector. As the economist Ziad Abdelnour put it, "The Arab world is not a great place to do business and it's not getting any better."[50]

Take the banking system, for example. Financial capital represents power, and the state is reluctant to let others have it. These semigovernmental banks—four of which in Egypt control half the market—lend mostly to the state and to those with political connections. Private firms are kept from expanding to avoid competition with state monopolies or companies owned by the rulers and their allies.[51] In short, the economic system—like the ideological and religious ones—is one more factor blocking change.[52] Michel Kilo, a Syrian liberal, warns that "there can be no economic reform without political reform."[53]

The story of Sainsbury's involvement in Egypt illustrates this broader principle. Sainsbury, Britain's second-largest supermarket chain, decided to go into business in Egypt starting in April 1999. Its one hundred stores provided 2,500 jobs in a country with massive unemployment, and it planned to create more, making Egypt its base for manufacturing goods to export throughout the region. But Egyptian customs blocked its import of goods, competing small retailers convinced Islamic clerics to put a religious ban on shopping in its stores, and militants spread false rumors that the company's owner was Jewish and had given huge donations to Israel's West Bank settlements.

This campaign resulted in organized shopping boycotts, mob attacks on stores, destruction of its signs, and beating up of employees. The company responded with ads saying it had nothing to do with Israel and decorated stores with Quranic verses. The government did nothing to help. After big financial losses, the company left Egypt only two years after arriving there with ambitious plans. The anti-Israel boycott groups rejoiced at still another victory over the alleged forces of Zionism and imperialism—and also defeated any chance of improving Egypt's economy, job supply, efficiency, and living standards.[54]

Having shown the problems of the existing situation, what do the liberals themselves stand for? What system do they see as preferable for the Arab world? In general, they rarely discuss details. There is not a great deal of original or systematic thinking, much less comprehensive programs or philosophical overviews. But if one wants to find a broad credo of what liberals are trying to do, a good outline has been presented by Heggy.[55]

Identity. Heggy suggests that the main Arab self-image should be as citizens of individual states whose heritage includes—but is not limited to—Arab and Islamic civilization. This view contrasts with the Arab nationalist or Islamist definitions of identity that have undercut the individual Arab state, providing instead a framework that has been the basis of success for all other societies in the last thousand years. Moreover, because these two dominant Arab worldviews insist that achievement of Arab or Islamist unity must precede major internal reforms, they postpone progress—including the building of stable, developed states—until some distant future. Reformists emphasize that the state and society already exist and their problems must be dealt with now.

Attitude toward the world. While acknowledging that other societies sometimes have enmity toward Arabs or Muslims—and always seek their own interests—the main source of Arab difficulties is domestic. In Heggy's words: "Our problems, in their entirety, originate inside our country and can only be solved internally. We alone are responsible for those problems and for the fact that they remain unsolved." Emphasizing conspiracy theories, he warns, is a self-fulfilling prophecy that guarantees impotence and inferiority.[56]

A moderate political doctrine. As Heggy puts it, "The values of liberalism, democracy, general freedoms and human rights [are] the most noble, sublime and civilized achievements of mankind." A strong civil society is "the most effective mechanism for public participation in public life."[57]

The role of women. As half the population, women must enjoy equal treatment. This is not just a matter of justice but an absolute precondition for social and economic progress. He asserts, "A society that does not grant its women full rights in all fields cannot hope to realize its full potential."[58]

A rational decision-making program, incorporating modern management techniques and a pragmatic approach to problems. It is not sufficient to proclaim that right and justice are on the Arab side or that victory is inevitable if they struggle long enough. Costs, the likelihood of success, and the balance of forces must be taken into account. Here, too, democracy is essential so that dictators do not make whimsical choices or decisions based on the narrow self-interest of a small portion of society.

Resolving the Arab-Israeli conflict. This will require compromise, which is in the Arabs' self-interest, especially since that issue "has been used for too long as an excuse to delay democracy and development."[59]

Educational and media reform. Schools must produce people possessing both the technical skills needed for modern life and the values required to build a free and democratic society. This open system also requires free speech and an independent, accurate media to encourage rationality and point to problems that must be fixed. As Saghiya wrote, when the state controls the press, journalists "will choose what seems to be the easiest way to please [their] ruler."[60]

The triumph of moderate Islam. The prevailing version of Islam must be based on its tolerant and peaceful aspects. This is in accord with the way that the religion has usually been practiced and is faithful both to its original intent and the needs of the modern age. Those who use Islam for terrorism, jihadism, extremism, and so on are the true deviationists.

Respect for minority rights. Non-Arab and non-Muslim citizens should be treated on an equal basis.

Willingness to borrow from the West. Despite its shortcomings, Western culture is an essential tool for progress. "To oppose Western culture is to oppose science, development and civilization."[61] Arabs should take from the Western model what is useful and retain from Arab-Muslim tradition what is essential.

Readiness to engage in self-criticism and assess one's situation accurately. If a society thinks itself superior and assumes it can learn nothing from others, it cannot devise workable policies or achieve progress.

In more formal contexts, the reform plan has been presented in many meetings of liberal, mostly human rights, groups beginning in 2004. The two most important statements were the March 2004 Alexandria Declaration and the September 2004 Beirut Declaration.[62] In both cases, the meetings enjoyed official state sponsorship—itself a sign of the regimes' power—but liberals then took the opportunity beyond what the rulers intended.

The meeting in Alexandria, Egypt, "Arab Reform Issues: Vision and Implementation," was organized as a government maneuver to quiet international pressure toward democratization. The goal was to show that Arab societies were perfectly capable of reforming themselves. Mubarak himself addressed the gathering of two hundred Arab activists and intellectuals, although some of the most outspoken dissidents—including Ibrahim—were not invited. Yet afterward, Ibrahim was able to describe the resulting declaration as "a sort of Arab Magna Carta." Its tone is very much one of issuing a Bill of Rights for the Arab world.

A second, largely parallel, liberal statement was developed at a September 2004 conference in Beirut entitled "Partnership for Peace, Democracy and Development in the Broader Middle East and North Africa,"[63] which was attended by scores of Arab liberal intellectuals and human rights groups. It was organized to present an Arab position to a Forum for the Future meeting in New York that would bring together Western and Arab states. The resulting resolution was far more receptive to international involvement in promoting Arab reform than was its Alexandrian counterpart.

Both statements suggested that resolving such regional conflicts as the Palestinian-Israeli one and others in Iraq, Kashmir, and Afghanistan would enhance reform efforts while weakening autocratic governments and radical movements. At the same time, though, they noted that governments, in the words used by the Beirut statement, "have often used these regional security issues to delay political, economic and social reform, as if solving these issues can only come at the cost of suppression and oppression."

According to the declaration issued at the end of the Alexandria conference, the goal of reform is "genuine democracy," which is defined as a system in which freedom is given the highest value, the people have sovereignty, and political pluralism is enshrined. This means a division of powers among an elected legislature, an independent judiciary, and an executive branch subject to both constitutional and political accountability. There must be respect for all the rights of all the people, including freedom of thought and expression, as well as the right to organize political parties and other groups.

These freedoms are to be safeguarded by an independent media and fair elections, with a peaceful transfer of power to those successful at the ballot box. The rule of law must prevail, meaning the abolition of special courts and emergency laws. On the economic front, the market must be allowed to function with less governmental interference. Unlike the current situation, a proper economy must be open to foreign investment and capable of growth, providing jobs, and reducing poverty.

The reformers also understand that successful change cannot be limited to politics alone. Other elements needed for democratization include such things as the empowerment of women, a family structure in which free individuals are allowed to take responsibility for their choices (in place of a current norm based on what was called at Alexandria "submissiveness and obedience"), the elimination of outdated social customs, and media that support "equality, tolerance, accepting the other," and other positive values.

Another priority involves placing a higher value on innovation, high-quality education, technology, and science. As the Beirut conference concluded, what is needed is "a thorough revision of education generally, and of religious education where intolerance is actively advocated in its name, where basic and high quality skills are trained and critical inquisitive thinking is promoted."

How are these and so many other reforms to be accomplished? The proposals were largely for more conferences; discussions with the Arab League, the establishment club of Arab states known for its ineffectiveness; and partnership with the Arab regimes. The Beirut Declaration went a bit further, proposing a partnership among governments, the international community, and civil society groups.

What is most strategically significant in these and other such statements is that the movement was proposing to work through existing regimes rather than creating an opposition movement to them. This may be the only available approach, or perhaps it is an early phase in a long-term struggle. At the same time, though, despite the reservations and safeguards that the authors of such declarations attempt to include, the enterprise is also subject to manipulation by the regimes that organized and funded these meetings and permitted them to take place.

On the agenda-setting front, however, the reformers have clearly identified the steps needed to advance the Arab world into the twenty-first century: build democracy, ensure social peace, and raise living standards. But what a monumental task this is! Even the optimistic Shafiq Ghabra warns that Arab nationalist statism and Islamism are mutually reinforcing roadblocks. Only reformists backed by the "moderate silent majority" can bring progress. But that group—if it indeed exists—is, he admits, at present paralyzed, weak, and unable to influence events.[64]

5

Whose Islam?

F undamentalists are trying to Islamicize" our society, said a liberal
Kuwaiti businessman, "while we're trying to privatize Islam."[1] The
Egyptian liberal Sayyed al-Qimni stressed a different aspect of the issue:
"We have an ongoing problem without a solution, as everyone is talking
about the proper Islam without us truly knowing what this proper Islam
is."[2] These statements are good summaries of the liberal position on
Islam. Unable to criticize religion itself or call for secularizing society—
the historical approach of most Western liberals—their main point is to
stress that religion be a personal matter detached from politics and
denied a monopoly on social and intellectual life. They also insist that a
moderate interpretation of Islam is correct and the radical Islamist one
is false.

Regarding this all-important issue, liberals use three pairs of arguments interchangeably, despite the fact that they are somewhat—though
not irretrievably—contradictory. The first set relates to the relationship
of radical Islamism and Islam. On one hand, they argue that radical
Islamism is a historical deviation from mainstream Islam, arising from
various heretical movements in the past and from Wahhabist extremism
today. On the other hand, they say that there has always been a debate
between two versions of Islam and the radicals won this contest, to the
detriment of the Arabs, centuries ago.

The second set of claims relates to the relationship between radical
Islamists and society. On one hand, liberals say that radical Islamists are
simply practicing what they were taught in schools and mosques. As a
result, educational reform is the most important element in reducing
extremism and terrorism. On the other hand, liberals insist that radical
Islamism arose in opposition to society, as the sole permissible outlet for

popular frustration at the lack of democracy and change. The masses had no other or way to express their grievances outside the mosque. In this case the most important task is to expand democracy and meet social needs as a solution to the radical Islamist threat.

Finally, there is a third set of positions regarding the relation of politics to radical Islamism. On one hand, liberals argue that revolutionary Islamists threaten the existing regimes. Thus, they urge rulers to ally with liberals against the subversive challenge. On the other hand, liberals claim that the regimes use Islam as a way of distracting the masses, mobilizing support for themselves, and blocking reform. Thus, it is a weapon of the Arab nationalist dictatorships that must be taken away from them.

There are several complex factors that help to explain these contradictions. An especially important one is the fact that while many Muslims are Islamists and almost no very pious Muslims are liberals, most Muslims remain conservative, traditional believers. This group includes the majority of clerics and ordinary people. This mainstream Islam generally supports the status quo and opposes both democratic reform and Islamist revolution, but in recent years it has been leaning far more toward Islamism than toward liberalism.

Thus, liberals have to decide among several strategies. Should they ally with moderate Muslims—including the conservatives—against the radicals? As Kuwaiti liberals put it, "Secularists and liberals cannot fight the radicals alone; only moderate Islamists can adequately fight the radicals, by engaging them in a dialogue."[3] Should they demand a new, progressive interpretation of Islam in conflict with both conservatives and radicals? Should they offer themselves as friends of the regime to cooperate against the Islamist threat? Or should they try to make use of that threat to demand democratization as the only way to stave off Islamist revolution?

In addition, liberals are handicapped by the need for extreme caution on anything concerning religion, as they try to ensure that they cannot easily be accused of opposing Islam, though of course Islamists and regimes have still charged them with doing so. As an Arab diplomat, writing anonymously, noted, anyone who dares challenge the obsessive desire to imitate blindly the way ancestors lived, without regard to contemporary circumstances, is "charged with apostasy and heresy, or at the very least with secularism."[4] The liberals' ultimate problem then will be not how cogent they can make their arguments—or justify them using historical Islamic practices and texts—but whether they could convince most Arabs that their interpretation of Islam is the correct one.[5]

Basically, the liberal position is so weak that it makes sense to try all these approaches simultaneously. That is why the same liberals use these different arguments without apparently being aware of their inherent conflicts. In contrast, for the regimes and conservative clerics there is an easy minimalist way they can combat radical Islamists. Focusing on the issues coinciding with their self-interest, they have frequently proclaimed as illegitimate violence against the regime or fellow Muslims. At the same time, they can agree that attacking even civilians from nations deemed responsible for "aggression" against Muslims—for example, Israelis or Americans—is an acceptable practice. On actual reform measures such as more democracy, women's rights, or civil liberties, they have either remained silent or actively opposed to change.

What the liberals prefer is something far more extensive, to create a model of Islam that supports their program for Arab society. As Qimni puts it, Judaism, Christianity, and other religions have done well in adjusting to the modern world because they have recognized the need to alter laws or practices that are no longer appropriate. Muslims simply need to do the same thing.[6] Ironically, of course, creating a new version of Islam is not substantially different from what liberals have criticized the Islamists for doing. But the Islamists have a big head start and a stance that better fits the way most Arab Muslims have been educated. In addition, the group interests of Islamic clerics are much better served by an Islamist approach that offers them more power and insists on Islam's central importance in society. In contrast, the liberals want to reduce their influence and increase the secular space in society.

One important way in which liberals have pushed for their interpretation has been to insist that the reforms they want are fully consistent with Islam and express its true essence. "Democratic change has become a non-negotiable choice that cannot be postponed," said the June 2004 Doha Declaration of Arab human rights groups. Many non-Arab Muslims live in multiparty democratic systems that experience has shown "are not the sole monopoly of any given culture or civilization. Neither

Arab culture nor the Islamic religion are in any form or shape contradictory to democratic practices and values."[7]

Indeed, they sometimes justified their desire to have democracy or other modern practices by insisting they were really Muslim inventions, not an import from the West. This was the route taken, for example, by Prince Hassan bin Talal of Jordan, who claimed that for centuries Islamic civilization was the "world's melting pot . . . a refuge for those escaping from religious and intellectual discrimination. Islam in those days supported scientific discoveries, respected the environment, and valued both education and civic responsibility."[8]

According to Hassan, pluralism and respect for diversity—the trendiest contemporary ideas—were supported by Islam's founders and early leaders. Muslims today should emulate this true model rather than the radical Islamsists who use "Islamic teachings to pursue non-Islamic programs." Their violence against innocent people is "absolutely immoral" and un-Islamic. Hassan points out that the Qur'an prohibits aggressive war, which is acceptable only for defensive purposes.[9] The problem he does not acknowledge is that bin Laden and his colleagues justify their war in Islamic terms precisely by arguing that it is a defensive one against Western-Zionist, Christian-Jewish aggression.[10]

While Hassan's approach views liberal Islam as normative and Islamist views as heretical, Tarek Heggy takes a more balanced approach. He recounts the great debates within Islam between liberal interpretations, like those of medieval philosophers such as Ibn Rushd (Averroës) and Ibn Sina (Avicenna), versus the hard-line interpretations of Abu Hamid al-Ghazali, Ahmad bin Hanbal, Ibn Taymiya, and later Muhammad ibn Abd al-Wahhab.

The liberals argued that precisely because humans do not understand God's nature and ways, religious texts and rulings made by people can be debated and reinterpreted over time. Logic, not blind faith, is the key tool in that process. But their challenge was short-lived, and few Muslims of the time were even aware of their existence, much less their ideas. Meanwhile, the hard-liners won, and their views were accepted by millions of Muslims, determining the course of Islam thereafter. As Europe embraced reason and advanced on every social, political, and economic front, Muslim societies were handcuffed by tradition.

While Europe rang with intellectual debate and new forces challenged the rule of despotic rulers and religious authorities, Arab lands remained

in the grip of those who opposed the free pursuit of knowledge and sti-
fled creativity. Fanatical movements "interpreted the doctrines of religion on the basis of tradition alone and imposed a scholastic, doctrinal
brand of Islam that left no room for the exercise of reason."[11]

In Akhdar's words, European Christianity—under criticism from
Copernicus to Freud and challenged by heresies and revolutions—had
to be modernized while "Islam has remained sheltered from any sort of
subversive criticism." Even well-informed Muslims do not know the most
basic facts about "scientific absurdities" in the Qur'an or the changes the
text underwent over time. The Arab world faced no Reformation,
Renaissance, or Enlightenment, no French or American Revolution.[12] In
that region, the word *renaissance* was translated into the name of the
Baath party, while revolution manifests itself as Arab nationalist coups
or the Islamist uprising in Iran.

What explains this situation? Officially, the Islamic heritage suggests
that the Arabs are the best nation in the whole world, yet this clashes
with a reality in which the Arabs have suffered so many defeats and are
behind almost everyone else in a number of ways. For Islamists the answer
is obvious: when the Arabs gave up their religion, they were abandoned
by Allah. If they return to proper Islam and reject the Western ways of
doing things, Allah will grant them victory and prosperity. The problem
is not only with the Islamists but also with the mainstream conservative
Muslims, whose view of Islamic religious law is that it prohibits "resem-
bling or imitating 'the infidels,'" which means that all Western institutions, sciences, values, and technology are akin to heresy. Everything
imported from outside the Arab world requires a fatwa [religious rul-
ing] permitting it—including coffee, running water, Western-style hats,
Coca-Cola, television, sciences, human rights, and democracy.[13]

But that was not the end of the story, according to Heggy. He posits
the existence of "two Islams"—a more "gentle and tolerant" version
dominating the Ottoman Empire and Egypt and a version prevailing in
more isolated, less sophisticated regions. The struggle is between Islam
as "a system of spiritual beliefs" and one that would be "a system that
ruled all aspects of life and governed the affairs of society."[14]

This is a sensible model. Traditional Islam, as practiced in Egypt and
elsewhere in the nineteenth and early twentieth centuries, was quite
moderate compared to the radical Islamism of today. Clearly, radical
Islamism has been growing. Unsuccessful politically at seizing power,

extremists have had many victories in the ongoing cultural and intellectual struggles, capturing and transforming the strongholds of moderate
Islam.[15]

Just as the Saudis "export" the blame for their radical Islamists to
Afghanistan and elsewhere, other Arabs pin the responsibility for their
own extremists on Saudi Arabia. The subtext here is that no social, educational, or political changes are needed in their own societies because
the deadly flowers of radicalism are not rooted in local conditions.[16] For
example, Wael al-Abrashi, deputy editor of *Roz al-Yousef* magazine in
Egypt, falsely states that "there was a Saudi connection in all the major
terrorist attacks in Egypt during the 1980s and 1990s in terms of their
ideas and funding." He adds, "Saudi Arabia created the monster, exported
it abroad, and then lost control of it. Then, the monster turned on it."[17]
While Saudi Arabia's doctrine and money certainly played an important
role in encouraging terrorism and spreading extremist ideas, the whole
issue cannot usefully be reduced to using Saudi Arabia as a scapegoat.

Merely to identify, as some liberals do, the intolerant form of Islam
with Saudi Wahhabism is certainly misleading. After all, the thinkers
Heggy lists as fathers of the hard-line view have had a huge influence
throughout the Sunni Muslim world. Wahhabism also has little to do,
for example, with the history of Egyptian Islamism—which began with
the Muslim Brotherhood in the late 1920s—or the Iranian revolution
and Shia Islamism.[18]

Equally, the mainstream officials and institutions of Egypt's Islamic
establishment, although they never challenge the government, spread ideas
quite close to Islamist ones. These include clerics from the government-
controlled Al-Azhar University and the state-appointed mufti. Ahmad
Abd al-M'uti Higazi, a poet and former leftist who became a liberal during a ten-year residency in France, criticized these official Islamic institutions for promoting ideas that encouraged terrorism and blocking
progress by inhibiting dialogue, prohibiting independent thought, and
subverting democracy.[19]

Instead of being enslaved to a narrow reading of old texts or rulings
made for conditions in earlier times, he suggests, Islam should be kept "a
living and constantly self-renewing experiment." As history develops and
new issues arise, so must religious rulings adapt to these conditions. For
example, Higazi continues, Islam originally improved women's status over
what it had been in earlier eras, but now "human society has developed

and the status of women has changed." These rulings from another era "no longer express the position of Islam with regard to women." The texts must "be reexamined in order to derive from them new rulings that will suit the intentions of Islam." Restricting a man to four wives was once considered progress, but it is now clear that such a situation does not work and fosters oppression, which is against Islam. He concludes by asking, "Who is closer to Islam, those who make a woman prime minister or those who make her an adulteress if she puts on makeup?"[20]

In dealing with the sensitive issue of religion, the Alexandria Declaration provided what might be the most comprehensive expression of the liberal strategy toward Islam. The careful wording of this proposal is worth quoting in full. It urges

> encouraging the continuous revision and renewal of religious discourse to reveal the civilized, enlightened aspects of religion such as promoting intellectual freedom, allowing interpretation of religious matters to benefit the individual and society and [challenging] all forms of rigidity, extremism and literalism in comprehending religious texts. The reform of religious discourse should be consistent with the spirit of science, rationality and the requisites of contemporary life. This will eliminate pernicious contradictions between the freedom of thought and creativity on the one hand, and the tutelage, imposed in the name of religion, on the other. Religion calls for persuasion through debate and does not impose intellectual terrorism on those who may disagree."[21]

In short, it calls for a modern, open-minded, rational, moderate, pluralistic, and flexible stance toward religion. This kind of thinking sounds self-evident to Westerners, where attitudes toward religion have gone through very similar processes, but it is a revolutionary notion in the Muslim world. Winning acceptance for such a sweeping change will be difficult. Ironically, the doors of interpretation can be opened only by a double-edged sword. For the Islamists have done precisely what Higazi advocates, whether or not they admit it. They have reinterpreted an Islam that they saw as decadent and unsuited to contemporary conditions. Such key Islamist doctrines as defining some fellow Muslims as heretics who might justifiably be killed; insisting that clerics should control, or even directly rule, the state; letting radical Islamists lacking proper credentials issue fatwas; or sanctifying suicide terrorism are at odds with the way Islam was preached and practiced for a thousand years.

In contrast, Higazi calls for a new, liberal reinterpretation of Islam in which Muslims use their "brains to arrive at the appropriate rulings for the needs of each generation." The new version of Islam must be able to endorse democracy, "separate religion and state, make man and woman equal, and adopt human rights in practice." This is instead of merely backing the "corrupt and evil" regimes that rule Muslim lands and that distort and violate Islam's principles and enslave its people.[22]

One of the most articulate liberal analyses of the problem was penned by Ahmad Bishara, leader of Kuwait's National Democratic Movement. Bishara said Islam, like other religions, views God "as a force of love, peace, compassion and a motivating force to the individual." But now Muslims need a war "to save their faith . . . [from] fanatical cults and muftis who have hijacked Islam for their own ends." He called for a "body of enlightened clergy" to serve as "the sole interpreter of the faith," banning "the practice of obscure individuals issuing haphazard fatwas on behalf of all Muslims." Secular authorities and "enlightened Islamic scholars" should root out materials "prejudiced [against] women, insensitive to human rights and intolerant to other faiths and cultures" from religious school textbooks and the media. Instead, the emphasis in Islamic education and sermons should be "the ideals of peace, tolerance and coexistence if Muslims aspire to fit in a multi-cultural and multi-ethnic world."[23]

"Many well-meaning Muslims think Islam is misunderstood in the West," Bishara explained. "Well, maybe to some extent that is true. But it is the failure of Muslims to understand the fundamental message of their own religion, practice it properly and accommodate it to the modern world that is at stake." Modern society is simply impossible without a separation between religion and state or the basic liberal principles of democracy and human rights. No modern state has "succeeded without this model. None will ever, either. Muslim societies cannot continue a self-deception that they are different. . . . They are not."[24]

Bishara's call for governments to exercise tighter supervision over the religious establishment made sense in terms of fighting proterrorist forces, but it also contained significant problems. As we have seen, a situation already exists in Egypt and Saudi Arabia in which mainstream official institutions actually encourage extremist ideas and work against liberal interpretations. Regimes also prefer an Islam opposing change in order to ensure their own survival. Religion has been an effective tool against the left (for example, in Egypt in the 1970s), Arab nationalism (for instance, in Saudi Arabia and Jordan from the 1950s onward), and reform or democracy (everywhere) while also stirring up hatred and blame toward foreigners as the cause of the nation's problems. Bishara's approach made more sense in Kuwait, where the rulers were relatively moderate and there was some role for parliament. But in general giving the existing governments more power over religion would only strengthen the status quo.

At the same time, Bishara's approach, like Higazi's, also represents a threat to the leaders of traditional Islam, who are the governments' main allies in fighting Islamists as well as being a significant force. Another problem in winning support for liberal arguments, true both for Bishara's and Higazi's views, is the invocation of the Western model of development as being the only one possible. This may very well be true, but it has also been a taboo concept in the Arab world's public discourse. No matter how often critics admit precisely this point in private, they know that this is a great issue for manipulation by nationalist and Islamist demagoguery. Thus, the most likely supporters for the liberal argument would be a small minority of intellectuals who face the opposition of the state, clerics, and traditionalist or radical Muslims, who together make up the great majority of the population.

One of the liberals' more promising tactics is to try to split traditionalist Muslims from radical Islamists by condemning the latter for issuing fatwas without proper clerical credentials and with a content that violates normative Islamic law. This tactic puts liberals on the side of conservative clerics, but it is in conflict with a truly reformist argument. Demanding change requires criticizing the religious establishment and insisting on a new orientation that focuses on the spirit of Islam rather than the letter of its laws as interpreted traditionally.

Liberals are thus left with a difficult choice: should they defend the conservatives against the radical Islamists or criticize the conservatives and demand reform?[25] If liberals uphold the power of the Islamic clergy

against Islamists, they cannot easily challenge it themselves. This is especially a problem because often—Egypt and Saudi Arabia are prime
examples—establishment clerics take some radical Islamist positions. In
almost all cases they strongly oppose reform. If liberals insist that only
qualified, high-ranking clerics can make decisions based on historic
Islamic precedent, this also means that liberal reforms depend on these
people's approval, which dooms any hope of a move in that direction.
This stance also conflicts with liberal claims that each individual Muslim
should use reason to reevaluate old ways of doing things.

An example of this inherent contradiction can be found in the way
al-Afif al-Akhdar defends the conservative establishment. He cites fatwas
by extremists justifying the September 11 attacks, the use of nuclear
weapons against the West, and a coup in Tunisia. Clerics compete in issuing rulings authorizing murders of Israelis, Americans, or non-Muslims
in general. Akhdar, himself a strong secular, even antireligious, intellectual, ridicules these fatwas as contradicting clear, hitherto virtually universal, Islamic standards. These include Quranic injunctions prohibiting
blood vengeance, punishing an innocent person for someone else's deed,
or killing civilians. This is an effective argument against radical Islamists.
But to stop the radicals Akhdar calls for all such rulings to be left in the
hands of Islamic courts, while those issuing improper fatwas inciting
murder, hatred, and war should be tried as criminals.[26] What happens,
however, when "legitimate" government-backed Islamic courts condemn
liberal reforms and even attack the liberals themselves?

Other liberals also point out how radical Islamists deviate from accepted Islamist rulings in obvious ways. Writes Khaled al-Ghanami in
Kuwait, "They ignore the words of Allah: 'There is no coercion in
Islam.'" They claim that "non-Muslims' presence in the Arabian Penin-
sula is sufficient reason to kill them," ignoring the fact that Muhammad
and his successor allowed them to be there. He recalls an accepted tradition about an early Muslim hero, Abd Al-Rahman bin 'Auf, who threw
himself on a pagan friend during a battle to save the man from being
killed by Auf's own comrades. Ghanami enjoins the "child-murderers"
of today to see how Auf "did not renounce his humanity or his love for
his 'infidel' friend. . . . Their claim that you must hate anyone who is a
non-Muslim cannot be true. The Prophet loved Abu Taleb, who died
while still clinging to idol worship. . . . [He] . . . recommended to the
Jihad warriors: 'Do not kill a woman, a child or an old man.'"[27]

Once Islamists insist that any ruler who does not do what they want is illegitimate, the result will be anarchy. Those who think music is forbidden will blow up stores that sell recordings, and so on. Ghanami warns, "This is no exaggeration; the day is not far off when they open fire on satellite dishes."[28] Clearly, then, it is in the interests of regimes and conservative-traditional Muslims alike to rein in such people.

Another issue critical for liberals is the need to reform the educational system. There is a lack of secular-oriented teaching regarding history, philosophy, civics, and attitudes toward the non-Muslim world. The responsibility for filling this vacuum is left in the hands of strongly religious, often Islamist, teachers and textbooks. Seven out of twelve subjects taught in Saudi Arabia's fifth grade classes are religious, and while statements made to Western audiences often imply or claim there have been reforms, more authoritatively a senior Saudi cleric exclaimed, "Educational systems of atheist nations and civilizations cannot be like the systems of a believing nation. This country represents the power of Islam. . . . Any attempt to change this status will be vehemently opposed."[29]

While the exact situation varies among countries, generally there is much raw material in the classroom that can be interpreted as legitimizing radical Islamist arguments. There has been a lot of talk about changing textbooks, but little or nothing actually seemed to be revised.[30] A high-ranking Egyptian cleric estimated that at the current rate of retraining to ensure moderation and consistency, 160 years would be needed to change the orientations of all the country's preachers.[31]

In the early 1980s, Ibrahim, who interviewed many violent Islamists in prison, was already warning about how the social and political order was manufacturing terrorists. The mass media spoke of such extremists as if they came from Mars and had no roots in Egyptian society, he explained, but they were products of Egyptian life. Many were well-educated, middle-class young people who were frustrated and feeling powerless. They came to see an idealized Islamic social order as the only protection against a corrupt, confusing, rapidly changing society. Only if they are given an alternative vision and hope for the future will they reject such ideas.[32]

Akhdar presents a particularly cogent critique of existing religious education, which promotes memorization of texts and a demand for blind obedience, rather than encouraging rational analysis. When faced with a choice among alternative interpretations of sacred texts—for example, one calling for the beating of woman and another urging love and compassion toward a wife—the mainstream emphasizes the former one. Consequently, "the grown-up bin Laden echoed what little Usama learned" in his classroom. He was explicitly taught, for example, that Muslims would kill all Jews on the Day of Judgment, that Muslims would conquer the world no matter what the odds against them, that only strict adherence to religious laws would make God grant them victory, and that Jews and Christians were inevitably enemies of Islam.[33]

One of the few qualified Islamic authorities who openly sides with the liberals is Abd al-Hamid al-Ansari, former dean of shari'a and law at Qatar University. He sees the educational system as one of the main forces promulgating "suicidal and destructive" ideas that lead the Arabs "blindfolded towards destruction."[34] Students are taught attitudes of hatred and fanaticism against women, non-Muslims, or even Muslims who hold different views. As examples he cites the practice of teaching that all non-Muslims must go to hell and interpreting jihad as justifying an aggressive war against them. These were contrary, he said, to proper Islamic teachings, which offered all human beings the right to choose their beliefs. The type of Islam that breeds terrorists "is a crime against the true Islam."[35]

Following the September 11 attacks, many liberals voiced similar sentiments, especially in Saudi Arabia. Adel Zaid al-Tarifi wrote that Islam is taught in his country through an extremist interpretation that leads to terrorism.[36] Raid Qusti asks: "How can we expect others to believe that a majority of us are a peace-loving people who denounce extremism and terrorism when some preachers continue to call for the destruction of Jews and Christians, blaming them for all the misery in the Islamic world? . . . Why are more and more Saudi young men being fed with radical ideas? Who are the people brainwashing them? How are they being radicalized?"[37]

Another Saudi writer, Abdallah Thabit, explained that radical Islamists naturally grew out of the government educational system. Millions of Arabs "have learned since childhood that anyone who is not with me is the enemy of Allah." They were taught "that whoever shaves his beard, changes the [style of] his clothes, and thins his moustache is a secular [person] who wants to control me, my family, my society, and my country with his Western ideas. And whoever disagrees with our predecessors in any way, and asks for something different, is a modernist who attacks the [Muslim] faith and plots day and night to destroy it."[38]

Sermons and teachers taught young people that hating, vilifying, and murdering non-Muslims as well as secular or modernist Muslims represented proper behavior. And secularism can be defined—in Saudi Arabia at least—as "watching satellite television stations, listening to music, teaching English or [letting[women drive." "Why," he concludes, "should people be different from their environment and what they have been taught?"[39]

Arab leaders and establishment intellectuals do not hesitate to conceal the truth about their version of Islam when it suits them to do so. For example, students in Saudi, Egyptian, and other schools are told that Muslims will kill all the Jews on judgment day, but the Saudi foreign minister told the American interviewer Barbara Walters that he had never heard of such a tradition, though it has been taught in every Saudi school.[40]

An especially interesting Saudi liberal is Mansour al-Nogaidan, one of the few radical Islamists who changed his ideas to embrace moderation. He describes how his education led him to set fire to video stores and even to the offices of a charitable society for widows and orphans in his village, in the belief he was fighting Western values and culture, which included equality for women. In jail, he read some of the medieval liberal philosophers, who made him realize that other interpretations of Islam were possible.

As a result, he concluded that Saudi Arabia could rid itself of terrorism only by domestic reform to remove the "deep-rooted Islamic extremism in most schools and mosques, which have become breeding grounds for terrorists." Only when, he concluded, "we see ourselves the way the rest of the world sees us—a nation that spawns terrorists—and think about why that is and what it means will we be able to take the first step toward correcting that image and eradicating its roots."[41]

From Tunisia, human rights activist and former minister of education Muhammad Charfi wrote in similar terms. Schools teach that Muslim law is sacred, and they have idealized Islam's early era, the period Islamists say they want to re-create today. Students learn that all non-Muslims are wrong and that a Muslim empire will conquer the world and spread Islam everywhere. This approach has had disastrous results on young people's minds. For after learning that proper Islam means a religious caliph should be running the state, adulterers should be stoned, and no money should be lent at interest, they find they are living under a secular government with a Western-influenced penal code and an economy based on banks.[42]

They are thus being systematically led to the conclusion that the existing system is contrary to Islam's teachings, that its failure may be attributed to that fact, and that changing this situation is their sacred duty. Similarly, they can logically conclude that non-Muslims are enemies of both Islam and God, so that making war against them is required. Saudi Arabia is more extreme, but far from unique in this respect.[43]

Tunisia is the only Arab state that really reformed its educational system to include the study of liberal Muslim thinkers, introducing students to a form of Islam that allows a free discussion of gender equality, human rights, and democracy. Students also learn about non-Muslim aspects of the country's history, which include the ancient Carthaginians and the Christian writer Saint Augustine. Darwinian views of evolution and modern theories about the creation of the universe are taught in secondary schools. As a result, radical Islamism has remained a marginal phenomenon in Tunisia.[44]

In fact, the Tunisia case shows that Islam can be taught in a liberal way without subverting its traditional beliefs and structure but putting an emphasis on teaching religion rationally while encouraging open discussion.[45] At Zaitouna University, the highest institution of religious teaching in the country, the many moderate teachings and traditions that exist in Islam, ignored by radicals and often conservatives alike, are highlighted. Education focuses on three central concepts, as the Tunisian liberal Akhdar explains. They are: "the promotion of ijtihad [the interpretation of texts] without any restriction on rational thinking; the reliance upon rationalist thought and the humanities . . . as part of learning about religious texts; and realization that Islamic consciousness must reinstate the other, particularly the Jew and the Christian."

Among the courses required at the university's Higher Institute of Religious Fundamentals, students must "understand the historical and scientific difficulties" of turning religious texts into legislation. On each subject, the classes stress that Islamic scholars have had different opinions, as in one case saying, "Each doctrine has its own perception, closely related to the society" in which it was formulated "with respect to time and place."

Another course, "Introduction to Scriptural Religions," is defined as teaching about "Judaism and Christianity . . . in a manner which respects the words of their founders." This is, of course, far different from the hostile image inculcated into students in virtually every other Arab country. Aside from a thorough grounding in Islamic sources, there are also courses on the Judeo-Christian Bible, comparing Western and Muslim concepts of freedom, human rights in Islam, both liberal and conservative Islamic theology in the past, and the varying interpretations of different Muslim sects.

In one final exam, students are asked to analyze the important Quranic saying "Let there be no violence in religion." The task is "to elaborate on the *Quran's* stance on the freedom of belief, and the question of accepting the other who is different in religion." They are told to discuss these issues "in accordance with modern requirements to found the civil society, which prerequisites tolerance and coexistence in order to guarantee progress and security, and in accordance with the aspirations by global community to build interactions on a base of the exchange of interests, regardless of colour, sex or religion." The Tunisian experience shows that moderate Islam is possible, but only if Arab states and societies teach their children that it is legitimate and give them the tools needed to live and believe that way.

Education reform alone is insufficient. Unless there is a more democratic, open society, Charfi suggests, radical Islamism will become powerful as "the last refuge of the discontented."[46] This has been another important liberal argument regarding Islam. By not offering other ways to understand, discuss, or solve problems, governments, in the words of Alia Toukan, a Jordanian businesswoman, push people toward extremism because they run societies in which there is little democracy or legitimacy but a great deal of corruption and frustration. Islamist parties fill this vacuum "by taking over civil society and becoming the real leaders of the masses."[47]

Yet while the state's shortcomings give rise to the threat of Islamism, this very factor also means the regime must manipulate the powerful weapon of religion in order to survive. As Akhdar explains, behind the modern façade, Arab states are still highly traditional. Religion, along with the power of the military, "is the glue, the crutch, that holds them together." Islam then is "an ideological weapon for paralyzing the social dynamics, blocking the intellect of the masses, maintaining the sub-animal status of women and mystifying the class struggle." The Arab nationalists have checked the independent power of Islam, but they have also used it to control power and win over the masses.[48]

Syria provides a good example of the way that religion is both a government tool for retaining power and combating liberalism while being a revolutionary threat to the regime itself. The government ferociously represses both radical Islamist groups and the reform movement while building big mosques in the belief that this will prove its pious credentials and strengthen conservative antireform forces. The regime also works closely with Islamists in inciting the anti-American, antidemocratic insurgency in neighboring Iraq. Religious observance grows because people have no other outlet for their dreams and frustrations. Even this trend, however, has its advantage for the rulers, for if Islamic forces seem strong, the regime can demand support by warning that the only alternative to the current government is an Islamist state.[49]

This is also, however, a dangerous game that might be a self-fulfilling prophecy. Young radical mullahs avoid direct attacks on the government, focusing instead on U.S. plots to take over the world. Yet they are also laying a foundation to subvert the regime, as when an influential prayer leader first praised President Bashar al-Assad in his sermon, then added that presidents should tremble because Islam is mightier than any power on earth and will triumph in the end.[50]

If an Arab nationalist–Islamist showdown seems inevitable, however, who should the liberals—by far the weakest side—seek as allies? Neither option is promising. In general, liberals offer their services to the regimes, hoping to talk them into reform as a defensive measure. Sometimes they see Islamists as a potential ally, because this group also suffers from repression and might favor free elections because it hopes to win them. The latter position is advocated by Ghabra, who argues, "We cannot lump all Islamists in one basket; they have varying positions on issues."[51]

At the same time, of course, Islamists are at the forefront in opposing liberals, both through vilification and direct attacks, even beyond what governments are ready to do. In Egypt alone, for example, the assassination of Farag Fouda, the wounding of Naguib Mahfouz, and the disappearance of Ridha Hilal have already been mentioned. The case of Nasr Abu Zaid provides a cautionary tale—which must have intimidated many—about what can happen to those who merely raise uncomfortable questions about contemporary Islamic beliefs.

In 1993 Abu Zaid's application for tenure was rejected at Cairo University despite his impressive scholarly credentials. Behind this decision was the accusation of apostasy against him made by Islamists on the faculty and outside the university. Then, in August 1996, Egypt's highest court ordered Abu Zaid to divorce his wife because it found him to be an apostate from Islam, meaning he could not then be legally married to a Muslim. But Abu Zaid considered himself a devout Muslim who simply wanted to analyze the Qur'an's text using scholarly methods.[52]

After graduating from Cairo University in 1972, Abu Zaid taught in its Arabic department. There were vacant faculty positions in Islamic Studies, and his colleagues pressed Abu Zaid to focus on that area. Abu Zaid was reluctant because he knew what had happened to previous graduate students who tried to apply accepted academic standards to this topic. Finally, though, he accepted their request. As he worked on his thesis, Abu Zaid tried to apply the medieval rationalists' approach to the Qur'an's language. He pointed out an idea generally accepted by Western scholars, and for which there is much evidence, that there had been a fierce debate about the Qur'an's final text when it was being formulated. This stance collided directly with the mainstream Islamic, and Islamist, claim that the Qur'an is entirely the direct word of God, not a compilation from human authors or editors.

From their standpoint, both conservative Muslims and Islamists understood the vital consequences of Abu Zaid's obscure scholarly work. Abu Zaid was providing a basis for the liberals' effort to make Islam more flexible and, in the end, liberal. If the historic development of the Qur'an's contents can be debated using reason and analysis, it thus becomes equally valid to analyze Islamic texts in order to obtain new rulings that fit with modern-day needs. Of course, radical Islamists had done precisely that—or, at least, chosen interpretations they wanted while rejecting other, equally valid ones, which amounts to the same thing.

Aside from their hatred of the liberals, then, Islamists also know they are extremely vulnerable to the criticism of traditionalist Muslims, who believe that because only what has been practiced for centuries is valid, anything new can easily be branded blasphemous. The mere fact that Islamism is new is sufficient proof of that crime. Islamists base their new interpretations on the thin rationale that they are merely returning to even older ones dating back to Islam's origins.

Abu Zaid carefully tried to avoid any offense to mainstream Muslims. He never implied that the Qur'an was not the word of God, but simply suggested that it was received in a specific time and place and thus dependent on a context for its interpretation by humans. He also pointed out a rather obvious, though nonetheless controversial, fact: Islamic texts had always been interpreted differently by various schools of thought. Indeed, though he did not say so, conservatives and radical Islamists are sensitive on that point precisely because it raises questions about the claim that their interpretations are indeed the unchallengeable word of God.

There is an interesting detail about Abu Zaid's denial of tenure that throws further light on this issue. In the introduction to one of his books, he criticized Islamic investment companies that had attracted massive amounts of money by claiming to adhere to Quranic injunctions on how to do business in a proper Muslim way. The member of the academic committee most energetically opposing his tenure was the religious adviser to one of these companies, which had been accused of swindling investors. Self-interest, in the broad or narrow sense of the word, is a major factor in the opposition to liberalism by regimes, Islamists, and conservative Muslims.

Far from appeasing the Islamists, though, the university's decision inspired further attacks on Abu Zaid. In April 1993 Abu Zaid was denounced as an apostate in mosques throughout the country, including his home village. One preacher came up with the idea of challenging Abu Zaid's marriage in court. Islamist lawyers took the case; money was easily raised to finance it. An editorial in the regime's own Islamic weekly endorsed the lawsuit and urged that Abu Zaid be fired—or even killed—a good example of how government works with Islamists against any threat of liberalism.

Although a lower court ruled that the plaintiff had no personal standing to bring the case, this decision was overturned and Abu Zaid was found guilty. Egypt's highest civil court confirmed the verdict. One expects it will be many years before another Egyptian academic dares raise detailed liberal arguments for changing the way Islam is interpreted.

In Saudi Arabia, the margin of freedom is even narrower. Nogaidan, the radical Islamist turned liberal, was sentenced to seventy-five lashes by a religious court because of his article calling for freedom of speech and criticizing Wahhabism. He also received death threats and hate mail, though authorities ignored his request to take action against those inciting against him. Instead, the regime established a committee to get rid of teachers suspected of liberalism or even moderation. Many clerics gave sermons denouncing liberals while they said nothing against the radical Islamists responsible for terrorist attacks within the country, and even they themselves called for killing non-Muslims.[53]

Even in Saudi Arabia, though, liberals occasionally won a round. In December 2003, for instance, a Saudi judge sentenced a man who accused a Saudi liberal of secularism in his writings to sixty lashes. The author forgave him, canceling the sentence. But such victories are small and often evaporate on closer inspection. For instance, a tenth-grade Saudi theology textbook was revised to remove statements that Muslims should hate "foreigners, their religion and everything they represent." But a new lesson was added warning against removing Islam from politics and insisting that anyone advocating Western methods of government deserves excommunication.[54] This was a euphemism, implying that proper Muslims could kill liberal Muslims. Governments are eager to teach that proper Islam means not rebelling against themselves, but they are equally eager to claim that it requires opposing liberal reform. They are less interested in eliminating material that justifies the killing of non-Muslims.

As a result, progress is blocked, most noticeably by radical Islamism but also by conservative-traditionalist Islam. An Arab diplomat writing under a pseudonym says Arabs live under "a culture of submission suckled from the clerics of past and from the idols of today." Elsewhere in the world, he notes, people fight to improve education, infrastructure, health, environment, human rights, and other such things while Arab thinking remains fixated on matters of religion.[55]

How can the situation be changed? On this issue, the truth is that the Arab world has gone more backward than forward since the 1980s. While radical Islamism is denied political or military victories, its ideas engage more Arabs than ever before. The conservative-traditionalist clerics and the mainstream definition of Islam have moved in an Islamist, not a liberal, direction. Any effort to rethink Islam has barely begun and faces large obstacles blocking even the most minimal progress.

As a result, liberals focus on the task of stopping radical Islamism rather than reforming conservative-traditional Islam. They mainly criticize the most extreme views that promote violence and hatred rather than those that block progress. Viewing the regime as the lesser of two evils, some liberals even support antidemocratic practices to undercut the Islamists' power. Ahmad al-Jarallah, a courageous Kuwaiti liberal editor, proudly stated that "Kuwait's democracy protects the rights of citizens to freely express their opinion." He then added that because the Jihadists were such a small and unrepresentative minority, the government should make citizens feel more secure by using the courts to crush them.[56]

It is understandable, but probably not profitable, for liberals to seek an alliance with regimes and mainstream clerics. After all, rulers have a stake in preserving conservative Islam—to avoid terror directed against themselves and weaken radical antiregime elements—but no interest in a systematic effort to liberalize Islam, which would turn more people against them than it would win over.

Consequently, the liberal strategy on Islam is not going to produce, at least for a very long time, a breakthrough to a future closer to that of other regions, where both secularism and liberal religion are commonplace. Liberals understand the problem, but their lack of supporters and persuasive arguments makes it impossible to do better. And if Islam does not become more flexible, the broader prospects for liberal change will remain weak. While there is some serious rethinking among Muslims in the West and non-Arab countries, there is virtually no sign of real debate or development of a liberal theology in the Arab world itself.

The greatest need for today, says Jarallah, is fitting the proper type of Islam into a reform movement. Only such a development, led by prominent religious figures and scientists, can bring success to a war on terror.[57] Says an Arab diplomat writing under a pseudonym, a peaceful society can be established only if the Arabs "examine our history, our books, and our stories with an open mind [and] without hatred of the other."[58]

The tide seems to be flowing in another direction, however. Toukan, like many others, notes that while extremists are effectively persuading the masses, moderates are failing to do so. Her suggestion was for people to support moderate candidates in parliamentary and professional associations' elections and also to ally with moderate religious leaders. Such a strategy, not even possible in most countries, is hardly a devastating threat to the regimes and militant Islamists.[59]

It is generally recognized that any progress on this front will take a long time. During a lecture in Beirut, the Palestinian American professor Hisham Sharabi passionately insisted, "We have to change the social and political systems in the Arab world and establish equality among people." Then a student asked him how such equality could be achieved when it conflicted with religious beliefs. Clearly, Sharabi responded, change was not going to happen "overnight."[60]

Responding to this enormous problem, some liberals argue that only democratization can moderate the Islamists. In Egypt, for example, the Muslim Brotherhood has roughly 20 percent popular support and is gaining because, says Abd al-Mun'im Sa'id, it profits from the government's mistakes and the Islamists' own ability to avoid any responsibility for the country's problems. Once entangled in a democratic process, he insists, the Brotherhood would have to deal with the real world. Instead of talking about jihad and Palestine, it would have to come up with programs for education and economics. Faced with real electoral politics, it would split into a number of parties.[61] Such a strategy might work, or it could leave the Arab world in far worse shape.

In fact, what is the Islamist attitude toward democracy? Much publicity was given to a January 23, 2005, statement by the al-Qa'ida leader in Iraq, Abu Mus'ab al-Zarqawi—who himself was not even an Iraqi— condemning democracy as intrinsically heretical by giving authority to the people instead of to the deity, to human law instead of to divine law.[62] While some other extreme Islamists thought the same way, this is not inevitably the Islamist position. After all, Zarqawi's Sunni Muslims knew they could not win the elections that were about to take place there. Meanwhile, his Shia counterparts were telling their people that it was a sin not to vote. More than half of those elected in the January

2005 Iraqi elections were on the Shia Islamist ticket, and indeed the expectation by both politicians and voters that this would happen was probably the single most important cause of those elections' success.

When Islamists see that they can win elections, they may quickly change their tune. For example, Qaradhawi endorsed democracy by claiming that the vast majority of Arabs wanted an Islamist state. In Iran, he recalled, a referendum after the revolution won a vast majority for this faction. Pro-Islamic voters would overwhelm a tiny minority that was Western- or secular-oriented.[63] The example of Turkey, where an Islamic party took power through elections, was also noted by some Arab Islamists as a model.

Thus, an increasing number of radical Islamists are coming to see elections as the road to power. In Lebanon, the Shia Islamist Hezbollah group did well in parliamentary elections and used its position to gain even more political leverage. After successes in 2005 local council elections in the Gaza Strip, the Palestinian Hamas group reversed its decade-long policy of refusing to participate in Palestinian Authority elections. Syrian, Jordanian, and Egyptian Islamists began to demand democratic elections, too, apparently disagreeing with the liberals' predictions either that they could not win or that they would be moderated by such a strategy.

In October 2004 in Cairo, Saad Eddin Ibrahim organized a seminar designed to develop a liberal strategy on Islam and reform. All of the twenty participants were Muslims, though three came from Muslim groups in London, Paris, and Washington. Ibrahim called their effort a jihad against the extremists and terrorists who had hijacked Islam. The seminar adopted a resolution calling for an Islam that took into account the changes in its societies during the last thousand years. It urged a battle with all those claiming a monopoly over interpreting Islam, refuting the version presented by radical groups, and a dialogue with moderate elements in the West to encourage peaceful coexistence among civilizations and nations.[64]

On a strategic level, the meeting presented several important ideas for furthering reform. One of them involved using Muslim groups in the West—where some Islamic theologians have been especially active in developing modernist interpretations. Another was establishing an Islamic Democrats movement to organize pious people and moderate Islamists who favor democracy. In addition, the seminar suggested a return to the original Quranic sources, a Protestant-style approach in which nonclerics could develop their own, fresh interpretations rather than depend on a religious hierarchy overwhelmingly loyal to the status quo.[65] This was, then, a critique of not only radical Islamism but also conservative, traditionalist Islam.

The reaction from Al-Azhar University was sharp and distorted, though its perception of a direct challenge to its own authority was accurate. Muhammad Sayyed Tantawi, Al-Azhar's head and Egypt's most important religious figure, directly threatened Ibrahim, whom he called a traitor to Egypt. Those participating in the seminar, Tantawi said, should be put on trial. He called the proposed emphasis on the Qur'an a deviation from proper Islamic practice being promoted by enemies of the Muslims. Other Al-Azhar officials went further, suggesting the meeting was part of a Zionist religious war against Islam being directed by the U.S. government. The implication was that the foreign participants—all leaders of Muslim groups—were non-Muslims meddling in the affairs of Islam.[66]

As always, the question was whether the masses of Muslims would believe the demagogic accusations or comprehend what the reformers were really trying to do. But the current ways in which Islam is most often represented by clerics, manipulated by politicians, and understood by the masses pose the main roadblock to Arab intellectual development and social progress, a factor that might nurture an even more entrenched, antiliberal political situation in the Arab world. The liberals have a hard time coping with this issue and—by definition—foreign non-Muslims cannot help them do so.

6

America: Satan or Savior?

"No liberal can be anti-American. America is the jewel of liberty," said the Lebanese writer Hazem Saghiya, "but this does not mean supporting everything America does. In fact, it is liberalism to criticize the United States," because this would be an example of independent thinking, a contrast from the dominant Arab political culture in which everything a regime does is enthusiastically endorsed.[1]

The question remains, however, as to what type of criticism is being offered. This issue, like so many others, offers at worst a trap and at best a tough challenge for Arab liberals. The distortion of U.S. policies and society is, after all, not just another aspect of the regimes' propaganda system but one of its central features. The United States is the great Satan whose alleged evil is used to justify their behavior and explain away their failures.

Even Saghiya himself, when not speaking before an American audience, was not so moderate in his criticism. The radical Islamists and U.S. government, he explained, are actually quite similar. They have often cooperated, and both have stimulated violence and terrorism while opposing humanitarian values. In Iraq, he claimed, the United States implemented "implicit racial superiority theories . . . accompanied by ideas of unilateralism, pre-emptive strikes, and evangelical missions to civilize the 'barbarians.'" Khomeini wanted to return to Islam's early days, agreed Saghiya, but British prime minister Margaret Thatcher, who allegedly wanted to return to the Victorian Age, was the same.[2] Saghiya also argued that while it was foolish to reject reform just because the United States proposed it, the United States had no interest in building democracy, because it was too weak, greedy, and selfish to do so.[3]

Thus, whatever legitimate grievances Arabs have toward the United States, the anti-American card usually goes well beyond that point. It is a bias simply too useful, too popular, and too widely believed to be abandoned, even by many liberals. At the same time, though, many Arabs clearly admire the United States and, as polls show, would themselves like to live there. The Lebanese American analyst Fouad Ajami points to the strange contradiction in "an Arab world that besieges the American embassies for visas and at the same time celebrates America's calamities."[4] This apparent paradox in fact makes perfect sense. The more attractive is the United States, the greater the need of Arab nationalists and Islamists to discourage pro-U.S. feelings, especially if they might translate into a desire to imitate that country or to support its policies.[5]

This pattern of fomenting anti-Americanism now has to be adjusted for the unexpected complication of accounting for a United States whose highest foreign policy priority has become to promote democracy in Arab states. No one in the Arab world could ignore this dramatic new orientation, as manifested in the underpinning for the U.S. war on Iraq and President George W. Bush's November 6, 2003, speech at the National Endowment for Democracy, in which he called for a "forward strategy of freedom in the Middle East." Saad Eddin Ibrahim, a leading Egyptian liberal, remarked that while he had various reservations about Bush's implementation of such plans, "I could not have written a better speech."[6] For many other Arabs, however, the fact that the United States had become the main international actor promoting democracy and liberalism in their countries was simply taken as one more proof of the evil, subversive nature of both the United States and at least its vision of democracy.

Nor was this the end of the problem. On one hand, the United States was criticized for pursuing its foreign policy goals by dealing with existing Arab regimes. This was perceived as accepting, or being responsible for, the repressive governments in the Arab world. On the other hand, when the United States did press rulers for change, this was labeled as imperialism, offering proof of an American desire to control the region and destroy Arab independence.

Bush himself played into this problem in a November 2003 speech at Whitehall Palace in London. He put a "commitment to the global expansion of democracy" as the basis of the U.S. foreign policy strategy, along-side a willingness to restrain aggression with force and a dedication to working with other responsible governments.[7] But how could the United States support democracy when the "responsible governments" it had to work with in the Arab world were dictatorships, albeit usually milder ones than its enemies?

The president explained that his innovative approach was intended to "shake off decades of failed policy" in the Middle East in which the United States had been "willing to . . . tolerate oppression for the sake of stabil-ity. Longstanding ties often led us to overlook the faults of local elites. Yet this bargain did not bring stability or make us safe. It merely bought time, while problems festered and ideologies of violence took hold."[8]

This remarkable apology and endorsement of the liberal Arab view-point, however, made relatively little impact because it was filtered through the powerful system of Arab media, ideology, and discourse designed to reinterpret it in a negative light. Thus, for example, the journalist Sala-meh Nematt could charge that the United States was the real reason for the failure of reform in the Arab world. All Arab states were either de-pendent on the United States or too busy defending themselves from attack by it. The U.S. accusation that Arab countries lacked democracy was just an excuse Washington used "to intervene in the states' domes-tic affairs." No wonder progress was impossible. From this standpoint, reforms might be useful as a way to free Arab states from U.S. control, but they were not possible because of U.S. power and the oppression it supported.[9]

The claim that the United States was responsible for Arab dictator-ships gave rise to delicious ironies. Egyptian intellectuals denounce U.S. calls for democracy as interference at the same time that they claim their government's repressive policy is underwritten by U.S. aid.[10] Saleh ibn Humaid, president of the Saudi Shura Council, complained in a presen-tation to the Arab Thought Forum that it was hypocrisy for a country to call itself a citadel of freedom, democracy, and human rights when it supported autocratic and oppressive regimes.[11] Yet he was an appointed official of a Saudi regime that was arguably the prime example of a non-democratic government backed by the United States. Did this mean that Humaid wanted the United States to oppose the government he served, or was he just using this as a slogan to bash the United States and negate his own rulers' responsibility for their country's shortcomings?

A case in point was the State Department's criticism of the Saudi government's arrest of thirteen liberal dissidents in March 2004 as being "inconsistent with the kind of forward progress that reform-minded people are looking for." The Saudi government falsely protested that those mild liberals taken into custody had jeopardized the survival of state and society, weakening the country at the very moment when unity was needed to fight the terrorist threat. There were no cheers in the Arab media for this U.S. initiative on behalf of free speech in the Arab world, challenging one of the regimes it supposedly always supported. Instead, governments and media reacted angrily to such efforts, mobilizing their people against any U.S. attempts to encourage them toward reform.[12]

It is interesting to contrast the Arab world's situation with that of Latin America. In that region's history, there has been a constant alternation between democratic and dictatorial systems, a long history of multiparty states with full citizens' rights, and a strong liberal opposition even under military juntas. In short, a viable alternative to dictatorship always existed. To press against coups or try to get the army back to the barracks was a real option for the United States, and one enjoying considerable, organized local support. Thus, U.S. policies that supported Latin American dictatorships can justifiably be criticized. This was simply not the case in the Middle East, where Arab governments generally enjoyed far more popular support than did any of the real alternatives, which were even more antidemocratic. Fair elections anywhere in the Arab world during most of the second half of the twentieth century would have been won by radical nationalists or Islamists who would have imposed their own dictatorship. Generally, the ruling dictatorships owed neither their power nor their survival to the United States. If the United States had refused to have any dealings with dictatorial regimes, there would have been no Arab government at all with which it could work.

Moreover, at the same time, virtually all Arab intellectuals, including almost all of those who are liberals today, supported either the incumbent government or a more radical alternative nondemocratic regime. They are thus criticizing the United States retroactively for dealing with these same governments when, in earlier days, they would have virulently attacked U.S. policy if it had opposed them. Many a contemporary Kuwaiti democrat, for example, was a Saddam Hussein fan before 1990. If the United States had pressured, opposed, or subverted Arab dictatorship, these Kuwaitis would have been among the first to condemn this as imperialistic, anti-Arab, and anti-Muslim.

Those using this argument against the United States also never mention any particular regimes as having wrongly benefited from U.S. support. Nor do they suggest how there could have been any different U.S. policy in this regard, given the lack of a moderate or democratic alternative.[13] For example, given that the Nasser regime was a repressive dictatorship, was the United States wrong in not backing the Anglo-French-Israeli effort to overthrow it in 1956 during the Suez War? Yet U.S. opposition to this plan is cited by Arabs as its finest pro-Arab moment. Similarly, anyone who criticizes the United States for cooperating with oppressive regimes should see the U.S. overthrow of Saddam Hussein as a good thing. But many of those who condemn U.S. policy as a friend of reactionary forces opposed the war. Or would those who criticize the United States for working with Arab dictatorships in attempts to resolve the Arab-Israeli conflict prefer that Washington had refrained from negotiating efforts because of the nature of those regimes?

Are Arab liberals seriously suggesting that their preferred U.S. policy would have been to cut off all aid to an Egyptian regime or to refuse to defend the Saudis and Kuwaitis from Saddam Hussein in 1991 unless they instituted thoroughgoing democratic reforms? Do they mean to suggest that the United States should not have helped Jordan survive subversive efforts by radical states in the 1960s and 1970s, or Iraq against Iran in the 1980s, unless they first made substantial reforms? Was it wrong in Arab eyes to engage the Palestinian Authority in a diplomatic effort and give it aid despite Arafat's dictatorial proclivities? The only alternative factions in a position to assume leadership under such circumstances would have been radical Arab nationalist or Islamist ones that would have moved no closer to, and probably further away from, the type of polity and society liberals want. The greatest ironies are that the servants of dictators complain that the United States was helping their masters, or that those criticizing the United States for not having tried to change Arab dictatorships in the past are equally critical of its efforts to do so at present.

This is why no one explores in detail the implications of blaming the United States for the dominance of Arab dictatorships. From the liberals' standpoint this attributing all Arab problems to U.S. interference is

also a counterproductive argument. First, it relieves the Arabs themselves of responsibility for the current state of affairs, one of the main
myths the liberals are trying to break. Second, it reinforces the ruling
doctrine's hold over the minds of millions of Arabs who have been
taught to blame the United States for all the problems of the Arab world.
Once again, the United States is said to be an enemy because either it is
fighting against Arab rulers or it controls those very same governments.
Either way, this definition of the United States as subversive enemy or
all-powerful puppet-master has promoted anti-American hostility and
ignored local responsibility for the shortcomings of polity and society.

Yet liberals often repeat such claims. As sophisticated an analyst as
Rami Khouri has argued that Arab ruling elites and governing oligar-
chies are "mostly dependent on Washington for financial and military
aid and, in some cases, direct protection." As a result they are supposedly
paralyzed, unable to oppose the United States and at odds with their
own anti-American citizenry. This is the reason, he claims, the regimes
are so ineffective. In contrast, the street represents the poor, angry, and
frustrated masses who feel humiliated by their own governments and
"exploited, manipulated, or ignored by the United States and other foreign powers."[14]

This, as always, begs the question: who told them that this is so, and is
it actually true? Moreover, the implications are that the dictatorships
would like to be good and democratic but the United States is holding
them back. The rational response for those who believe such nonsense
would be to support their local dictator. This is precisely the mainstream
establishment argument.

It is difficult for the United States to have any influence in promoting
democracy or anything else when there is a knee-jerk reaction against
whatever it does by the mainstream Arab nationalists and Islamists. This
response is inevitably based not just on an honest misunderstanding or
an independent examination of facts but on the anti-American card's
usefulness for stirring up nationalist and religious anger. The practical
result is to strengthen the existing regimes as the alleged champions in
the battle against the American threat.

Such distortions are not limited to those unfamiliar with the United States. Professor Hisham Sharabi, who taught at Georgetown University in Washington, D.C., for many decades, was a veteran critic of Arab society. Yet despite his ferocious attacks on the Arab system, he reinforced its main defense by telling an audience in Lebanon that the region was under "neocolonial attack" by the United States, which wanted to treat the Arabs as it had Native Americans. "The Americans have entered the region to possess the oil resources and redraw the geopolitical map of the Arab world" and to help the Jews control the Arab world, he explained.[15]

A good example of this phenomenon of an ideologically determined anti-Americanism unresponsive to fact was the reaction to U.S. ambassador to Egypt David Welch's op-ed piece in *Al-Ahram* on the first anniversary of the September 11 attacks. Welch's article was a masterpiece of cultural sensitivity, flattering the Egyptians and thanking them for their kindness to the United States but asking for one small favor in the politest way: that the (state-controlled) media stop claiming the United States or Israel was behind the attack when bin Laden's responsibility was clear, even from his own words.[16]

The response was an outpouring of anti-American hatred. The regime-controlled Egyptian Journalists' Union not only criticized the statement but claimed Egypt had greater press freedom than the United States because the U.S. press would not publish such a critical article as Welch's piece.[17] A petition by dozens of Egyptian intellectuals, authors, and journalists condemned the ambassador as treating them like "slaves" or subjects rather than as the "voice and conscience of the Arab nation" whose culture was the basis of world civilization. How did a foreign ambassador dare "dictate to free Egyptian intellectuals and journalists" how they must think and write, demanding they must agree with everything the United States says, "even if it is lies. . . . Even if America thinks that it has conquered the globe, it will not succeed in conquering and subduing the free wielders of the pen." Instead, the U.S. ambassador should be ashamed of Israel's crimes, equal to those of Hitler. It would be better for him to go home than to interfere in Egypt's domestic affairs.[18]

The fact that the United States, which is in mainstream parlance the Arabs' chief enemy, promoted democracy served as an additional argument against it. The United States, it was claimed, was simply ordering the Arabs to do something else in order to further its own interests and extend its own control. But the heroic Arabs would never grovel before the United States. There was a humorous aspect to this, of course, in that the Arab intellectuals were rejecting freedom in the name of freedom, flaunting the independence of those who in fact were subservient to their dictators' every demand. No matter how much the United States, or the West in general, tried to speak as a friend to heal the Arabs' wounded pride, explained the American diplomat Hume Horan, "we will not be listened to. . . . The foreigner's extended hand receives no response; indeed, the gesture is likely to be rebuffed or misconstrued."[19]

At the same time that they reject America's advice, though, Arab elites can easily claim they are already engaged in reform and enjoying the benefits of democracy. The most establishment reaction of all is simply to say, as did Egypt's foreign minister Ahmad Maher, that Egypt was already a model democratic state and that "we do not need anyone to teach us."[20]

An *Al-Ahram* editorial also claimed Egypt was already a democratic state with multiple political parties along with freedom of both expression and the press. Indeed, *Al-Ahram's* sister newspaper, *Al-Gumhouriyya*, suggested that Egypt's democracy under Mubarak's wonderful rule should be a model for other countries.[21] Because democracy was the people's rule, any external attempt to change their system was inherently antidemocratic. Even worse, it was a manifestation of the imperialist concept of a "white man's burden" to liberate other people "from ignorance and backwardness." Such attitudes and the resulting colonialism, the state-directed newspaper explained, was the true cause of the Arab world's problems.[22]

As for the Wafd, the political party that supposedly represented liberalism in Egypt, Ahmad Alwan, a member of its supreme council, explained that it would never agree with a tyrant like Bush, who only understands force and uses it in an attempt to achieve his greedy ambitions.[23] The strategy, then, was not to benefit from U.S. support for democracy but to make gains by manipulating anti-Americanism. Yet how could any democratic opposition beat the regime and the Islamists at this game?

Indeed, this approach of attacking the United States for advocating democracy reflected the antireform forces' main theme that the United States was merely using democracy as a trick to conceal its evil policies. Salameh Ahmad Salameh, an *Al-Ahram* columnist, warned that modernization was simply an American trick to install its own puppets. Any real democracy would have to fight "American hegemony." An editorial in the Kuwaiti newspaper *Al-Watan* said the United States hypocritically wanted to promote democracy in some countries while destroying it in others that opposed U.S. interests, for example, to subvert the rulers of Saudi Arabia because that country opposed a U.S. takeover of the Gulf's oil.[24] Rajah al-Khouri, a columnist for *Al-Sharq al-Awsat*, wrote that U.S. proposals to support democracy in the Arab world were the idea of "Zionist circles" that wanted to pretend Arabs hated the United States because they lacked democracy, needed to modernize, and suffered from poverty. The real reason for antagonism, he said, was that America's policies were so terrible.[25]

Of course, even if the main complaint about the United States concerns its policies, the problem is that exactly what those policies consist of is subject to enormous distortion. This is a point far too often missed in Western discussions of this issue. If Arabs are told and convinced of such falsehoods as that U.S. policies show no interest in establishing a just Arab-Israeli peace or that they seek to enslave Iraqis, it is hardly surprising that people are going to find them objectionable.

There is also a high level of hypocrisy involved in the critiques of the United States by the regimes and their supporters. For example, one well-known Egyptian radical, who demanded that his own country become an Islamist state, attacked President George W. Bush for allegedly using religion to obtain his political goals. Qaradhawi, a powerful Islamist cleric who likes to pose at times as a moderate, issued a fatwa permitting the killing of American and British civilians in Iraq at a time when he had one son studying at a university in Florida, a daughter studying in Texas, another son in the American University in Cairo, and three daughters at school in Britain. None of them, wrote the Egyptian liberal Sayyed al-Qimni scoffingly, seemed destined to sacrifice their lives as jihad warriors.[26]

Qimni also pointed out other cases of the distortion and hypocrisy used in examining U.S. policies. For example, he explained, many Arabs spoke as if the Iraqi insurgents were defeating the United States without comprehending that if the United States wanted to do so, it could wipe whole Iraqi cities, like Fallujah, where there was heavy fighting, off the map at a push of a button. As it was, concern for the remaining civilians in Fallujah made the U.S. army risk and receive casualties by fighting from house to house instead. If the kinds of weapons of destruction possessed by the Americans were in Arab hands, he continued, they would have used them to destroy everyone in an enemy city.

Rather than have contempt for the United States, he concluded, Arabs should understand that "this world that we fight against, covet, and hate has in the past sacrificed 40 million [people] to defend its freedoms—[freedoms] that we do not understand—and is more zealous about them than we are about our Islam. . . . We all know that they obtained their rights in the past and that they know how to obtain them [today], and are capable of doing so."[27]

Of course, since Arab liberals wanted the same kind of freedom and were making an analysis of the Arab world's problems roughly similar to that of U.S. policy, the new version of the anti-American campaign was designed to brand them as tools of Zionism and imperialism. Most disturbing in this connection was the equating of the reform movement with treason against the Arabs and Islam. The Saudi writer Khaled al-Suleiman wrote that the real U.S. goal was not for Arabs to become good at computers or physics but to destroy "the moral bonds of our social behavior." They would then become just like the United States: "A society in which the marriage of minors is a crime, but sexual relations with minors is permitted! A society in which drinking alcohol is like drinking water, and inhaling marijuana is like inhaling air. . . . A society stripped of its identity, its values, and its virtues—an ugly society with no connection to its roots, which is only a pale mirror image of the West."[28]

Al-Ahram equated the American effort to promote democracy to the means used to undermine the Soviet Union during the Cold War, employing such alleged weapons as a controlled U.S. media, Hollywood films, and all the techniques of advertising and systematic propaganda. The United States was creating false enemies "to justify U.S. warmongering." Of course, it insisted, all Arabs want "the right to live in freedom and democracy," but "those aspirations should not be cheapened by being turned into a gimmick to serve U.S. interests."[29]

The kind of democracy the Americans really want in the Arab world, claimed the Jordanian Khaled Mahadeen, was a puppet regime to rubber-stamp whatever the United States wanted. Parliaments and media would serve U.S. interests, "glorify Washington's arrogance, applaud its wars on Arabism and Islam," and keep silent about U.S. involvement in the Zionist annihilation of the Palestinians and the American destruction of the Iraqi people. Other U.S. goals are to destroy the Arab school system and Islam, "to abolish religious education, Islamic modesty . . . Jihad, and charity."[30] A more polite but essentially identical establishment response came from Mustafa al-Feki, chairman of the Egyptian People's Assembly foreign affairs committee. The U.S. democratization campaign is based on a total misunderstanding of Arab society and education, including the ridiculous idea that the region needed any new values or ideas.[31]

In short, U.S. sponsorship of democracy as such did not necessarily win it more favor in the Arab world. This did not mean, however, that the proreform camp became any weaker than it would have if the United States had said or done nothing on the issue. U.S. efforts strengthened the cause of reform, though by how much is a question impossible to answer. Certainly, the new U.S. policy—not to mention the war in Iraq—sparked more debate over these issues than would have occurred otherwise. Even if the United States had not developed its new policy, the same accusations would still have been used by the mainstream forces against liberals.

Still, unhappy about the problems they felt U.S. policy created for them, and desperate to minimize any claim that they were puppets of U.S. imperialism and Zionism, some liberals responded bitterly. For instance, the Jordanian Fahd al-Fanik warned that the U.S. effort "is likely to damage the popularity of these reforms and silence those advocating them out of fear that they will be seen as America's propagandists."[32]

Liberals also used ingenious—and often ingenuous—counterarguments to turn this problem into an advantage for themselves. One such approach was to insist that indigenous Arab reform was the best way to avoid U.S. domination and intervention. Daoud Shirian, a Saudi columnist for *Al-Hayat*, suggested that if the Arab media became more independent of their governments, the United States would have no justification for interfering in the Arab world and violating its sovereignty.[33] Michel Kilo, a Syrian journalist and reform activist, claimed that only reform could rescue Syria from U.S. domination. If there was no reform, the United States would invade and take over. The danger was so great, he warned—getting away with his remarks by quoting

American sources—because there was some truth to claims that the regime tortured its own people and kept them in a state of poverty and unemployment, that the health and education systems were declining, and that the economy was in bad shape.[34]

A parallel approach came from the Egyptian Usama al-Ghazali Harb, editor-in-chief of *Al-Siyassa al-Dawliya*, in an article entitled "With Our Own Hands, Not Those of America." Arabs don't want foreign interference, he explained, but they know that thoroughgoing reform is needed "not because . . . foreigners demand it, but because of our real needs." Every Western criticism has already been made by Arabs themselves. The enemies of reform use the foreigners' support for it as an excuse to dismiss the liberal agenda by saying change is merely a foreign gimmick to undermine "our traditions and beliefs." But liberals, says Harb, must confront and defeat these lies.[35]

Harb agreed that historically the United States had little credibility with regard to its intention to spread democracy, but September 11 brought a change, making the leaders of that country see that "political despotism and socio-economic problems in the Arab and Islamic world are a threat to their national security." At any rate, Arabs needed to remind the Americans that they were the ones really demanding democracy.[36] Harb suggests that the new U.S. prodemocracy policy should show that it is actually heeding Arab demands. Historically, the support for traditionalists against reformers, opposed to the "long-term interests of the Middle East's people," was intended to "further U.S. interests in fighting communism, protecting the oil supply, and defending Israel's security." This was justified by saying that stability was more important than democracy in the guise of "deference to the 'traditions and local traits'" of traditional societies. And if the struggle against Israel was manipulated by regimes "to justify domestic repression and delay definitely the process of democratic reform," this was partly the West's fault because it allegedly did not do enough to resolve the Arab-Israeli conflict.[37]

These claims are debatable. First, Harb uses a neat trick that is easy to miss. It is true that the West supported traditional regimes in the Arab world—like the Moroccan, Jordanian, and Saudi monarchies—but it also supported the traditional liberals as well—like the parliamentary regimes in Egypt, Syria, and Iraq. Those who, in Harb's description, were the "reformers" whom the United States was opposing were radical Arab nationalists and Islamists. These forces did in fact overthrow the rulers in Egypt, Syria, Iraq, and Libya, among other countries, in the 1950s, 1960s, and 1970s. Far from complaining that U.S. policy was not supporting electoral democracy, the masses and the intellectuals cheered as radicals dismantled formal multiparty democratic systems and silenced liberals. Even in Saudi Arabia and Jordan, where the United States sided with traditional regimes, these regimes had enjoyed considerable popular support and their enemies were hardly liberal and democratic forces.

Equally, the West did far more in trying to resolve the Arab-Israeli conflict than did the Arab side, which for many years made maximalist demands, complained about U.S. diplomatic efforts, and sabotaged every initiative. For example, the eight-year-long effort of President Bill Clinton to bring a negotiated peace and create a Palestinian state is literally never mentioned.

On one level, then, Harb and other liberals who make such arguments reinforce the existing system, which defers real debate by blaming the United States for everything wrong in the Arab world. At times, even Harb repeats the key arguments of the hard-line mainstream ideology. He criticizes, for example, the U.S. response to the September 11 attacks, claiming incorrectly that when Americans asked who was responsible for the attacks, "the official answer was as rapid and assertive as it was misleading and rash: the Arabs and Muslims did it. We're going to get them." He claims that the main debate in the United States came between those who blame "the pro-Israeli bias of U.S. policy in the Middle East" and those who claim "that Arab and Muslim societies are naturally prone to 'terror.'"[38]

All the careful admonitions of the U.S. government and the media about not generalizing the blame and expressing their explicit exoneration and respect for Islam are simply ignored. By suggesting that the American response was full of racism and hate, Harb intensifies anti-American stereotypes and hostility. "Unfortunately," he concludes, "we see no sign that the United States has learned anything from the cataclysm that befell it. . . . If the death of over 3,000 Americans and the destruction of major symbols of American civilization is not enough to make the U.S. administration see the trouble with its policy, what is?"[39]

At the same time, though, Harb is also trying to manipulate mainstream arguments to justify support for change. Thus, he concludes by saying that while the United States has followed "selfish, unprincipled, and shortsighted policies," it is good if it now speaks about modernizing Arab societies, developing democracy, and resolving the Arab-Israeli conflict because these are all things Arabs "have been seeking to achieve for a long time."[40]

The Arabs should not give up on their dream of democracy just because "the fall of the [Iraqi] dictatorship is mixed with occupation," or "because the call for democracy is made in foreign tongues."[41] The central issue is that "internal tyranny, the lack of democracy, the decline in freedom, these are the roots of the problem. They are more important than any external threat. Indeed, they are what make such threats possible."[42]

A similar approach was taken by the Jordanian Jamal al-Tahat, who suggested that the main thing wrong with American initiatives is that the Arabs themselves should have undertaken them. He also tries to turn the tables on mainstream nationalists by pointing out that the regimes often brag about "achievements resulting from cultivating relations with America," so why shouldn't they support reform efforts that might improve their relations? If the U.S. approach damages the Arabs, it is only because they did not themselves already carry out reform.[43]

Another way of separating reform from U.S. policy was used by Nader Fergany, the lead writer of the Arab Human Development Report, seen by many in the West as a central liberal document. Fergany, a political science professor at Cairo University, is himself a staunch Arab nationalist of fairly traditional views. As he points out, much of the report stays in the Arab mainstream—reinforcing traditional antidemocratic ideas—by putting much of the blame for lagging development on U.S. policy and on Israel. Fergany asserts that the report proves the Arabs are capable of criticizing their own societies as a defense against the "explosive mix" of ignorance and arrogance that seeks to "impose reform on Arab countries from outside—even by force," as manifested in such mistaken policies as the U.S. overthrow of Saddam Hussein.[44] Instead, he calls on the United States to leave reform to the Arabs and, for its part, to stop violating human rights and cease supporting Arab repressive regimes and Israel.[45]

These views might be called the more cautious liberal approach regarding the United States, though one must always bear in mind that what someone thinks privately and says publicly are not necessarily the same thing. A bolder, rarer approach is to advocate explicitly a change in

Arab views of the United States. This is the road taken, for example, by Saad Eddin Ibrahim, who points out that the United States acts in its own interests, as do all countries, including the Arab ones. But the Arabs are simply not very effective in coping with frictions that arise when their interests clash with those of the United States, thus generating even more American hostility toward themselves.

It is rare that anyone in the Arab debate goes beyond polemical-type arguments to do the type of analysis so common in the West when writing about Middle East matters—a serious, detached attempt to understand the basis and nature of another party's behavior. Abd al-Hamid al-Ansari's view, from Qatar, thus comes across as a remarkable exception. Ansari insists that America's response to the September 11 attacks was a relatively moderate one in the context of legitimate self-defense. Other countries faced with such an assault would have been far more aggressive and destructive. While regretting innocent victims of the U.S. attack on Afghanistan, he points out that there was no other way to deal with the Taliban, a "group of fanatics who rejected all calls for mediation" and had provided a safe haven for terrorists. Moreover, Afghan refugees reported that the Taliban hid tanks and heavy guns near mosques and heavily populated areas. If this is true, they were responsible for the civilian deaths. He concludes, "We must have the courage to admit that what happened in Afghanistan was the liberation of our Muslim brothers—even if, unfortunately, it was by non-Muslim hands."[46]

Ansari considers the Arab and Muslim tendency to view the United States—and the West in general—as hostile to be one of that society's most harmful mistakes. To fight these alleged enemies, Arabs are ready to sacrifice real achievements and live poorer lives. Yet America's government and people are not hostile to Islam or to Muslims. Muslims practice their faith freely there. What the United States is hostile to is the "destructive" form of radical Islam, which Muslims should also oppose.[47]

Reviewing the history of American-Arab relations, Ansari finds that "the positive aspects vastly outweigh the negative ones." He mentions such events as U.S. opposition to European colonialism in the Middle East; saving Egypt's regime in 1956 when England, France, and Israel were close to overthrowing it; liberating Kuwait from Iraq and Afghanistan from the Russians; saving Bosnia and Kosovo from Yugoslavia; defending Gulf Arab states against Iran and Iraq; giving $52 billion in foreign aid to Egypt; helping Egypt regain the lands it lost in the 1967 war; and diplomatic and financial efforts to help the Palestinians in the peace process. Much of the Arab world benefits from U.S. aid, trade, arms, technology, and training. The negative aspect, U.S. support for Israel, should not be allowed to outweigh all the many positive ones.[48]

What would be the situation, Ansari asks, if the United States had listened to Europeans who opposed military action in Bosnia and Kosovo or in Iraq? Those places would not be liberated today. Iraq's Arabs would be worse off if the United States had followed European advice and said, "Democracy is not suited to the Arabs, their culture is contrary to it." He concludes that the Arab people cannot defeat their dictators without "powerful external help."[49]

All of these factors are rarely mentioned in Arab discourse. The same point applies to another neglected issue: the cost of hostility to the United States. Ansari notes that the Arab world has always lost by following the ideas of "revolutionaries mouthing slogans." There is nothing to gain by "waving bin Laden's picture and burning American flags." Instead, the Arabs should act like other countries and "win over America" by understanding its mentality and communicating effectively. The way for the Arabs to win U.S. support is by reform—more democracy, respect for human rights, and openness—because "the American people do not respect anyone who doesn't respect his own people."[50]

Ahmad Bishara has a similar view. In an English-language article he explained that few have told of the positive aspects of the United States, which include idealism, noble sacrifice, and nurturing human freedom. Like Ansari, he referred to its growing Arab and Muslim communities, who have been given haven from persecution and economic deprivation in their homelands. Many Arabs have been educated in the United States and have used this training to develop their own countries. Yet across the Arab world the media have constantly spread anti-American propaganda. The only way to combat this is to give Arabs a more accurate perception of American society and not leave the field to "despotic regimes, the media, and Islamist propaganda." A better view of the United States is in the Arabs' interest, he concluded, for only by defusing the stereotype of an American bogey can they successfully struggle against despotic regimes and extremist Islamist oppositions.[51]

Other liberals—especially in the smaller Gulf monarchies that have fond memories of U.S. help on a number of occasions—have proposed a changed position toward the United States. "There is much in U.S. policy to condemn," said an editorial in the Saudi *Arab News*. "There are many aspects of Western society that offend. . . . But anti-Americanism and anti-Westernism for their own sake are crude, ignorant, and destructive [ideas]" that lead to terrorism and must be stopped.[52] A Kuwaiti, Khalid al-Khater, used the analogy of learning how to drive a car. Because democracy, like cars, is a Western invention, Americans can act as driving instructors to help people to ensure their own societies' success in building such institutions.[53]

A Bahraini writer, Ahmad Jum'a, put the appeal for better relations in a pragmatic context. It was worthwhile for the Arabs to try doing something different toward the United States since their earlier strategies had failed so badly. Germany and Japan benefited from cooperating with the United States after World War II, while the Arabs failed in fighting the United States as a Soviet ally during that same period. Saddam Hussein fought the United States, and one sees what happened to him. The Arabs have gambled on the USSR, Nasser, war with Israel, and Islamic revival—none of which have worked. Since the Arabs are not going to vanquish the United States through radical Islamism, why keep trying it? They could try making friends with the United States, and if that does not work, Jum'a said jokingly, the Arabs could still "throw America into the sea."[54]

Another writer, Anas Zahid, ridiculed the Arab media and intelligentsia's constant calls for war or economic boycotts against the United States and the West. "How," he asked, "do we fight countries from which we buy weapons and beg for a loaf of bread?" The West has supplied the Arab world's medicine, food, aircraft, computers, clothes, diapers, and chocolate. The problem, he concluded, was not an East-West, Muslim-Christian, or Arab-Zionist struggle. "The issue is that we are backward . . . and do not want to face ourselves. Without facing ourselves we will not move one step forward."[55]

Iraqi dissidents also concluded that close cooperation with the United States was indispensable if they were ever to get rid of Saddam Hussein. They could expect no support in the Arab world or even sympathy from its media or intellectuals. As one exile put it, they understood "that the battle of Baghdad can only be won after winning that of Washington. . . . We are in dire need of the help of all Americans who believe that U.S.

national interests lie in promoting democracy and human rights beyond its borders."[56]

If, then, the United States is not such a terrible enemy—or at least one not worth fighting—perhaps, said liberals, its ideas and criticisms for Arab society should be given serious consideration. Getting this simple idea across is very difficult, however.

First, while the most outspoken liberals see the United States in a positive light as a strong advocate of the democracy and reform they want, some have worried that its involvement will discredit them. Their enemies have attacked them in Arab nationalist or Islamist terms as American agents or apologists. Thus, they have tried to distance themselves from the United States, for example, through the suggestion that reform should be left to the Arabs, that the United States is really the enemy of democracy, and that the Arabs should institute reforms in order to defeat the nefarious plans of that country.

Second, other liberals have continued to be hostile toward the United States because they retained a strong element of Arab nationalist thinking themselves. They were more ready to join in with mainstream criticisms that U.S. policy in general, as well as its stance on democracy, constitutes hypocritical and imperialistic interference in Arab affairs.

Third, some liberals have copied their enemies' approach toward the United States. Just as Arab nationalists and Islamists have used the United States as a scapegoat for their failures, liberals could blame U.S. policy for their own movement's weakness and inability to transform the Arab world. By supporting existing regimes, the United States, they said, helped to preserve the Arab world's status quo. Consider, for instance, Toujan Faisal, the first Jordanian woman elected to that country's parliament, in 2002, and who was thereafter imprisoned for four months after accusing the government of corruption. "To promote real democracy in the Arab world," she wrote, "the United States needs to begin encouraging its regional allies to tolerate internal opposition from all sides and give it a legitimate outlet in free and fair democratic elections."[57] This was a reasonable position, but it must also be noted that she supported Saddam Hussein, a personal friend whom she called "an old-fashioned knight. . . . Compared with him, the other leaders of the Arab world are small pygmies."[58] After Saddam's fall, Iraqi documents showed she had received payoffs of hundreds of thousands of dollars from his government, for acting as an agent in the sale of three million barrels of Iraqi oil.[59]

On these as on other matters, most liberals' writings show how far apart American and Arab perceptions are, whether liberals were expressing their personal views or simply adapting their language to what was necessary if they were to have even a chance of being effective. An example is the effort of Rami Khouri to use a mirror-image approach that simultaneously tries to advance, while it also, presumably unintentionally, undermines the argument for reform and better Arab-American relations.

Khouri tries to balance Americans' feeling of victimization by September 11 with a parallel Arab feeling about the 2003 Iraq war: "Americans have had enough of Arab states that take their money and protection and allow anti-American terrorists to operate from their soil; Arabs also have had enough of Western powers that speak of peace and democracy but routinely use their capabilities to maintain an Arab autocratic and oligarchic order that has shunned democracy and maintained internal and regional orders defined by chronic inequalities and tensions."[60]

Like the hard-liners, though, Khouri attributes the post–September 11 and prodemocracy U.S. strategy to the machinations of anti-Arab forces: a coalition of Republican conservatives, pro-Israel hawks, Christian fundamentalists, global supremacists, and free marketers who have taken over the White House. He equates Bush and bin Laden as two ruthless men who want to use force to get their way but are unrepresentative of their societies.[61]

Yet how can one avoid the conclusion that if an American prodemocracy strategy is the product of terrible people who want to hurt the Arab world and Muslims, it cannot be a good thing? Where are the Arab nationalists and Islamists wrong when they condemn the United States and its policies, and warn against friendship or cooperation? This is a serious pitfall for liberals: by trying to fit into the existing discourse, use its language, and not become pariahs, they may often reinforce its basic assumptions. Yet if they break completely with the dominant concepts— which they may or may not sincerely believe—they face the danger that no one will listen to them and many will attack them.

On top of this is the fact that there are many paradoxes in the situation from the U.S. standpoint. First, there is the unavoidable conflict between devising a policy that can promote democracy while dealing with dictatorial Arab regimes. No Arab state is democratic, yet the United States needs Arab government allies for the war against terrorism, resolving the situation in Iraq, preserving access to Middle Eastern oil, solving the Arab-Israeli conflict, and many other purposes. Far from being soft on Arab dictators—a stance more characteristic of European policy, which is generally more popular among Arabs—the United States has put sanctions on more Middle Eastern dictatorships than any other country in history, at considerable cost to itself. While such pressures have been placed on Libya, Iraq, and Iran because of conflicts regarding terrorism and other international issues, these countries also happen to be among the region's worst human rights violators and dictatorships, too.

But each case is difficult and different. Take, for example, the tiny country of Qatar, whose strategic value for the United States was enhanced by its providing the Al-Udeid air base and other facilities for U.S. forces in the Gulf. Even liberal American newspapers quite divorced from the Bush administration's thinking had nice things to say about Qatar, which the *New York Times* called "one of the most liberal, democratic countries in the traditionally tribal ruled neighborhood."[62]

Yet while milder than most Arab regimes, the Qatari government censored the press and barred political parties and national elections. Qatar also subsidized and hosted the Al-Jazeera satellite television network, giving it free rein to attack the United States while ensuring that it never criticized Qatar itself. Clearly, the regime saw the U.S. presence and support as a way of ensuring its own survival, a factor made even more attractive in that the United States did not interfere with Qatar's ability to use anti-Americanism as a political tool. As one American observer summarized the situation, even if Qatar was liberalizing faster than its neighbors, the U.S. government was still allying itself with a "closed regime that is most concerned with protecting a small ruling elite."[63] So by working closely with Qatar on strategic matters, did the United States encourage or set back the cause of reform in the Arab world?

Tunisia is another case in point. In February 2004 Bush hosted Tunisian president Zine al-Abidine bin Ali at the White House. Tunisia in some ways had been the most socially progressive of Arab states, for example, in its handling of women's rights and education. Yet it, too, has been a dictatorship. Kamel Labidi, a human rights activist and journalist, criticized this meeting in an article entitled "The Wrong Man to Promote Democracy," an ambiguous phrase intended to invoke both presidents in this category. He called bin Ali a "ruthless autocrat" whose "police state" had silenced Tunisia's once active civil society. The official welcome given him, said Labidi, demonstrated that the idea of the United States promoting democracy in the Arab world was hollow.[64]

While Labidi's description of bin Ali is reasonably accurate, by these standards there is no Arab leader with whom the United States can meet or work. Moreover, U.S. officials used meetings with bin Ali to urge him to make reforms. If he was unlikely to listen to such advice or encouragement, neither was any other Arab leader. These problems, then, are endemic to the situation of bilateral relations, a built-in paradox.

Another paradox was the way Arab rulers manipulated the U.S.-led war on terrorism for their own antireform agenda. Labidi complained that the Tunisian government passed a tough antiterrorism law it used against peaceful critics, whom it labeled terrorists though they had never committed violence. Such measures, he suggested, would increase the level of support for radical Islamism and terrorism. "The absence of free speech has . . . made extremist clerics on satellite TV stations look like reasonable alternatives to the government, leading more young Tunisians to the mosques and more young women to wear the veil."[65]

But could the United States be held responsible for this behavior? Certainly, the United States was not happy with a situation in which democratic dissenters were harassed while anti-American incitement was everywhere and money flowed freely to terrorist groups. The most anti-American regimes also used the war on terrorism as an excuse for cracking down, too, insisting that they had to put down peaceful dissenters as pro-American traitors who were cooperating with a U.S. effort to subvert the legitimate rulers. For their part, in suggesting the United States was the factor blocking reform, some liberals—and their rivals—were using the typical Arab world excuse for a failure to succeed. Perhaps as well, those reformers were trying to give themselves a mainstream cachet by suggesting their program frightened the United States and was contrary to its interests.

In addition, there was still a third paradox regarding bilateral relationships. For the United States, Labidi remarked, the most important considerations in its relationship with Tunisia were that it was moderate, a U.S. ally, "a model of relative prosperity for the Arab world," and a supporter of the Israeli-Palestinian peace process. But even here U.S. policy tried to strike a balance. When he visited Tunisia, Secretary of State Colin Powell urged the government to adopt "more political pluralism and openness" while praising it as well. This method would not work, Labidi said, insisting that only international pressure could gain reform.

But how did people like Labidi react at a time when the United States did push strongly in trying to change Arab dictatorships into democracies? In effect, he blames the continuing domination of dictatorships and lack of freedom in the Arab world on the United States. After September 11, he claims, the U.S. government undermined change in the Arab world because it decided "to hold itself above international law and adopted some of the same tactics in its war on terror as police states use to silence opponents." He suggests that Egypt justified extending its emergency law because Powell stated, "We have much to learn" from Egypt's antiterrorist methods. The war against Iraq, according to Labidi, united liberals and their dictatorial rulers into an anti-American alliance.

In contrast, but with little evidence, Labidi insists that the Middle East had been moving in a prodemocratic direction before the United States did anything. His only example was that Morocco pledged to abide by the Universal Declaration of Human Rights and that other rulers were starting to pay lip service to such principles.[66] This does not amount to very much. It could be more easily argued that Arab regimes gave far more lip service to democracy after the Iraq war, though this did not mean they were doing much to implement it.

The point is that U.S. policy faces tremendous paradoxes in implementing any prodemocracy policy, more from the nature of international affairs, regional issues, and the existing regimes than from any degree of American hypocrisy. Such a strategy of supporting democracy did not automatically produce pro-American sentiments among masses suffering under dictatorships, because those same regimes had the power to manipulate their subjects' perception of America's goals and behavior. Even liberals were split over whether this strategy was helpful and about the very nature of the U.S. position itself.

Indeed, liberals often sounded similar to mainstream Arab nationalists on such issues. The way Khouri put it was to say that the United States was now "the 800-pound gorilla sitting in our laps, inside our living rooms, with its quarter of a million troops in the region and its stated policy of wishing to reshape the politics of the Middle East to become more America- and Israel-friendly." The basic choice for Arabs, as outlined by Khouri, was either to hope the United States might have awoken from its past evil policies or conclude that it was merely making empty promises.[67]

While Khouri says both sides are to blame for misperceptions involving Arab-American relations, he provides an excellent example of just such a misunderstanding on his own part. He quotes Secretary of Defense Donald Rumsfeld saying that he thought Iraqis would figure out a way of ruling themselves within the parameters laid out by the United States. In context, Rumsfeld was simply suggesting that the Iraqis would adapt ideas like democracy and human rights to their own conditions. It was both a vote of confidence in their ability to manage their affairs in a democratic manner and an assurance that the United States was not expecting them to copy blindly its own system. For Khouri, though, this was an example of "arrogant Roman-like rhetoric" that combined "award-winning incompetence and insensitivity."[68] In this case, as with mainstream Arab nationalist or Islamist attitudes, it is the assumption of U.S. hostility and the distortion of U.S. behavior that ensure the very conflict that Khouri decries.

If this kind of response comes from someone like Khouri, a graduate of Syracuse University who grew up in the United States (his father was a UN employee in New York) and is a fan of the New York Yankees baseball team, how much hope is there for communicating a positive image of the United States to others?

It is hard for even relatively open-minded Arabs to break with past tendentious assumptions rather than actually reexamining the evidence and history involved.

There are both full and partial exceptions to this rule, but they are relatively few. A number of elements are needed for a more coherent alternative version of the United States and its policies. This includes a better understanding of American society and political culture; an Arab taking of responsibility for their own problems and shortcomings; puncturing the myth of Arab resistance to the United States as a central element of ideology and behavior; reevaluating stereotypes about U.S. policies on the Arab-Israeli conflict; putting in context the accusation of U.S. backing for Arab dictatorships; and a willingness to believe that the United States can have good intentions toward the Arab world.[69]

In each case, only the barest beginnings have been made by a handful of people, compared to hundreds of repetitions—even by liberals—on each point in the hard-line Arab nationalist-Islamist discourse. The main fortress of this intellectual system has been built on the argument that all Arab problems can be blamed on external villains. It is hard to see how the liberals can really make any change without challenging this worldview. Yet fighting this battle is both dangerous and difficult.

Angrily reacting to the Islamists' murder of a Saudi prince touring Algeria, Muhammad Talal al-Rasheed wrote: "We have bred monsters. We alone are responsible for it. . . . We are the problem and not America or the penguins of the North Pole or those who live in caves in Afghanistan. We are it, and those who cannot see this are the ones to blame." While Arabs seemed incapable of productive action, the United States at least had gotten rid of Saddam. "The majority of us are sick and tired of this carnage and President Bush, wrong on just about everything else, is right on this one."[70]

The respected Kuwaiti political philosopher Mohammad al-Rumaihi also took on the myth that Arab history has been one of fighting U.S. imperialism. Pointing out that President George W. Bush had just met with six Arab leaders, representing more than half of all Arabs, he noted that while the United States was the Arabs' main partner in every aspect, they simultaneously talked of "resisting" and even defeating it. He asked, "Is this not another Arab exaggeration?" Sudan, for example, requested U.S. help in resolving its civil war one day, and a week later bemoaned the fact that the Arabs do not fight the United States in Iraq. Others pose as militants but try to use the United States to their advantage, like a Syrian intelligence chief's justifying his country's occupation of Lebanon by claiming it to be in U.S. interest, or a government's pretending to cooperate in the U.S. war on terrorism as an excuse to crack down on moderate dissidents at home.[71]

A rare example of creative thinking about the nature of the United States itself has been the writings of Abd al-Mun'im Sa'id, director of the Al-Ahram Center for Political and Strategic Studies, on U.S. history. Although he cautions against having faith in a U.S. government whose views are allegedly based on dreams of a U.S.-dominated world, he also tries to understand the real roots of American success. The Arabs, he explains, have an incredibly poor knowledge and understanding of U.S. government and society.[72]

In contrast to the way Arabs think, explains Sa'id, Americans are strong because they view history not as Arabs do, as a way to assert that they have been heroes or complain that they have been victims in the past, but rather as a guide to do better in present and future. Again unlike the Arab world, Americans criticize and reassess their history on such controversial matters as the treatment of Native Americans or slavery because they are determined to avoid repeating mistakes. But the Arab and Islamic world lacks "such moral introspection and efforts to act on it." Americans have apologized for enslaving Africans while the Arab world pretends that it never did so. While America's international behavior may justify rancor against it, fabrications and distortions don't help Arabs deal with the world's sole superpower. Sa'id concludes, "We have concocted an American history tailor-made to the spirit of anti-American hostility that has swept the Arab world."[73]

Another aspect of the mistaken Arab assessment about the United States has been to underestimate its power and determination. As one writer put it, the mainstream idea that the Arabs will defeat or outwait America assumes the United States is a cowardly country that will withdraw from places where it suffers heavy casualties—as in Vietnam, Beirut in 1982, or Somalia. But the United States has shown in Yugoslavia, Afghanistan, and Iraq that it does not give up easily. It will continue its war on terrorism, and America's enemies are the ones "who ultimately will be consigned to the dustbin of history."[74]

Can the United States really encourage democracy in the Arab world? The views of liberals vary widely. Some enthusiastically say yes; others suggest that the United States should stay out of this issue and restrict itself to adopting policies more to Arabs' liking. The former group hopes that U.S. pressure will change the behavior of Arab regimes or overturn them altogether. The latter group puts more emphasis on a fear that regimes will effectively use U.S. involvement to discredit liberals. There are also many liberals who share the prevalent anti-Americanism of the mainstream nationalists.

Even those who hope for U.S. help do not necessarily believe it will be forthcoming. The Egyptian analyst Ahmed Abdallah claims the regimes know that the United States needs their help to fight terrorism and thus they do not take seriously the idea that it will pressure them on behalf of democratization.[75] But do in fact the regimes feel so sure that the war on terror will trump demands for democratization and that U.S. policy will pose no problem for them? Perhaps this has been true to some extent, but the degree of their nervousness, defensiveness, hostility, and pretensions at reform show that they have been truly worried.

More accurate, though, was Abdallah's point that in practice these distinctions might make no difference. The United States had a difficult choice, not only because of the war against terrorism but also because of the threat of Islamist revolution. He asked, "Is America going to help democratization of these regimes at the risk of an Islamist [anti-American] participation in power?"[76] The answer seems to be no. Abdallah also pointed to the limits of U.S. power. As a result, he predicts that "repressive regimes would survive, thrive and trample over democracy."[77]

The most common single point raised is the ritual denunciation of U.S. policy toward Israel and the demand that the United States solve, for all practical purposes single-handedly, the Arab-Israeli conflict. Yet how this can be done and the extent to which the Arab world can contribute to a solution have not been addressed, while the lessons of the failed 1990s peace process have been consistently ignored. Whatever the benefits of resolving the conflict, the argument that reform depends on resolving Palestinian grievances (on terms acceptable to the Palestinian leadership) echoes the traditional mainstream argument used to defer any real change.

Other frequently expressed concerns are objections to the U.S. war in Iraq or, among those who support the war, the need for assurances that the United States will turn power over to the Iraqi people in a way that encourages democracy. American success in Iraq has been clearly seen as an important step in changing the political atmosphere in the region to one more friendly toward reform.

Many have suggested that the United States should not support Arab tyrants, though how this should be carried out in policy terms is not clear. Khouri proposes that the United States be more willing to export the good values that it has hitherto kept mainly for domestic purposes, including such fundamental principles "as the consent of the governed;

the indivisible nature of liberty and justice for all; habeas corpus and impartial judiciaries; and term limits for political leaders."[78]

According to Ibrahim, the United States should deliver a "forceful" but not arrogant message that the United States will help in the democratization process. It should provide training for democratic life, help civil society groups, give aid without strings attached, and press Arab governments to reduce their restrictions on freedom. He promises that such a strategy would both avoid the need for future U.S. armed intervention and ensure that the region's people would gain democracy.[79]

When speaking in private, many liberals make clear that they would like the United States to be a deus ex machina, a force that solves their own problems by somehow forcing Arab governments to change even if this requires strong pressure or—in some cases—military action. An Iraqi-type response is attractive to many liberals, though no one would ever admit this publicly, as an apparent instant solution for their own countries. They also suggest that U.S. aid and other help to Arab regimes be conditioned upon their record regarding human rights and democratization. It is also possible, however, that such sanctions would encourage governments to crack down on dissidents even harder, escalate their anti-Americanism, and use nationalist appeals to mobilize their people even more effectively in support of themselves.

Some Arab liberals like Bishara, given their sense that—despite any shortcomings or drawbacks—U.S. help was indispensable, applauded Bush's reelection in 2004. Those in the region who wanted Bush defeated, he explained, were Islamists and dictatorial regimes like those of Iran and Syria. They used terrorism to scare the United States out of the region and pretended the United States was attacking Islam to discredit it and ensure their own domination. Reformers, he continued, supported the U.S. war on terror, wanted the United States to be fully involved in supporting democracy, and saw the violence in Iraq as the birth pangs of a new order rather than a sign of impending doom. Thanks to Bush's policies, women's rights have advanced in the Gulf monarchies and Afghanistan, regimes were forced to fight terror, human rights groups spoke out openly, calls for educational reform were spreading, and there was an active debate in which people demanded more liberty.[80]

If progress was slow, Bishara insisted, this was inevitable in handling such a difficult task. Moreover, if not "for the timid and opportunistic stance" of European states like France and Germany, "the results would have been much greater." If they had the opportunity, he concludes, liberals would have voted for Bush as a way of getting a better future for themselves and their families. While not all Arab liberals felt this way, many of the most energetic and consistent ones did.[81]

Fouad Ajami's assessment stands as a balanced, sober one regarding both the limits and the importance of U.S. involvement in trying to support the liberal cause. "In the end, the battle for a secular, modernist order in the Arab world is an endeavor for the Arabs themselves. But power matters, and a great power's will and prestige can help tip the scales in favor of modernity and change."[82]

One promise made by liberals—which is a reasonable hope though far from a guarantee—is that democratic Arab regimes would be more, not less, friendly to the West, despite what might be the greater appeal of anti-American demagoguery in a setting where political parties competed for votes or Islamists rule. As a meeting of Arab human rights groups put it, in terms often heard in Western discussions of this issue, "Democracies generally prefer peace and avoid aggression. Rarely do democratic countries go to war with one another."[83]

It can also be argued that the suspicion and hostility toward the United States, arising from both perception and cultivation, can undermine these efforts. But a remark made by Gamil Mattar, director of the Arab Center for Development and Future Research in Egypt, is also telling. In response to the U.S. prodemocratization policy, he explained, Arab governments have hurriedly claimed to support change, even while hoping to stall and do little in the hope the challenge will go away. Meanwhile, their people have been watching them more critically and might someday demand that those promises be fulfilled. He concluded: "If I were one of the architects of Washington's reform offensive, I would feel quite smug at the effect I produced."[84]

7

Israel: The Great Excuse

E ven more than the contentious issues of Islam or the United States,
the question of Israel forces Arab liberals to face extremely difficult
choices and unattractive options. Israel is almost always defined in the
Arab discourse as absolutely evil, not a state with interests or a people
with rights but a force designed to injure and destroy Arabs or Muslims.
A massive daily barrage in every institution of state and society ensures
that this image is perpetuated.[1]

The sole permitted standpoint defined as the proper Arab attitude
toward Israel has generally been one of condemnation, boycott, struggle,
and preferably its elimination. Tarek Heggy characterizes this dominant
school of thought among Arabs as "clamoring for war and for the Palestinians (and Arabs) to continue along the same path (opposition +
denunciation + blaming the United States + armed uprising 'Intifada' +
the culture of resistance + random acts of violence, etc.)."[2]

Any statement questioning these principles draws a massive retaliation intended to silence and discredit its author. This is the paradox
faced by Arab liberals. The easiest route for them is to join in this chorus, proving their participation in the orchestrated passion, protecting
themselves from accusations of treason on this most sensitive issue. It is
easy for them to excuse their hypocrisy by arguing that this leaves them
freer to speak on less controversial matters. Many do take this road.

This strategy, despite its ease and superficial attractions, also demands
of them a high price, for the manipulation of the Arab-Israeli conflict is
one of the most powerful weapons in the arsenal of the antireform regimes, hard-line ideologues, and radical Islamist opposition. They argue
that there can be no internal change, no softening of autocracy, and no
cooperation with the United States unless this issue is first solved in a

way that satisfies their stringent demands. Nothing can be done until Israel is defeated or destroyed, and since this does not happen, then nothing else can be done.

While many realize, and some openly state, that this issue has become the Arab world's excuse and the regimes' way of distracting attention from failures, persuading people on this point is very difficult. The issue is never really discussed rationally, because to do so would be too dangerous for the survival of the dominant Arab narrative and the use of the issue as a political weapon. For example, Tarek Heggy points out that not a single Arab writer has questioned what would have happened if the Arabs had accepted the 1948 partition plan creating both Israel and a Palestinian state. The same applies to asking what would have happened if the Arabs had cooperated with Egyptian president Anwar Sadat's call for comprehensive negotiations following the Camp David accords in the late 1970s.[3] With a few exceptions among Arab liberals, the same silence applies to considering how events might have developed if Arafat had accepted the offer of a Palestinian state in 2000.

The same critique applies to the Arab states' obsessive use of the conflict as their demagogic cover and excuse. An Arab diplomat writing under a pen name asked:

> Why don't the officials who organize demonstrations on the Palestinians' behalf ever protest or act to mend the terrible state of health, education and social services of their own countries. . . . What would have happened if, from 1948 onwards, every Arab country had dedicated itself to domestic construction and not made the Palestinian problem its main preoccupation and relentless concern? . . . What would have happened if every Arab country had concentrated on educating its citizens and improving their standard of living . . . health and culture?[4]

Similarly, he points out, Islamists demand jihad against Israel but never speak of a jihad for moral improvement. The rulers, then, keep their societies on a permanent war footing even if they have no intention of actually fighting. At the same time, they generally act in a way to ensure that the conflict will not be resolved, perpetuating it as their asset. As a result, criticisms of society are dismissed, dominant ideologies reinforced, and liberals discredited. No voice should rise above the din of battle, goes their slogan. How can these irresponsible dissidents destabilize a society locked in life-or-death combat against such a dreadful foe? How can liberals advocate cooperation with, much less imitation of, the West—or at least the

United States—which sides with the enemy? And aren't reformers secretly Zionist agents, or agents of Zionist agents, or too soft on Zionism?

The extent to which this system shuts down the reform movement is best illustrated by a remark from Kanan Makiya, a leading Iraqi exile intellectual: "The spectrum unfortunately of what it is possible to talk about in Arab politics these days runs from Palestine at one end to Palestine at the other with no room for the plight of the people of Iraq," or any other country for that matter.[5]

Gamal Mubarak, the son of Egyptian president Hosni Mubarak and a supposed advocate of reform, laid out the regimes' basic position in a single sentence. There could be no reform, he said, as long as the Israeli-Palestinian fighting dragged on.[6] More candidly, his father stated the rulers' real fear: "If we open the door completely before the people, there will be chaos."[7] Since both ending the conflict and fighting Israel are so dangerous, the regimes prefer to keep the conflict going, but only in terms of rhetoric or, at most, by covertly supporting and openly cheering anti-Israel terrorism, thus allowing the regimes to encourage violence at no cost to themselves.

Some liberals respond that while this issue must be solved for democracy to succeed, the existing dictatorships have proven incapable of resolving it. Only democratic regimes can conclude the conflict on terms acceptable to Arabs and Muslims. The current rulers cannot do so.[8]

This is, of course, the same claim made by other contenders for power in the Arab world. Arab nationalists in the 1950s and 1960s, Marxists in the 1960s and 1970s, and revolutionary Islamists in the 1980s and 1990s argued that the road to Jerusalem was through Cairo, Baghdad, Damascus, and Riyadh. In other words, only domestic revolution could create the conditions needed to destroy Israel. The failure of internal Islamist revolutions, in turn, made possible the rise of bin Laden's concept of jihad that reversed this formula and proclaimed that the road to power in the Arab world lay through terrorist attacks against Washington, D.C., New York, and Jerusalem.

Liberals argue this situation in both ways. On one hand, solving the conflict is necessary in order to remove a key pillar supporting the current regimes. The supposed need to keep the Arab world on a permanent war footing serves as a principal excuse to preserve dictatorships. On the other hand, reformers suggest that only moderate democratic regimes can gain the domestic support required to make the compromises vital for reaching a peace agreement. In addition, only democratic governments will really be motivated to end the conflict and able—though this is rarely said—to win full cooperation of the United States and Israel to reach that outcome.

This is, of course, a dilemma—and not the sole one—for which liberals have no solution. The Arab governments and the Palestinian leadership do not want to make real peace, and the liberals cannot force them to do so. As long as there is no real peace, it will be hard to establish stable democracies. Yet perhaps peace will be possible only after such regimes have already come into existence.

How can liberals respond to this paradox? One way is simply to endorse the mainstream interpretations while avoiding this issue as much as possible. Of course, liberals are far more likely to view the conflict as wasteful and to favor a negotiated peace concluded on the basis of compromise. But they don't have to say so. Usually, though, no liberal can write an article on any subject without devoting a sentence or two to a ritual criticism of Israel.

Consequently, the absolutely ideal solution for liberals in rhetorical terms is to urge or demand that others solve the problem for them, hoping the United States and the West can produce some kind of negotiated conclusion that will sweep the issue off the agenda so that it no longer interferes with their efforts to change the Arab world. The liberals can do nothing to help this process, but they very much want to see it happen, taking away the regimes' and Islamists' best weapon of mass persuasion. In a sense, though, this is a deferral paralleling that of their enemies, a partial acceptance of the impossibility of progress until a distant, uncertain future.

The next-most-attractive variation is to try to turn this question against the status quo. Liberals, like Islamists, are aware of how much cynicism and hypocrisy—or one might say, pragmatism and good sense—shape the policies of Arab states, which are not eager for war with Israel and whose militancy manifests itself with words rather than action. While Islamists argue for an escalated struggle, liberals suggest that the failure to reform has weakened the Arab world in the face of the Israeli threat and is the main reason for its defeats. If one really wants to beat Israel, democratization is the best way to do so. In contrast, terrorism and promoting anti-Semitism are portrayed as bad tactics that discredit the Arabs and play into the Zionists' hands.

According to the June 2004 Doha Declaration of Arab human rights groups, for example, "Historical experiences have proven beyond doubt that liberation movements throughout the world . . . which grant people their freedom of expression are the best way to liberate the land and the nation." The real traitors are the Arab nationalist regimes that "are unable or unwilling to deal seriously with outside threats and hegemonic designs." Rather they are the ones sometimes "ready to surrender their sovereignty to ensure their own survival."[9]

A third approach, the toughest and least popular, is to confront the issue head-on, denouncing the conflict as being unnecessarily perpetuated in order to save the regimes. These liberals call on their people to view Israel in the same way other countries are perceived, with understanding as well as measured criticism. But this is a courageous choice that can bring ostracism and persecution.

The first Arab intellectual to advocate this publicly was Muhammad Sid-Ahmed in a 1975 book.[10] Sid-Ahmed is both an establishment insider and an outsider. The scion of a powerful family who became a Communist and spent some time in jail, Sid-Ahmed argued that the opportunity for peace opened up by the 1973 war must be grasped lest the issue become more explosive in the future. In later years, he urged Arab intellectuals to support Israeli peace groups. He called for negotiations to be held on ending the conflict, developing security arrangements, eliminating weapons of mass destruction, and economic cooperation.[11]

Yet during the 1990s peace process, Sid-Ahmed noted that most Arab groups—even in Egypt—boycotted Israel and viewed the negotiations as a temporary truce required by the Arabs' weakened position in the world and region. Once circumstances changed, they would then be ready to renew the struggle for eliminating Israel. Part of the reason for this stance was that the consequences of accepting Israel were so potentially devastating for the Arab ideology, self-image, and political system. As a result, while individual moderates can always be pointed out, it is no exaggeration to say, as Ahmad al-Jarallah did, that the Arabs "are still living in the 1960s when they threatened to throw Israel into the sea."[12]

Those who advocated a real peace did so in large part because they argued that continuing the conflict was too damaging to the Palestinians

and dangerous for the Arab world. They justified their stance on pragmatic grounds, urging the achievement of the best possible solution
rather than the chimera of achieving total victory if enough lives and
decades were spent in more fighting. Khaled al-Kishtainy, an Iraqi intellectual exile living in London, mused that for a half-century Arabs have
viewed pictures of death and destruction yet did not put a priority on
ending that suffering. The conflict—and hence suffering—was continued through their intellectuals' idiocy and their leaders' arrogance,
which brought more suffering in that land and catastrophes on their
own people.[13]

At the moment the peace process was breaking down completely, in
October 2000, al-Afif al-Akhdar urged, in an op-ed appearing in a Palestinian newspaper, "In this volatile situation, the voice of cool reason
should be heard." The Palestinians needed peace as much as the Israelis
in order to have a state and fulfill their needs. Time is not on their side
as problems become more complex and suffering prolonged. Those who
demand a new war, he warned, will produce a new Arab catastrophe.[14]
"Every Palestinian demand beyond a two-state solution is political
suicide."[15]

A prime example of the rare direct challenge to Arab thinking about
Israel came from the Egyptian playwright Ali Salem in his book *My
Drive to Israel*. Salem ridicules the Arab version of the issue and shows
in detail how it provides indispensable underpinning for the existing
political system.[16] In addition, he points out that this battle—however
emotionally satisfactory and possible to justify—leads to Arab defeats
and an incredible wasting of resources, which retards progress.[17]

Both sides are responsible for this tragedy, he told an interviewer. "It
is futile to describe Israel as the only one who is wrong." Baited with the
question of whether he had seen pictures of Muhammad ad-Durra, a
Palestinian child falsely said to have been killed by Israeli fire, Salem
responded, "Of course, but I also saw the picture of the Israeli soldiers
who were butchered, and their corpses burnt. I also saw the kidnapping
of Israeli soldiers in Lebanon. Why do you ignore this?" He added that
when Arab intellectuals or groups, like the Union of Egyptian Writers,

make demagogic cries for endless struggle it is others—particularly the Palestinians—who pay the actual cost.[18]

Defeating Israel, Salem notes, has been the great delusion of modern Arab history. Each costly failure has ended in defeat only to be replaced by a new theory of how to succeed, from the PLO's debacle in Jordan in 1970 to Iraq's invasion of Kuwait in 1990, supposedly for the purpose of uniting the Arab world against Israel. In the latter case, he remarks sarcastically, "our losses were trivial, several hundred thousand casualties and several hundred billion dollars."[19]

Even when no one is actually fighting, the Arab states maintain "a mental state of war" whose purpose is to persuade their people to give up all their rights. When things are quiet, the regimes say that this is the most dangerous moment of battle because the enemy is preparing a new conspiracy with Western imperialism to destroy the Arabs. The purpose of this incitement is to blind the people to every other issue and to suppress criticism or even thought. "In a state of war, no one argues . . . or asks questions." They are told that this is not the right time to talk about free speech, democracy, or corruption, then ordered, "Get back to the trench immediately!"[20]

Another way the Israeli threat is used, Salem continues, is to discredit directly the very notion of freedom, democracy, and cultural openness. Any steps in this direction, claim the regime's supporters and Islamists alike, will ensure defeat. Even if there is no Israeli military threat, the great danger is that of an imaginary "cultural invasion." Fearful of phantoms, "we waste our lives building fortresses and citadels to defend ourselves against them."[21]

To discuss this alleged cultural invasion seriously is to show how ridiculous it is. Salem ponders how this attack will work: "Israel will launch Hebrew banners into the skies over Arab capitals and scald us by pouring ashes from them. They'll mount Hebrew novels on rockets so as to penetrate our minds and . . . hearts and souls" to expel all the great works of Egyptian writers and musicians. The ultimate weapon is an Israeli "nuclear eraser, capable of wiping out your own history of creativity and wisdom."[22]

What, Salem asks, is the proposed solution for this cultural danger? "Don't speak with them, listen to them, or read them. Convince yourself that they don't exist. Imagine that Israel is the temptress of the folk tales, the voice of seduction luring you to desire and destruction, the siren of Greek mythology and of the *Thousand and One Nights.*"[23]

Even this is insufficient, however. The only truly safe defense is to shut down your mind, plug your ears, and close your eyes. When a distinguished, relatively moderate political science professor told Naguib Mahfouz that Israel might destroy Egypt's heritage, the great writer responded contemptuously that if Arab culture was so despicably weak, the Arabs would be better off dead.[24]

Yet of course such behavior in fact does great harm to the Arabs themselves, closing off their own creativity, making them too fearful to adapt ideas from the West or benefit from its cultural advances. These are notions, Salem concludes, promoted by demagogues who manipulate Arab feelings of inadequacy about themselves and ignorance about others.[25]

Such suppression, even in states formally at peace with Israel, can only deter intellectuals and artists, setting limits to their exploring or voicing different ideas. In 2003, for example, Egyptian filmmakers pressured the organizers of the Cairo International Film Festival to withdraw Khalad al-Hagar's film from the competition because ten years earlier he had made a movie that allegedly promoted normal relations with Israel—the story of a love affair between an Egyptian man and a British Jewish woman. Hager defended himself by condemning Israel.[26]

Ultimately, such treatment is a form of blackmail, forcing everyone to support the regime and reject change. The way Israel is dealt with provides a pattern followed in many other aspects of life and thought, including attitudes toward the West, Islam, and reform. But this effect is precisely the intention. All the chest-beating, aggressive rhetoric greatly benefits the Arab world's status quo by furnishing it with the ultimate all-purpose excuse, but it does not really benefit the Palestinians or harm Israel. That is why, ultimately, it has less to do with Israel or the Palestinians than with the requirements of the Arab system.

For example, in 2002 the United States launched an initiative to encourage Arab countries toward democracy. Obviously, this was not something governments wanted to do. How to explain their rejection? From Egypt, Salameh Ahmad Salameh wrote in *Al-Ahram:* "America cannot act for reform in the Arab world as long as it tramples the rights of the Palestinian people underfoot" and wages war on Iraq.[27] Simultaneously in Saudi Arabia, Abd al-Karim Abu al-Nasser explained that the United States was only advocating democracy "to divert attention from the . . . Israeli problem which makes the region insecure and unstable . . . and provides some Arab regimes with justification for repressing their citizens." Why should Arabs listen to anything the United States says when it ignores Israel's alleged plan to take over the Middle East?[28]

Two years later, in 2004, when the United States proposed to help Arab civil society groups through aid and training, this program was rejected on the same grounds. Even the moderate Sid-Ahmed wrote that the U.S. plan was really intended to wipe out the Palestinian cause and its centrality in Arab thinking. Former Arab League secretary Esmat Abd al-Meguid told the United States, "If [President Bush] would like to see democracy that means equality, liberty, respect for others, then this should be applied to what is happening in Palestine."[29] Yet why should that issue block an attempt to promote a better educational system, fair elections, freer speech, and less corruption in Arab states unless one was to assume that such changes were only a favor that the Arabs were doing for the United States?

In Jordan, civil society groups worked hardest not on demanding democracy or civil liberties but to cancel that country's peace treaty with Israel. Even the government's own spokesperson, Asma Khader, a civil society and women's rights activist, publicly supported this campaign.[30] Such a priority left civil society little time or energy to fight for its own rights or compete with militant forces that could easily outbid liberals in stirring up passion on that issue.

Even the much-praised Arab Development Report, which bemoaned the Arab world's failures to achieve economic and democratic progress, attributes much of the blame to the same issue, asserting that Israeli control of the West Bank and the Gaza Strip "casts a pall across the political and economic life of the entire region," which somehow "freezes growth, prosperity and freedom in the Arab world."[31] Aside from the exaggeration on causation, it is as if the Arabs themselves had no responsibility for the continuing conflict or the failure to reach a peaceful negotiated solution.

So obvious is manipulation of the issue—though few say so publicly—and so devastating its use within Arab society, that some liberals have felt compelled to remark on it. An Egyptian writer, Hassan Hafez, wrote in an opposition newspaper, "I wonder why we blame Israel for every fault in [our] society. This is the logic of the weak, who seek a peg on which to hang all their mistakes in order to evade a true confrontation with reality."[32] The alternative, he concludes, is "to grab those responsible for our failures by the collar instead of blaming Israel for all our problems like cowards. [Blaming Israel] causes us to look ridiculous before the world and it makes the small Israeli state look great. We have to be honest with ourselves before we blame others! When we blame others we are being untrue, we mock common sense and we scorn our people."[33]

Another Egyptian writer, Amin al-Mahdi, one of Egypt's best minds and most articulate liberals, revealed the great secret outright. The factor dictating the agenda in the Arab states' handling of the conflict was its value as a domestic diversion: "To cover up the inability of the Arab regimes to adapt to modern life, and to justify territorial ambitions in the region."[34] Muhammad Farid Hassanein, a former member of the Egyptian parliament turned liberal oppositionist, spoke in similar terms. "Egypt's rulers are afraid of peace," he explained after a trip to Israel, "since peace pushes us towards democracy, and they are not interested in that. Nor are they interested in our becoming acquainted with the cultural reality which Israel has created or with the democracy that the Israelis . . . have implemented."[35]

There were rarely open debates in which liberals challenged the conventional wisdom on the issue, but one such interesting exchange was between the Syrian-Palestinian author Hisham Dajani and the famous Syrian poet Mamdouh Adwan (best known by his pen name, Adonis). Dajani argued that most Syrian intellectuals supported peace, and he gave three basic reasons why. First, a realistic examination of the situation showed that negotiations and compromise were the only way to get back the Golan Heights. "Due to the balance of power," Dajani explained, Arab states and the Palestinians could get land back only by making "some concessions on the issues of water, security arrangements, and normalization of relations." There could be no illusion of capturing the Golan Heights by force; it could return to Syria only through negotiations.[36]

Second, the restoration of Syria's territory would be a sufficient incentive to warrant making peace. The destruction of Israel was not a necessary objective. Regaining all of Syria's land would restore Arab pride.

Third, Syria need not fear peace with Israel. It was silly to believe that Israel would swallow up the Arabs if there was peace. This has not happened with either Egypt or Jordan after they signed treaties with Israel. Indeed, peace would strengthen Syria by allowing it to devote its resources and energies to solving its domestic problems like corruption, democracy, and economic backwardness.[37]

Yet there is much counterproductive fallout from Dajani's linkage—common among liberal Arabs—between peace, on the one hand, and reform, democracy, modernization, economic change, and the struggle against corruption, on the other hand. Such ideas are not exactly music to the ears of the establishment and its supporters. If peace promotes all the things they dislike, why should the rulers support it?

Aside from this problem, Dajani faced an uphill battle in breaking old attitudes, which were strong even if irrational and destructive of real Arab interests. All Adwan had to do to win the debate was to reiterate the traditional Arab arguments with all the passion and power they invoked. Moreover, those taking such positions could look forward to material benefits for doing so. Despite the fact that Adwan had often been critical of Syria's government in the past, he knew the regime would support his viewpoint. Indeed, after his attack on Dajani, the regime lifted its ban on Adwan's writing for the state-owned newspaper *Tishrin*.

The return of Syria's territory and even the creation of a Palestinian state would not settle the issue, because compromise was unjust, Adwan responded. Moreover, Israel would never be satisfied with peace and would strive to conquer the Arabs. "These are murderers and nothing more," Adwan insisted. No Israelis really favored peace, and they looked at Arabs as subhumans who should be killed. This argument showed the high political value of making Israel an irrational evil entity incapable of normal political behavior, for if peace was impossible, the battle must continue. If that held true, discussing alternatives or promoting change was either foolish or treasonous behavior.

In answering Adwan, Dajani used the type of rational, realpolitik, national interest approach that might win arguments elsewhere in the world, but not in the Middle East. Adwan, he explained, "speaks in the emotional language of a poet," but this kind of thinking "turns us into a nation that lives in dreams. . . . I deal with politics, the art of the possible, and the art of the pragmatic."

The Arab-Israeli conflict, he insisted, was like other historical enmities. Once peace was made, frictions would gradually decline. He pointed out how Germany twice invaded France but today those two countries are allies. In Japan's war with the United States, two atomic bombs wiped out cities and killed hundreds of thousands of people. Yet now these former combatants are allies. Why? Because their leaders dealt rationally with the situation and, inasmuch as they pursued rivalry, turned to peaceful economic competition instead. "There is no such thing as eternal enmity. . . . True, our generation at least cannot forget, but we cannot fight forever against those who are stronger than us and are supported by the entire West. . . . Instead of sending our forces to lose the battle, let us turn them inward: to the battle for political and economic reform."[38]

To a reader who asked whether Arab countries should be seen as extremist if they promise to liberate the land through war if negotiations fail, he responded: "Yes. . . . There is no one single Arab state that wants or is capable of fighting. The sole meaning of war has been more and more catastrophes and defeats Saddam style."[39]

A similar approach was taken in the *Arab News*, albeit only to its "safer" English-language audience—soon after the start of the 2003 Iraq war.[40] The Arabs were harmed by their obsession with Israel on whom "every problem faced by Arab societies was blamed, in however obscure or far-fetched a way." Both journalists and regimes preferred that Israel be the subject of passion in the Arab street rather than issues closer to home. The article goes on to praise Saudi Crown Prince Abdallah as seeking to combine peace with Israel and reform in the Arab world. The editorial concludes: "The days when the Arab world could just scream 'Israel,' as if that one word were sufficient answer to every question about every problem that came its way—as though saying that one word could deflect all further inquiry—are over. The time for peaceful coexistence, internal reflection and healthy, progressive thinking has come."[41]

That view, though based on some discernible trends, also seemed to arise from a certain amount of wishful thinking. Even more heartbreaking was a flaw in Dajani's argument. He had predicted that the struggle would be resolved because enmity was declining in each generation. But the tremendous increase in anti-Israel incitement after 2000, coupled with the new appeal of bin Laden's worldview, could be read as actually increasing the level of hatred and encouraging additional decades of conflict in the Arab world.

Aside from cynical exploitation of the Arab-Israeli conflict, however conscious or otherwise, there are also genuine misunderstandings at the root of the Arab obsession with hostility toward Israel. An aspect of this attitude is the belief that Israel is collapsing from external pressure and internal conflicts. One guest on an Arab satellite television program claimed that such things as the existence of conscientious objectors, drugs, and crime in Israel showed that the country was disintegrating.[42] In part, this analysis was due to misreading democracy and internal dissent as weakness, the same belief that leads many people in the Arab world to reject having a more open system for themselves.

A liberal Arab critic of this approach noted that underestimating Israel is an example of how "ideology kills knowledge." In fact, he continued, Israeli society is stronger because of its democratic norms such as free elections, a strong civil society, a free press, and an independent judiciary. Assuming that open debate and self-criticism is a sign of collapse reveals an Arab political culture that, in contrast, conceals differences and rejects pluralism. Indeed, he continued, the Arabs would be better off if Israel had no democratic system, as it would be weaker and more easily wiped off the map. He concludes, "Our strategic goal should be to weaken this democracy—not censure its shortcomings."[43]

Other liberals also occasionally use Israel as an example for Arab regimes, though they must be cautious lest such an argument expose one to harsh attacks. Two Kuwaiti writers found original ways to do this. The more "shocking" approach in terms of Arab discourse was an article by Fuad al-Hashem comparing Sharon to Iraqi leaders. Perhaps only a Kuwaiti, given that country's experience with Saddam, could dare produce such an article proposing "that the Palestinian people should thank God twice a day for having the Israeli army as an enemy," for it is far less brutal than the Iraqi army that occupied Kuwait. If Israel had behaved like Iraq, he continues, it would have used chemical weapons on the Palestinians. Saddam killed as many Kuwaitis in one day as Israel did [Palestinians] in two years.[44]

A Kuwaiti college professor, Ahmad al-Baghdadi, takes an equally daring approach. Of course, he writes, Sharon is a terrorist, but he does not terrorize his own people or imprison its intellectuals and writers. At least, unlike every leader in the Arab world, he was democratically elected. In comparison, Arab rulers terrorize their own citizens, trying intellectuals for heresy (something that actually happened to Baghdadi himself), attempting to break up marriages because one spouse is charged with apostasy (which happened in Egypt), and so on.[45]

Arab regimes kill hundreds of dissidents, Iraq is in a constant state of terrorism against its own citizens and neighbors, and the Palestinians invented airplane hijacking. Baghdadi asks, "Isn't this terrorism?" "The Arabs and the Muslims," he concludes, "claim that their religion is a religion of tolerance, but they show no tolerance for those who oppose their opinions." These things did not happen in the West or in the "Zionist entity."[46]

Still, only a Palestinian might make the ultimate comparison about this event. Having lived under both the Israeli occupation of the West Bank and the Iraqi occupation of Kuwait, Taufiq Abu Bakr stated, "I have refrained from comparing the two . . . because the result would have disgraced and shamed [the Arabs]."[47]

A few liberals even criticize the Palestinian movement for its strategic mistakes, neglect of its own people's interests, and its subversion of reform in Arab states. Some Arab liberals privately celebrated Arafat's death in 2004.[48] After all, they had a right to consider themselves to be among the victims of his policies. Since Arab regimes insist that internal change and good relations with the West depend on solving the Palestinian issue, Arafat, by rejecting a peace agreement and going to war in 2000, determined the fate of all the Arab people in a way damaging to any hope for reform. His policy strengthened the regimes at a critical moment when they might have been vulnerable. Thus, Arafat's policy and the new intifada served the reactionary cause in Arab countries. As Amin al-Mahdi, an Egyptian writer, put it, Arafat "turned the Palestinian people into a human shield protecting the Arab regimes from the 'aggression' of modernism and freedom."[49]

This problem was further intensified by the fact that bin Laden and other radical Islamists ready to use terrorism against Arab regimes simultaneously justified its use against Israeli citizens. It was an easy matter, though, for the majority of Muslim clerics and Arab intellectuals to distinguish between "justifiable" and "nonjustifiable" indiscriminate attacks on civilians. The easy way, which is what bin Laden had used, was to say that "terrorism" was justifiable as a defensive measure. Since Israel (or the United States) was an aggressor, all their citizens were fair game for murder. For example, the influential Egyptian-born Sheikh Yousef Qaradawi said that "Israeli society was completely military in its make-up and did not include any civilians."[50]

Some, however, rejected such an analysis with what was arguably the real traditional Muslim position. For example, even in Saudi Arabia Sheikh Mohammad bin Abdullah al-Sabil, a member of the Council of Senior Ulama and prayer leader of the Grand Mosque in Mecca, condemned "attacks on innocent people [as] unlawful and contrary" to Islamic law which required Muslims to "safeguard the lives, honor and property of Christians and Jews." Sheikh Muhammad Sayyed Tantawi, head of Egypt's Al-Azhar University, also condemned "all attacks on civilians," though at other times he has endorsed suicide bombings against Israelis.[51]

Aside from the merits of the case, one reason why some Arab liberals have criticized suicide bombings even against Israel was as evidence that radical Islamists have routinely taken positions in conflict with historic normative Islam. This stance of accusing radical Islamists of being "un-Islamic" could promote an alliance between liberals and moderate clerics as well as delegitimize the Islamists' claim that they are the rightful interpreters of the religion. Another concern was the possibility that such terrorist methods might be used in revolutionary campaigns within Arab countries, as indeed did happen in Algeria during the 1990s and in Saudi Arabia later. While such uses lay outside the narrower definition of "just" terrorism, who knew how that category might be further extended in the future?

An Egyptian attorney, Ahmad Shawqi Iffat, wrote bitterly in condemning the strategy of terrorism. It did not benefit the Palestinian cause because the enemy always took a grave vengeance for each operation. In addition, terrorism lost the Palestinians international sympathy.[52]

Yet despite the uselessness of these attacks, most Arabs supported them. This issue was typical of how such problems are handled. The Arab debate revolved around a discussion of whether the attackers were committing martyrdom or suicide in an Islamic context. Moderates point out that Islam defined as a martyr someone who is killed by the enemy in battle and not by a deliberate decision to die. But that is beside the point, Iffat continues. No one has evaluated the tactic in practical terms: namely, did it achieve its ends, benefit the cause, or lead to something better?[53] He implied it was a failure.

A good example of the type of thinking about which Iffat complains was the sharp rebuke issued by the Qatar-based scholar, Sheikh Yousef Qaradhawi, who criticized Tantawi for once opposing suicide bombings since he insisted there were no civilians in Israel and all Israelis were criminal colonizers. Tantawi was thus betraying the brave warriors instead of "supporting them and urging them to sacrifice and martyrdom." A similar stance was taken by a large number of Arab intellectuals, who issued a communiqué applauding the attacks.[54] Not only did resisting occupation justify any means, it did not matter whether those tactics contributed to ending that condition. In reality, the real justification was that doing certain things provided revenge and made the Arabs feel better, not the best criteria for making political decisions. The fact that Israel had already offered to withdraw from the territories through negotiation—and thus no violence was necessary at all—did not even register with more than a handful of people in the Arab debate.

This kind of thinking was by no means the monopoly of Islamists. One of the main leaders of Lebanon's left, Walid Jumblatt, chairman of the Socialist Progressive Party and chief of the Druze community, praised a January 2004 suicide bombing by a Palestinian woman as contrasting with the terrible "silence, the helplessness, and the retreat" characterizing Arab society. "She offered hope . . . because the fall of one Jew, whether soldier or civilian, is a great accomplishment in times of [Arab] decline, subservience, and submissiveness." He concluded that it was a shame such fighters were so few and poorly armed "while the [weapon] depots of the Arab armies are full to the brim."[55]

This statement well illustrates the way the conflict has been used not only demagogically but also as a substitute for addressing Arab society's other shortcomings. Whether victory was attainable was not a serious consideration, given the therapeutic value of violence and terrorism. What the Arabs needed was not more scientists, better schools, or more modern hospitals but more battles, killings, and martyrdom. The fact that, judging by his own political record, Jumblatt probably did not believe what he was saying only shows more vividly the cynical manipulation of the issue. In fact, barely a year after making this statement he would claim to be a supporter of democratic reform and place himself at the head of the movement to force Syria's withdrawal from Lebanon.

Faced with this overwhelming consensus, some liberals came up with ingenious arguments trying to stay within the framework of the prevalent Arab discourse to make their points. One common approach was to claim that using suicide bombing or continuing the intifada played into Israel's hands. In other words, this approach employed the usual intolerant insistence that disagreeing with the author's own standpoint was "objectively" to help the enemy.

This is how the journalist and reform activist Michel Kilo made this case in Syria. "Every day," he wrote, "we hear shrieking corrupt voices that claim that the situation should not be reformed as long as the [Israeli] threat exists, as if corruption is the tool that will deflect" this danger. The people know the real fault lies with the country's leaders and that the Israeli threat has been used as a cynical excuse to deny reform and accuse its advocates of being traitors. But by refusing to make major changes and keeping Syria weak, the rulers are the real traitors endangering the Arabs. If Syria continues to support attacks on Israel, that country will launch a new war and defeat it. Don't let the backing for radical groups, he urged, "bring about the demise of Syria just like it brought about the demise of Palestine!"[56]

A similar idea was contained in an October 2002 column by the Egyptian Abd al-Ati Muhammad. Of course, he asserts, Israel and the United States do not want peace and demand unilateral concessions by the Arabs. Sharon deliberately escalates the situation to produce "martyrdom" operations. This then allows him to fool the world into supporting his policy, helps him stay in power, and ensures that the occupation continues. What is needed instead, then, is a diplomatic strategy that can succeed in making a real change so that the martyrs have not sacrificed their blood in vain.[57]

A parallel approach has been to criticize Palestinian leaders for betraying their own cause. Khaled al-Kishtainy angrily wrote, "Palestinian intellectuals do not really care about the suffering of their people." They have fancy houses in the West, drive luxury cars, and send their children to prestigious schools. "Every time a solution to the Palestinian problem is proposed they say 'No' [and choose] steadfastness, sacrifice, and Sha-hada [martyrdom]. And who is the shahid [martyr]? Not any of their sons. . . . Rather, one of the children of the unfortunate [poor Palestini-ans]."[58]

This is how the Kuwaiti liberal editor Ahmad al-Jarallah also accuses radical Islamist Palestinians of "playing into the hands of Israel." Islamic Jihad's terrorists are "our courageous comrades," but they are completely unrealistic. They act "as if they are superpowers with a mighty army at their command to blow open the gates of Palestine and take over Jeru-salem." As a result, their efforts strengthen Sharon and help him kill Palestinians and even to implement his supposed goal of expelling all Palestinians from the West Bank and Gaza in order to annex these areas. In addition, these militants make emotional speeches that send their people to their deaths while the leaders enjoy their luxurious lifestyle.[59]

While Jarallah blames the radicals in effect for backing their leaders, the writer Salameh Nematt complains that militant Palestinian groups are "blackmailing" and threatening the Palestinian Authority in order to prevent it from accepting a cease-fire. How could these factions oppose their own government possibly to the point of civil war? They should obey their government instead of subverting chances to achieve a Pales-tinian state.[60] That article was written during the period when then Palestinian prime minister Mahmoud Abbas (Abu Mazin) was trying to promote a cease-fire and progress in the negotiations. The argument still rested on the polite fiction that the Palestinian leadership wanted attacks to stop, even though the terrorists knew they had Arafat's support and encouragement.

Still, criticism of Arafat became increasingly common during the last years of his life, not only in private conversation among Arabs—which had long been true—but publicly as well. In an August 2003 article, Abd al-Rahman al-Rashed, editor of the London-based, Saudi-owned *Al-Sharq al-Awsat*, wrote an article entitled "The Palestinian Leadership Must Go." Disgusted by infighting and corruption, Rashed exclaimed, "Is it not shameful and distressing when a Palestinian woman sacrifices her children for these leaders who refuse to give up their seats? Is it not shameful that these are the figures who drag the entire Arab world into a struggle . . . controlled by personal interests?"[61]

While Palestinians are dying, he complained, their leaders "will nei-ther fight nor make peace" but rather spend their time fighting over jobs and money. Given that they cannot achieve anything, they should resign. Their bad behavior had led the U.S. government to demand a different kind of Palestinian leadership. "Is it with such a lame leadership that the Palestinians will free their land? Should we enter into conflict with the rest of the world for the sake of these individuals?"[62]

Hazem Saghiya, who lives in London, warned Palestinians that violence would lead to disaster, saying that it was better for them to win over Israeli public opinion by rejecting suicide bombings.[63] Al-Afif al-Akhdar, who lives in Paris, reflects a cogent Western-influenced critique of Hamas, which in itself means such views are easily dismissed by mainstream Arab thinkers. When Palestinians used terror and called for Israel's elimination, it allowed Israel to discredit Arabs as extremists. Such a policy "is not acceptable to international consensus" and leads to "diplomatic and media isolation" and more tragedies.[64]

This argument, however, includes some controversial points. Mainstream Arab writers argue there is no reason to compromise in the conflict because "right" and "justice" are on their side. Measuring strategies mainly by their ability to achieve success and gain Western support—rather than as a manifestation of a victim's right to retribution—is against the Arab consensus and smacks of treason. Why should Arabs kowtow to the demands of a treacherous and hostile West? This argument is often used against liberals, as when one radical Kuwaiti attacked liberals in general, who, he said, are always ready to applaud the West in exchange for whatever crumbs it throws them.[65]

Their opponents' effective use of the Arab-Israeli conflict against them gives liberals even more incentive to want it to be ended. Akhdar points out that successful national liberation movements—his examples are Algeria and Vietnam—used violence as a way to force an enemy to negotiate in order to reach a political settlement.[66] Like other liberals, he turns the "treason" argument against the radicals. The real treason, he says, was to demand total victory while rejecting negotiations that might bring it about. This "irrational nihilist behavior" increased repression, violence, and anarchy in Arab countries.

As a strategy it was both immoral and futile: by being indifferent to human pain and throwing away the future on the "naive illusion of 'liberating Palestine to the last grain of soil' expresses a hallucinatory paranoia that views murder and suicide as goals in themselves." He points out how Arab leaders have rejected previous opportunities for reasonable compromise, from the 1930s through the 2000 Clinton plan. Akhdar charged that a spate of terrorist attacks in Israel brought a conservative victory in the 1996 Israeli elections, toppling then prime minister Shimon Peres, who would have negotiated a peace agreement with the Arabs. So detached from reality was Hamas that its leader, Ahmad Yassin, claimed to have discovered mystically that Israel would disappear in twenty-five years. Akhdar ridiculed this kind of thinking as being at the root of Palestinian tragedies. Violence, he concludes, "will achieve no political reward whatsoever."[67]

This is precisely what most of the Arab world does not accept. The U.S. war on terrorism is deemed to be an offensive against the Arab world that must be fought. Acting in "self-defense" against a demonic enemy means that no action the Arabs undertake can be defined as terrorism. Victory is inevitable; enormous sacrifices are justified. Since the enemy supposedly never offers anything reasonable, violence is the only alternative.

Far from being self-evident, the liberal message has a great deal of trouble getting through, partly because it has to dilute the impact of its message by first insisting on its own acceptance of the Arab discourse's clichés on the issue. This is true for even the mildest dissenting views, as when Lebanese newspapers beg for their own government to have some say over Hezbollah attacks on Israel from its soil.[68] Of course, explains the Beirut *Daily Star*, such operations are justified, but there must be limits. Attacks, like one that had just occurred in which a mother and her children were murdered in Israel by members of Arafat's Fatah movement, were bad on both moral and practical terms, especially because they delay, or even prevent, the liberation of Palestinian land.[69]

One of the most coherent critiques of the Arab approach came from an Egyptian author, Amin al-Mahdi. He saw the Palestinian leadership's rejection of peace in 2000 as a key moment when the wrong choice was made. Not only did Palestinians lose the chance to have a viable state, but they also greatly worsened their situation. There followed a series of additional mistakes, such as making impossible demands like the "right" of Palestinian refugees to return to Israel (which would have turned that country into a second Palestinian state), turning to violence, allying with the Islamists, and giving free rein to lawless groups who disrupted order among their own people.[70]

At the very moment, following September 11, 2001, when terror was deemed by so many to be the world's main enemy, such behavior reminded the world that it was coming mainly from Arabs and Muslims. The Palestinians thus lost their moral advantage. True, Mahdi claimed, American leaders were prejudiced against Arabs, yet they had good reason to conclude that Arafat would not fight terror because he had already gone so far in the other direction.[71]

But why did this happen? One major reason that the Arab side rejected serious peace proposals was that "the Palestinian issue was always the main source of legitimacy" for radical Arab regimes. It was used to justify their hostility to the West, the war against democracy, and their dictatorial measures. None of the Arab regimes really cared about the Palestinians, he said. The real reason they opposed Clinton's 2000 peace plan was that they thought its success would bring down the "iron curtain" in the Arab world and "open the region to change."[72]

How do the liberals want to handle the issue? Their main strategy has been to ridicule the radical line while at least pretending to accept mainstream Arab assumptions. It is precisely because Israel and its leaders are so brutal and unrestrained, they claim, that using force against them is so dangerous. Palestinian suffering is so enormous that it must be brought to an end rather than extended by continuing the attacks. Those helping Israel are not liberal "traitors," but extremist hotheads. Diplomacy is a better strategy than violence as a means for the Arabs to outmaneuver their enemy. The policy of Arab regimes is invoked to portray the writer as being on the side of the mainstream against a radical fringe.

The same technique is used by Shafiq Ghabra, who brings in Saudi Arabia and the Arab League as alleged supporters of the liberal position by invoking the March 2002 Saudi plan endorsed by an Arab League summit. The plan said that if Israel withdrew from all of the territories it captured in 1967, accepted a Palestinian state, and let all Palestinian refugees live in Israel, Arab states would recognize that country. The statement was vague, or at least designed for public relations purposes, to the extent that Syria and Saddam Hussein's Iraq supported it. At the same time, Ghabra had some basis for claiming that this was a "historic shift" that "made official" the Arab leaders' desire for comprehensive peace and normalization.[73]

What was especially interesting was Ghabra's point that having once reached the conclusion that peace was both good and necessary, Arab leaders must pass on this message to their own people. An Arab street that is constantly told of Palestinian suffering is more likely to support radical Islamist forces which insist that peace is impossible or undesirable.[74] In short, he suggests that the regimes reverse their historic policy that inflaming the issue is in their own self-interest, and instead come to view the easing of tensions as beneficial to themselves.

This is clever but a difficult sell, to say the least. Usama al-Ghazali Harb explains why. Writing in the year 2000, at a moment when he thought a negotiated Israel-Palestinian agreement was imminent, he explained the conflict's past utility for Arab regimes in helping them "justify postponing or dismissing the question of democratization." He hoped that ending the conflict would convince these rulers to seek "more sustainable sources of legitimacy, rooted in the constitution and the law, and more in keeping with the spirit of the age." Indeed, he suggests that this is precisely what happened at the end of the 1970s, when Egypt negotiated peace with Israel, making possible the political liberalization, financial reform, and economic open-door policy of that era.[75]

Three years later, in 2003, when hopes for peace had been dashed, Harb wrote that since tyrants did not want to resolve the conflict because they used the Palestinian issue as the basis for their credibility, the United States must step in and end the conflict by itself. In doing so, he was ready to agree with the mainstream view that the region's economic woes and terrorism were largely due to Israel's presence, power, and belligerence.[76] Thus, once again, the Arab world's difficulties were passed off onto the United States and Israel, albeit this time from a liberal perspective.

A different approach has been presented by Khaled Kishtainy. The source of the Arab world's problems is not the Palestinian issue but a "backwardness" that has been exacerbated by the regimes' desire to keep the conflict going. Now, however, "most Arabs understand this, and they are angry about all the [suffering] that befell their land because of the Palestinian problem, and they do not want to continue to make sacrifices for it."[77]

It is doubtful, though, that most Arabs view the situation in these terms. If they don't want to fight the conflict, they are ready to cheer others who do and they choose their political preferences accordingly.

Those who are more moderate want the United States to solve every-thing for them while the Arabs remain passive, presumably by pressur-ing Israel to meet their demands. Those most moderate say the Arabs should themselves act to ensure that the conflict ends in a negotiated peace. Each of these groups finds a different mechanism for assuring success fairly soon: the hard-liners by military victory, the second group by U.S. action, and the last by believing the masses are ready to demand that their leaders make peace.

The critical question, however, as Ghabra outlines it, relates to the Arab need to address the issue realistically. He begins by insisting that if Arabs end the war by negotiating a just peace, Arab states can enter a new age of development. If they refuse, the future will be grim. It is nec-essary to reevaluate whether violence can bring success. Finally, the Arabs must choose whether they want to eliminate Israel entirely or make a diplomatic settlement based on Israel's existence.[78] Ghabra does not say outright what he favors—an explicit statement would be risky—but it is clear that his view requires significant shifts in Arab thinking and his-toric demands.

Clearly, liberals have the greatest interest in ending the conflict, which has in no way benefited them or promoted their vision of the Arab world. If they portrayed Israel as being the root of all Arab problems, it was more often—but not always—a reference to their rivals' manipula-tion of the issue rather than to a belief that the Jewish state is malevo-lent. In public they often accept the mainstream version of the conflict, trying to add a liberal twist. In private, they might be quite dovish, ready to ridicule the Arab discourse's claims,[79] but they could not organize a serious peace lobby or effectively challenge mainstream premises.

Another issue related to the Israel question was that of anti-Semitism, which mainstream Arabs often justify among themselves while at the same time denying its existence. There has been a rise in anti-Jewish sentiment and propaganda in the Arab world, often in government-sponsored newspapers and television stations, showing that spreading such ideas has been a tool not only for the Islamist opposition but also for the regimes themselves. At times, the material was explicitly anti-Jewish, while on other occasions the practice was simply to apply traditional anti-Semitic stereotypes to Israel and "Zionists," though this was often a scarcely concealed code word for Jews.[80]

Many Arab intellectuals supported, or even produced, this kind of material, regarding any criticism of it as false, foreign, and hypocritical Zionist propaganda. A few were appalled at anti-Jewish, anti-Semitic claims and conspiracy theories for reasons ranging from intellectual integrity and humanitarian considerations to concern that such statements cast Arabs in a bad light internationally and strengthened Israel's case. Thus, while the majority supported, or at least acquiesced to, such claims, a minority did not.

An example was the 2002 controversy over a forty-one-part television serial aired by Egyptian and Iraqi television entitled "A Knight without a Horse." The following year, the Syrians produced their own similar program. The theme of the show was a secret Jewish plan for world conquest along the lines of the *Protocols of the Elders of Zion*, a czarist forgery. Official Egyptian and Syrian sources praised the series as an accurate depiction of Jewish and Israeli traits and methods. But how would Arabs feel, asked Mark Sayegh in his *Al-Hayat* column, if Israel aired a program about an Arab conspiracy to take over the world? Israeli intellectuals and artists were, he claimed, horrible about violating Palestinian rights, but they had not reached such a level of idiocy. He then tried, as liberals often did, to exploit militant arguments against the radicals. Such publicity stunts were merely the regime's effort to conceal the fact that it was not really willing to fight Israel. If the Egyptian government was serious, it would cancel its peace treaty with Israel rather than air anti-Israel dramas on television.[81]

Another *Al-Hayat* columnist, Ibrahim al-Arabi, also relied on a self-interest argument. Using this reactionary forgery made it seem as if the Arabs were stuck in the nineteenth century, he complained. At any rate, it was a mistake because persecuting the Jews had always backfired on the Arabs. If Jews were treated badly they could claim that they need Israel as a national homeland.[82] While the Egyptian Organization for Human Rights complained that the series would stir up prejudice, a practice it opposed in general, its leader added that because Israel was behaving so badly in practice, the Arabs did not need to resort to forged documents to make their case.[83]

Hazem Saghiya, still another columnist with the same newspaper, strongly condemned "Muslim clerics who ceaselessly justify the murder of Jews" and the Arab media for pushing public opinion in that direction. Yet he, too, views this approach as a needless distraction from Arab inaction and Israel's evil policies. Militants "write and show solidarity with the Palestinian people, curse the Jews . . . and then sink into deep slumber."[84]

The newspaper's editor, Jihad al-Khazen, came up with another variation on this theme. Instead of denying that the Holocaust ever took place, a crime that occurred but that they did not commit, Arabs should use the event as a weapon for their own agenda, asking how a people who have experienced such massacres could then persecute and mistreat the Palestinians. Even this approach—like its counterparts based on anti-Israel slanders—was strongly criticized by many of his readers.[85]

Whatever the intentions of the authors, these arguments are not a ringing endorsement of the need for peace but only advocate a different means of struggling more effectively against the evil enemy. More straightforwardly, Hazem Abd al-Rahman wrote an *Al-Ahram* article stating, "We do not hate the Israeli people and we do not hate the Jewish part of this people." But even if one includes the statements that were far closer to mainstream views, these critiques of extreme incitement were still the minority, overwhelmed by a much larger number of articles justifying in effect that very same hatred and accepting the wild charges of historical anti-Semitism as accurate.[86]

One particular controversy revolved around a planned conference in Beirut to deny the Holocaust ever happened. This was condemned by still another *Al-Hayat* columnist, Joseph Samaha, as in effect defending the Nazis in the name of the Palestinians and Arabs.[87] Generally, though, those opposing the meeting, like another *Al-Hayat* writer, Abd al-Wahab Badrikhan, stuck to self-interest arguments concerned with the international horror such an event would provoke. A Lebanon trying to attract foreign investment would find that harder to do by hosting such a meeting.[88] In the same vein, Arab intellectuals known for opposing peace negotiations with Israel—like the Palestinian poet-politician Mahmoud Darwish, Edward Said, and the Syrian poet Adonis—signed a petition urging that it be canceled. But when criticized for allegedly bowing to Western pressure and being soft on Zionism, Darwish withdrew his signature.[89]

Ironically, there was a grain of truth in the radicals' accusation that the main motive of those criticizing Arab anti-Semitism was to avoid antagonizing the West. For if Arab governments or media occasionally pulled back from some extreme anti-Semitic statements it was due to Western exposure and pressure that made them fear such behavior would have significant costs. The apology of a Saudi government-backed newspaper, *Al-Riyadh*, for publishing a Saudi professor's article claiming Jews murdered non-Jewish children to use their blood for festive meals on religious holidays came only after U.S. government criticism. The editor, a member of the Saudi royal family, explained that Arabs should draw a distinction between anti-Israel Jews who opposed "Zionist racism" and those who were Israelis and their supporters, who should be condemned.[90] Presumably, only the latter ate the children.

The lack of empathy toward others to the minimal degree taken for granted in Western discussions showed an absence of tolerance that has undermined the foundations for any truly democratic society in the Arab world. At best, what was demonstrated was less a liberal alternative than merely a more practical version of traditional thinking. As a result, the majority of Arab commentators on these subjects continue to repeat similar statements in state-controlled media without penalty. The author of the Saudi blood libel article simply shifted to a different newspaper.

Perhaps the most single important denunciation of anti-Semitism, following the U.S. Congress's criticism of Egypt—and presumably jeopardizing Egypt's $2 billion in annual aid from the United States—was the December 2002 series of articles in *Al-Ahram* by Usama al-Baz, President Mubarak's political adviser.[91] Any Arab who attacks the Jews collectively "harms the interests of his nation," he explained. Israeli policy can be criticized without resorting to anti-Semitic claims.[92] He recommended that Arabs stop viewing Jews as engaged in a big conspiracy, expressing sympathy for Hitler and Nazism, or calling Jews "the sons of apes and pigs." He urged that the star of David symbol not be used in cartoons attacking Israeli policy since this was reminiscent of the Nazi era.[93]

As a result, the Egyptian Foreign Ministry asked high-ranking Muslim clerics to recommend that Jews not be called "apes and pigs." Tantawi, the state-appointed head of the Al-Azhar mosque university, led in this effort, though he himself had used such terminology in the recent past, labeling Jews as the enemies of God.[94] Egyptian diplomats also continued to defend the veracity of the *Protocols of the Elders of Zion*.[95] Articles violating all of Baz's "recommendations" continued to appear almost daily in the state-controlled Egyptian media.

Compared to this situation, there are relatively few examples of writings that strongly advocate a compromise peace with Israel as being in Arab interests, much less any attempt to treat Israel as a normal state, understand its concerns, or combat hatred of its people. This is especially remarkable in view of the fact that two major Arab states—Egypt and Jordan—are formally at peace with Israel. There is far more acceptance of the idea of recognizing Israel's existence after a negotiated solution creating a Palestinian state, but even this is often expressed in ambiguous language that does not rule out the goal of destroying Israel. Arab liberals, in public at least, usually feel a need to emphasize the value of apparent moderation as a better tool for fighting and defeating the enemy.

Nevertheless, liberals are very much aware of the fact that the Arab-Israeli conflict is an inflammatory issue used to discredit them on all their other points. This manipulation of the issue against them makes liberals especially eager for the conflict to be resolved fast and peacefully. But knowing better than anyone else that their own governments are so intransigent about compromise, they pin their hopes on the United States and Europe to deliver a solution for them. In Saghiya's words, "A peaceful, evenhanded, negotiated resolution is essential if future U.S. policies are to succeed in the region and if Arab liberals are to pursue reforms."[96]

This statement was made to an American audience, and some of Saghiya's points shoring up his emphasis on evenhandedness—pressure must be put on both Israeli and Palestinian leaderships, for example—did not make it into print in Arabic newspapers. Open calls directed to the Arab audience for such a peace with Israel are as rare as they are courageous. One of the most cogent was made by Heggy in an article for *Al-Watani* entitled significantly "The Arab-Israeli Conflict: Between Reason and Hysteria." For it is the irrational framework in which the issue is viewed—rather than an evaluation of specific rights or wrongs—that is the obstacle to peaceful resolution.[97]

The fact is, Heggy says, that the goal of destroying Israel "is not only unattainable" but one that brings tremendous loss and destruction upon the Arabs themselves. Heggy calls for Arabs to make a "sober reappraisal" of their own positions and policies that, notwithstanding Israel's "unforgivable excesses and atrocities," made the Arab side act against reason and fall into "a vortex of tragic losses and missed opportunities."[98]

For liberals, emphasizes Heggy, escaping from this cycle is imperative. Only by ending the conflict can the Arabs pass through the gateway toward solving their other problems; it is the only way they "can embark on a process of democratic reform, economic development and social peace and not fall prey to forces opposed to education, civilization and modernity, indeed, to the values of progress in general."[99]

But here is a huge catch-22. For if the regimes find the conflict so useful because they do not want to open the gateway to their own demise, what would induce them to change their attitude? Heggy himself is quite aware that this is a most difficult task. For decades, Arabs have been taught that they are the victims, "that everything negative in their lives is the result of conspiracies hatched against them by the outside world." What is required is the courage to reject this framework, teaching the Arab public to stop "blindly following the school of 'big talk,'" which has cost them so dearly, the slogans that enslave them "to a conflict that is destroying the very fabric of our societies."[100]

How can this be done if those responsible for shaping their views— leaders, educators, clerics, intellectuals, and journalists—continue to produce the same kind of analysis that has previously dominated their thinking? A new generation must be formed, Heggy suggests, "driven by reason rather than by volcanic passions fueled by voices [claiming] to speak in the name of religion or nationalism."[101] Yet how can this happen if the current generation in the Arab world has been more strongly influenced by radical Islamist ideas and more urgently bombarded by systematic incitement to battle than any previous one? The Arab liberals can only hope that somehow the conflict will be resolved.

8

The Challenge of Terrorism

I s the dominant Arab policy of resistance, defiance, and confrontation toward the world, asked Tarek Heggy, a means to an end or an end in itself? If permanent struggle is a way to achieve goals, does it have a chance of succeeding, and if it is an end in itself, are the costs worth it?[1]

This is an especially critical question regarding the tactic known in the West, but far more rarely in the Arab world, as terrorism. There can be endless discussion of whether an action like suicide bombing or deliberately targeting civilians is right or wrong. But the underlying assumption shaping this debate is whether certain categories of people—Westerners, Americans, Israelis, and secular or liberal Arabs—are so evil that they merit destruction and deserve death. Thus, the use of terrorism, whatever the details, is deemed justified, a valid means in itself or at least when defined as self-defense, which is a permissible rationale for jihad in Islamic doctrine.

A strategy of terrorism also rests on the belief that it is the only way to defeat demonic forces that cannot be dealt with through dialogue or compromise, that these nations, people, or ideas are inevitably enemies. The resort to terrorism is also based on knowing that a large constituency exists in the Arab world that is ready to justify, finance, and assist such behavior. Terrorists can expect that violent attacks, on non-Muslims at least, will bring them popularity and increase their base of support.

Finally, the most controversial, least popular type of terrorism—using it as a revolutionary method within the Arab world—can only be defended to the satisfaction of a much smaller but still sizable group. Radicals can argue that Arab society is in terrible shape, there is no other way to change it, and the rulers are so corrupt and traitorous as to deserve death. They can also claim—based on what many Arabs have been taught in school—that the proper interpretation of Islam is a value so exalted that it must prevail over every other consideration.

The problem, then—as liberals point out—is that the mainstream Arab political worldview provides premises that can be used to justify, or at least excuse, using terrorism as a tactic. After all, the foundation for terrorism's popularity is the widely accepted idea that Arab societies' problems and the conflicts in which Arab states are involved come from the enmity of the West and Israel. Why shouldn't these places be subject to "defensive" violence in every possible form? In turn, this stance develops and enjoys virtual immunity from criticism in an atmosphere where the doors of compromise are closed: dissent is treason; foreigners are villains; liberalism is heresy; and conspiracies are everywhere.

To make matters worse, most of the regimes, the institutions they control, intellectuals, and media applaud terrorism to prove their own militancy. They may also provide money and other means of support to such groups in order to further their own interests. They push young people into violence by what they tell them about the world, then claim to have nothing to do with the outcome, blaming it on Zionism and imperialism. Sa'ad bin Tefla, Kuwait's former communications minister and himself a journalist, likened this behavior to that of someone who commits murder and then mourns at the victim's funeral.[2]

With almost all Arabs endorsing anti-Israel terrorism and a majority approving of anti-Western terrorism, a proterrorist position is useful to rulers in ensuring popular support. Those who like such a strategy do not have to back the Islamists, the regimes seem to say, but also get this same result by remaining loyal to the regime. In the struggle between rulers and Islamists, Ahmad Bishara points out, rulers and terrorists act as if they are "competing for the same audience." But this is precisely the point: they are.[3]

As a result, many Arabs fully endorse terrorist attacks (at least outside their own country); others decry certain aspects of the tactic, especially its use as a domestic revolutionary tool, but feel satisfaction when attacks succeed against others. The great majority of intellectuals are at least ready to characterize non-Muslim victims as receiving the wages of their sins.

At a minimum, even if condemning terrorism, they view such attacks as giving them leverage that might help ensure that their own demands are met. After all, they claim that terrorism arises due to their own legitimate grievances. Those who would want terrorism to end, then, must give the terrorists concessions and solve problems in the way that they demand. Consequently, the more terrorism that takes place, the more pressure there is to meet Arab demands.

In other words, whether or not it is correct to use terrorism against Americans, it is said to be an understandable response to U.S. misdeeds against Arabs and Muslims. The idea that the United States is an aggressive enemy of the Arabs is thus reinforced in the public's mind, even as the terrorist act itself is being criticized. All of these factors also intensify opposition to a liberal Arab approach based on a better understanding of others and reaching accommodations with them.

In this context, then, what effect did the dramatic events of the early twenty-first century have on prospects for reform in the Arab world? The sequence included the launching of a Palestinian war based on terrorism against Israel in 2000; the September 11, 2001, attacks on the United States; the retaliatory U.S. conquest of Afghanistan and overthrow of the Taliban regime there; the U.S.-led coalition's defeat of Saddam Hussein and his regime in Iraq; U.S. support for democratic reform in the Arab world; and a renewal of radical Islamist terror attacks within the Arab world.[4] Did this situation increase or decrease support for terrorism and its uses? There is no simple answer, and the results have been quite mixed.

It should be stressed that only a small minority of the Arab people have engaged in real self-criticism and soul-searching stemming from terrorist events, because these issues were mainly interpreted within the dominant worldview. Many cheered the attacks on the United States or, in this same basic context, justified them or claimed that Arab terrorists were not responsible. U.S. military actions in Afghanistan and Iraq have been heavily criticized—especially by non-Iraqi Arabs—as imperialistic. American backing for democracy is seen as hypocritical and subversive.

The liberal Arabs' reaction reflects a horror at seeing reactions so much at odds with their own thinking. But given peer pressure, censorship, and repression, liberals were more easily able to make their points openly and strongly in the Western media or English-language publications in the Arab world rather than in Arabic-language outlets, where they might have more effect on the people they were trying to convince.

Although at first glance it might seem that domestic terrorism within the Arab world would inevitably promote empathy and moderation toward others, the fact remains that the first round of Islamist revolutionary terrorism in the 1990s—including bloody insurgencies in Algeria and Egypt—did not have such an effect. And after the Jihadist Islamist campaign against the United States and other targets reached a peak, the experience of such violence being renewed at home usually did not inhibit enthusiasm about ongoing similar measures directed by the same people against foreigners.

Especially rare was the kind of forthright analysis leading to the conclusion that all terrorism is unacceptable. This was the analysis made by Abd al-Rahman al-Rashed, the Saudi who as editor turned *Al-Sharq al-Awsat* into the Arab world's most reformist newspaper and then did the same thing on television with the Al-Arabiya television station. "It is inconceivable for us to justify one terrorist bombing while denouncing another," he insisted. The attacks "are interconnected ideologically, if not by the affiliation of their perpetrators." But instead Arab intellectuals "not only are silent but even justify terror, for they in reality supply terrorism with what it most needs—propaganda and legitimacy." Only when such incidents take place in their own countries do they rush to "make distinctions and clarifications."[5]

Thus, on one hand, many regimes—especially Saudi Arabia—tried to export and buy off Islamist extremists, a decision that increased terrorism in the West and Asia. On the other hand, in such countries as Egypt and Algeria, the violence made liberals feel it more necessary to support the regime as the preferable alternative to an Islamist revolution.[6]

As it fought Islamist revolutionaries by clamping down on freedom, the Egyptian government enjoyed the support of the elite, including liberals, who were, in the words of Ahmed Abdallah, a former leftist who studied at the London School of Economics, "frightened at the prospect of an Islamic state denying them personal liberty and modern ways of life." As a result, "the regime has sensed no pressure to reform and democratize." The Islamic challenge ended by strengthening the system, disrupting reform, and justifying repression.[7]

While radical Islamists support terror attacks, regime supporters often suggest that they are conspiracies mounted by the enemies of Arabs and

Muslims or that at least they will be used to advantage by these enemies. For example, many writers warned that the United States and its allies used terrorism as an excuse for attacking Arab states.[8] Rather than seeing terrorism as a symptom of problems in their own society, the mainstream view has more often claimed that it was a foreign importation or an understandable, perhaps justified, Arab response to victimization by foreigners.

Instead of viewing terrorism as a phenomenon to be rejected entirely, many regimes struck hard against domestic, revolutionary terrorism, while trying to deflect—or even sponsor—it against foreign targets. Regimes wanted to convince potential supporters of domestic terrorism that the governments were on their side, ready to defend Islam against the American, Israeli, Western, and secular threats. They rejected efforts to suppress such terrorism on the grounds that it meant acting as the policeman of the "oppressor" against the "freedom fighters."

Even allegedly moderate Islamists, and liberals to a lesser extent, employed this doctrine of "good" and "bad" terrorism. For example, Sheikh Yousef al-Qaradhawi, a leading Sunni cleric, backs terror attacks against Israel and other places but condemns those within Muslim countries because they bring no benefit and topple no governments. He criticized the September 11 attacks but also called on Muslims in the U.S. military not to participate in the war to overthrow the Taliban in Afghanistan, on grounds that both operations injured civilians. Yet Qaradhawi also ruled as religiously proper the kidnapping and murder of American civilians in Iraq. He criticized the fact that one place damaged in a 2003 terror attack in Morocco was a Belgian club because Belgium had a pro-Arab policy of opposing U.S. policy and Israel.[9]

In contrast, many liberals have argued that terrorism—at least when not directed against Israel and sometimes even then—is an enemy of Arab and Muslim interests both because it damages their image abroad and it is the instrument of totalitarian forces seeking to seize power in the Arab world. Abd al-Hamid al-Ansari reminded readers that "terrorism has claimed more victims in many Islamic countries than in the West."[10] Ali Salem pointed out that long before September 11, Islamist terrorists killed more than a thousand Egyptians in the 1990s. They committed "crimes in order to establish 'the kingdom of God on earth' and have succeeded only in turning our lives into hell."[11]

Liberals assert that such violent behavior is a natural consequence of extremist Islamism and is even encouraged by regimes that finance radical groups or use them to deflect attention from their own shortcomings. For liberals, terrorism is less the result of foreign oppression than of domestic incitement, radical ideology, and a dictatorship that closes down democratic alternatives. The rule of a system that fosters frustration and offers no peaceful outlet for expressing grievances, they say, is bound to nurture terrorism. In contrast, freedom of expression and open debate weakens the appeal of terrorism.[12] They argue that if moderate opposition ideologies could compete with Islamism and people saw hope for more freedom and democracy, support for extremists would fall sharply. "Radical interpretations have emerged," said Kuwait liberals, "to fill that empty space and have penetrated all levels of life and society."[13]

Liberals also argue that extremists simply base their ideas on the indoctrination they received in state-controlled schools, mosques, and media.[14] It was mainstream ideology that preached an intolerant interpretation of Islam and political worldview that led to violence. They urged that governments and moderates carry out a thoroughgoing reform of education by governments, regulate Islamic practice, and act against radical Islamists.

For example, after blaming everyone for September 11, Alia Toukan emphasized that the regimes "bear a direct responsibility for pushing, and sometimes encouraging, some of their people into political and religious extremism." Such factors as dictatorship, corruption, and the people's feeling that they have no power or influence in their own societies have this effect.[15] While regimes alienate their own people, Toukan notes, Islamist groups take the role of protector, provider, and even leader for the masses. Every Muslim and Arab must ask how fanatics and terrorists have emerged from their midst to speak on their behalf with an interpretation of Islam that violates the religion's most basic principles.[16]

What is especially dangerous is that since radical terrorist-supporting views have established themselves as mainstream, they now are passed on to the next generation as the proper interpretation of Islam. Mundir Badr Haloum, a Syrian university lecturer, warned that young people are learning as normative Islam such ideas as considering the killing of others to be a religious duty and classifying non-Muslims or other types of Muslims as enemies. Even when forced by political interests or diplomatic pressure to condemn terrorism, "we wear a pained expression on our faces but in our hearts we rejoice at the brilliant success—a large number of casualties."[17]

In contrast, most liberals view terrorism as a common enemy that they share with the United States. Thus, they tend—though by no means always—to justify the U.S. war on terrorism as helping Muslims fight their own foe, a radical Islam that distorts their religion, threatens their freedom, and damages their people's image. But the same point also applies to the relationship between liberals and regimes, for which terrorism at home at least is also a threat. Thus, many liberals view this issue, like the danger of radical Islamist rule, as a motive for working with the existing dictatorships.

A major difference between liberals and regimes is that the former are more likely to analyze the causes of terrorism seriously. In contrast, proregime elements seeking to conceal the terrorists' real political goal of overthrowing the existing governments know that if the masses understood this reality they might sympathize more with the terrorists after all, or at least blame their own rulers for the violence.

One regime strategy is to claim that the terrorists are incomprehensible, irrational vandals. This could be an effective way of minimizing sympathy for them while not having to engage in arguments that their actions could claim sanction under Islamic law. As one editorial put it in the Saudi English-language *Arab News* after a particularly bloody attack in Saudi Arabia, "What [do] these barbarians think they are doing? How can anyone imagine that the butchery of fellow human beings in such a random and brutal fashion advances any cause one centimeter?"[18]

Thus, too, Jordan's minister of political affairs and information, Muhammad Adwan, said that the terrorists' attacks prove they "have nothing to do with Islam, not only because they targeted Arab and Muslim countries, but also because Islam rejects such hideous deeds." Another Jordanian minister said the assaults "have no aim other than to soil the image of Arab and Islamic civilization throughout the world."[19]

It can be a short step from such arguments to conspiracy theories that terrorism is a Western or Zionist plot to weaken or discredit the Arabs and Muslims. If the Jihadists have nothing to do with Arabs or Muslims, if they have no program to revolutionize the existing societies, then what are their motives? One journalist explains that the worst aspect of terrorism is that by making Muslims look bad, it helps the Zionists promote a Western struggle against Islam. Thus, the terrorists make it more likely that Arab and Islamic countries will fall under the control of the United States and international Zionism.[20]

Liberals have no problem, however, in pointing out the terrorists' Islamist ideology and revolutionary goals at home. They want to show that the violence arises out of domestic problems because they wish to stress the extent of these shortcomings, which they promise to fix through reform. Terrorism's roots, explained Bishara, are quite indigenous. Arab societies have become breeding grounds for terrorists and are more threatened by them than even the West. Bin Laden and his followers "are a menace, not only because they terrorized innocent people in the United States and brutalized the Afghanis, but also because they distorted the Islamic faith and endangered peace in the region."[21]

Many writers point out that unless Arabs and Muslims admit that terrorism has arisen out of their people and religion, they will never be able to address the problem. In Abdallah Rashid's words, "Not all Muslims are terrorists . . . but . . . almost all terrorists are Muslims. . . . Does all this tell us anything about ourselves, our societies and our culture?" A cure to the illness can come only after an honest self-assessment.[22]

Another important argument is that terrorism cannot accomplish anything, suggesting that liberals offer a more effective, less threatening way out of the Arab world's current mess. For instance, the Egyptian Muhammad Sid-Ahmed pointed out that if the West identifies terrorism with Islam, so do the Islamists, since they advocate terrorism in the name of Islam. Even from the Islamists' point of view, such violence is counterproductive, he claims, because many pious people who would be impressed by their arguments turn against them because of their behavior.[23]

Saad Eddin Ibrahim has observed that terrorism has brought no political change. Armed struggle is a legitimate tool in conflicts, he asserted, but violence directed against civilians was unlawful "thuggery."[24] The Kuwaiti liberal editor Ahmad al-Jarallah, whose criticism of terrorists and Islamist extremists earned him a letter-bomb attack on his office that left him wounded in December 2003, noted that a movement dependent on suicide bombers was futile. It had certainly not worked for the Palestinians against the Jews.[25]

Yet despite such reasonable claims, the liberals are painfully aware of just how popular terrorism, jihadism, and bin Laden are—certainly far more popular than their own movement. Abd al-Hamid al-Ansari blamed the Arab media for creating a cult of admiration around bin Laden. They stirred up religious hatred, antagonism toward the United States and Israel, and portrayed the U.S. war in Afghanistan as being against Islam.[26]

This approach also followed a traditional Arab and Islamic tendency toward hero worship. Whether the hero is in fact a liar, an adventurer, a tyrant, or a terrorist, his sins are covered by the sanctity of his fighting for the right cause. Arab intellectuals were ready to rewrite bin Laden's real views to make them more popular, for example, attributing his actions to the Palestinian problem, contradicting the fact that bin Laden and his group largely ignored the issue.[27]

In writings aimed at the West, though less often in Arabic-language articles, liberals have suggested that the region faced a choice between reform or a radical Islamist terrorist victory. Thus, after a May 2003 suicide bomb attack in Morocco—aimed at Jews but causing mainly Muslim casualties—a Moroccan liberal editor, Aboubakr Jamal, wrote in the *New York Times* that the violence "endangered Morocco's future as a democracy." In addition to the terrorist threat there was an equally anti-democratic threat from governments that made tough laws ostensibly against terrorists but really to prevent free speech and human rights. "To fight terrorism," Jamal warned, "Morocco needs more democracy, not less."[28]

Yet he also admits that most liberals disagree with him and support giving the government dictatorial powers in order to crush the threat of radical Islamism. They feel that "we have to delay democracy in order to save it from those who would use it to kill it. . . . We rely on the enlightened despot to preserve our future."[29] In practice, many or most liberals do support dictatorial regimes in the hope that they will defeat terrorism and the radical Islamists who use it as a strategy. This undermines the liberals' ability to urge what amounts to their own revolution against the regimes.

Liberals try to bridge this gap by urging the regimes to make changes that they believe will simultaneously reduce terrorism (and radical

Islamism) while laying a basis for democratic reform. Often, however, their proposals could also be claimed to reduce free speech for the Islamists. Certainly, they would enhance governmental powers.

For example, Ahmad Bishara, the Kuwaiti liberal leader, proposed a detailed plan for fighting terrorism in his country. The government should stop terrorism-promoting groups from raising money, ban hate literature and inciting sermons in mosques, and close down the 250 radical Islamist front organizations operating illegally in Kuwait. He pointed out that Sulaiman Abu Ghaith, bin Laden's spokesman, for many years preached in a state-run mosque in Kuwait and taught at a government school before coming out into the open with his revolutionary views.[30]

As with Abu Ghaith, the schools have been a real breeding ground for terrorism and should be purged of extremists. Textbooks "are laced with hate to non-Muslims and intolerance to other cultures." Islamist ideologues often teach the religious and Arabic courses in schools, which constitute almost 20 to 25 percent of the academic load. Both the teachers and the student associations have been controlled by the Muslim Brotherhood for two decades. Despite the fact that it was not a legal organization, the Brotherhood received a large state subsidy, and its annual meeting was sponsored by the crown prince and prime minister.[31]

Kuwaiti liberals were, however, relatively optimistic, given the somewhat greater level of activity and support they enjoyed compared to counterparts elsewhere. They were even hopeful about Saudi Arabia, which, according to Ahmad al-Jarallah, editor of the *Arab Times*, "was earlier ambivalent towards terrorism [but] has been forced to join the war on terror." The Saudi media, he said, "now proclaim terrorists violate the teachings of Islam."[32]

Even better, in Jarallah's mind, the reform effort was being led by defense minister Prince Sultan bin Abd al-Aziz, who he quoted as advocating that the kingdom become "a model for the Islamic world," highlighting Islam's core message of being ready to be forgiving, tolerant, and encouraging open discussion. Sultan said this is how "to eliminate fundamentalism and to be a moderate country." Jarallah believed Sultan's promise to modify the school curriculum to reflect development needs and Islam's proper values. The Saudi people, Jarallah concluded, wanted to save Islam from a band of terrorists who harm the image of Islam and Muslims all over the world.[33]

This was, though, an overoptimistic assessment, for if some members of the royal family wanted reform, many did not. The changes being contemplated were limited ones, and even these were not actually implemented. In no other country was the debate over terrorism so heated, but liberals remained a tiny minority, heard more often outside the country than within it. The most minimal gesture was fraught with controversy. Thus, after many Saudi clerics and academics issued a manifesto suggesting that Muslims might find common ground with the West, they were harshly criticized by those supporting, or at least justifying, the September 11 attacks.[34]

The situation is accurately summarized by Bishara, who notes that on the war of terror, the "Saudi official line continues to glorify the acts of mass terror in Palestine, Chechnya, and the sectarian fighting in Iraq as 'martyrdom.'" He suggests, "Obviously there is something odd and contradictory here: how can the state indoctrinate its citizens in 'martyrdom' ethos in one tongue, while calling the very same acts in Saudi Arabia as terrorism and sacrilegious?" He concludes, "Saudi Arabia looks like [it is] fighting terror in one hand while feeding it with the other."[35]

Of course, this is true. The Saudi establishment and its supporters oppose terrorism aimed at overthrowing the regime, but this is not the same thing as a consistent, principled rejection of the tactic, nor does it denote any agreement about the problem's root causes or solution. For example, although fifteen of the nineteen September 11 hijackers were Saudi citizens—as was bin Laden, the operation's mastermind—this fact was downplayed or denied within the kingdom. Some Saudi officials, and much of public opinion, blamed Israel for the attacks in the United States. The prevailing view about terrorists was voiced by Prince Sattam bin Abd al-Aziz, Riyadh's deputy governor: "Those people were in Afghanistan, they took their ideas not inside Saudi Arabia, but outside Saudi Arabia."[36]

Khaled Hamed al-Suleiman wrote in 'Okaz: "Ideological extremism is merchandise that was never manufactured or sown in this land; it is merchandise imported to this land, duty-free, and the one who exported it got nothing for it, except the pure souls harvested by indiscriminate acts of terror."[37] Many Saudis also blamed the United States for terrorism within their country, attributing it as a reaction to the war in Iraq even though the violence and the movements carrying it out had started long before that event.[38]

Liberals warned, however, that this extremism and violence were the result of ideas learned in Saudi Arabia. The columnist Raid Qusti wrote in an English-language Saudi newspaper that many denied that Saudis were involved in the September 11 attacks or terrorist bombings within the country, saying, "We Saudis would never do such things. . . . It's outside influence, for sure." Qusti responds, "What nonsense! . . . Who are we trying to fool?" To handle this problem, change must be far-reaching, including "all aspects of our life—the school, the mosque, the home, the street, the media."[39]

A particularly striking story was told by Badria bint Abdallah al-Bishr, a social science instructor at a Saudi university. Just after September 11, her son came home from fifth grade to tell her of what he had learned that day: Osama bin Laden was a great Muslim hero. Her other son, in third grade, was assigned to draw pictures of the planes crashing into the World Trade Center. Three years later, his fifth grade teacher was named as a participant in armed terrorist attacks on Saudi government offices.[40]

If changes were not made, liberals warned, the country would soon face great disruption and eventually a radical Islamist revolution. For them, a series of terrorist attacks within Saudi Arabia, particularly a large one in Riyadh on May 12, 2003, proved the truth of this assertion. Implementing more liberal, tolerant concepts was the only real way to guarantee the regime's stability.

In short, the moderates were not setting themselves up as rivals to both government and Islamists but rather as the government's ally against extreme Islamists. Liberals, suggests Bishara, are the "natural partners" of the Gulf monarchies' governments.[41] This was arguably the most pragmatic way liberals could promote themselves, but it was not likely to be an effective strategy and was certainly a far cry from calling for an altogether new system.

The regime, however, was well aware of the fact that extremists had far more supporters than liberals. As one hard-line Islamist put it in criticizing liberals, "You give the false impression that many people condemned the war against America. But the truth is that many people are happy declaring this war." Another cleric brought out the traditional, usually successful, use of xenophobia and treason charges against liberals: "You cry for what happened to the Americans . . . and you forget the oppression and injustice and aggression of those Americans against the whole Islamic world."[42]

Given this high level of opposition, proregime figures have usually—though not always—distinguished between "bad" terrorism aimed at Muslims or at least within a Muslim country and "good" terrorism targeting Israelis and the West. The columnist Abed Khazandar sought to differentiate between types of suicide attacks: "If I carry out suicide operations against an enemy occupying my land, killing my children, and expelling me from my home, this is legitimate Jihad. But if I carry out similar operations against innocent civilians who came to Saudi Arabia at the invitation of its government in order to serve the country and train its sons, then this is a criminal and terrorist act" forbidden by Allah. Indeed, one proof that the latter attacks were bad is that they hurt the homeland but "caused no damage to American interests."[43]

Similarly, al-Jowhara bint Muhammad al-Anqari said, "You want jihad? Wage jihad face to face with the aggressor. Don't use the tools in the hands of our enemies, and do not destroy your land with your own hands!"[44] In other words, jihad should be exported but never imported.

Most Saudi denunciations of terrorism were carefully worded to reflect such distinctions. In a major speech to pilgrims at Mecca, Saudi Arabia's top cleric, Sheik Abdul-Aziz al-Sheik, said that terrorism was giving the Muslims' enemies an excuse to criticize them. He inveighed against attacks on Muslims or guest workers in Saudi Arabia, asking, "Is it holy war to shed Muslim blood? Is it holy war to shed the blood of non-Muslims given sanctuary in Muslim lands? Is it holy war to destroy the possessions of Muslims?" By implication, though, other kinds of attacks on civilians—non-Muslims outside of Saudi Arabia—were legitimate. And the real villain was the enemy using terrorism as an excuse to hurt Muslims.[45]

The following year, Sheik gave a similar talk to the pilgrims, also appearing to condemn terrorism while actually endorsing its ideological premises. He denounced those killing fellow Muslims as having been "lured by the devil," but he identified the demon causing the problem as an anti-Muslim campaign waged by the West to discredit and destroy Islam. Don't be fooled, he urged his audience, "by a civilization known for its weak structure and bad foundation."[46]

The easiest response to the problem, and one often used by proregime figures in Saudi Arabia and elsewhere, is to portray the terrorists as crazy people and criminal elements. This can be an effective way of minimizing sympathy for them while not having to engage in arguments that their actions could claim sanction under Islamic law. As one editorial put it in the Saudi English-language *Arab News* after a particularly bloody attack in Saudi Arabia, "The question that comes back once again to all decent people is what [do] these barbarians think they are doing? How can anyone imagine that the butchery of fellow human beings in such a random and brutal fashion advances any cause one centimeter?"[47]

This does not prevent many of the same people, however, from arguing that similar tactics are justified and politically productive when used by the Palestinians against Israel. If terrorism is used against Muslims, however, it is easy to claim only the victims as martyrs while the killers are "common murderers." Clearly, the newspaper insists, "all decent people" view their deeds with "contempt and loathing,"[48] a claim not borne out by public opinion polls regarding terrorism if the victims are Israelis or Americans.

Still, in trying to prove bin Laden's men are purely nihilists, the editorial suggests that they are even worse than non-Muslim terrorists (the examples of Zionists and Christian Greek Cypriots are used), who at least "were acting for a specific cause, centered on a specific country." Al-Qa'ida, by contrast, is menacing international society with "a desire for anarchy and destruction." But this argument is somewhat disingenuous for, from a moderate perspective, to admit that the group seeks an Islamist state would not only be to associate their enemies with Islam but to suggest to some of their readers that these people might have good intentions and base their actions on shared beliefs.

Far fewer people, especially when writing in Arabic, opposed terrorism in principle and across the board. The English-language *Arab News*, many of whose readers were expatriates themselves and the target of terrorist attacks, warned that "those who gloat over September 11, those who happily support suicide bombings in Israel and Russia, those who consider non-Muslims less human than Muslims . . . all bear part of the responsibility for the Riyadh bombs. . . . We cannot say that suicide bombings in Israel and Russia are acceptable but not in Saudi Arabia." Whatever criticism U.S. policy or Western society deserves, "anti-

Americanism and anti-Westernism for their own sake are crude, ignorant and destructive." Not only the bombers but also "those who poi-
soned their minds must be crushed and the environment that created
them dismantled" to prevent even worse tragedies in the future.[49]

Due to censorship and the unfriendly domestic environment, comprehensive denunciations of terrorism were also more common among
Saudis writing in Western publications than in those directed at home
audiences. Sulaiman al-Hattlan, an *Al-Watan* columnist and a fellow at
Harvard's Center for Middle Eastern Studies, wrote in the *New York
Times* that it is time "to stop blaming the outside world for the deadly
fanaticism in Saudi Arabia" and start making real reforms. Otherwise
the eventual result might be "the Talibanization of our society."[50] He
warned:

> Saudis have become hostages of the backward agenda of a small minority
> of bin Laden supporters who in effect have hijacked our society. Progres-
> sive voices have been silenced. The religious and social oppression of
> women means half the population is forced to stay behind locked doors.
> Members of the religious police harass us in public spaces, and some-
> times even in our homes about our clothing and haircuts. A civil cold war
> is raging, one we have long pretended doesn't exist.[51]

Mansour al-Nogaidan, a former radical Islamist turned liberal, agrees
that some princes favor reform, but he has no illusions about the regime's
readiness to make such changes. After writing articles calling for free
speech and criticizing the Wahhabi version of Islam prevalent in Saudi
Arabia, Nogaidan, a small, roundish man with intense, protruding eyes
and a gentle voice, was sentenced to seventy-five lashes by a religious
court. After writing a *New York Times* op-ed piece, Nogaidan was arrested. The judge screamed at him, "How did you dare to write in the
enemy's newspaper?" As punishment, Nogaidan's column for *Al-Riyadh*
was also taken away from him.[52]

Nogaidan was born in 1970 and, as a young man, had been inspired
by mainstream Wahhabi doctrines to become an extremist preacher and
commit terrorist acts. He burned down video stores for selling Western
movies and a charitable society for widows and orphans for allegedly
challenging women's traditional role. In prison for two years, Nogaidan
read liberal Muslim philosophers from the Middle Ages. As a result
of his experience, he agreed with Qusti that what was really producing

terrorism was a "deep-rooted Islamic extremism in most schools and mosques. . . . We cannot solve the terrorism problem as long as it is endemic to our educational and religious institutions."[53]

Rather than go after the extremists, however, the government sympathized with them, and rather than joining hands with liberals, it persecuted them. The authorities did nothing to investigate or punish those sending liberals death threats. The ministries of education and of Islamic affairs established a committee to purge teachers accused of liberalism, one instructor being put on probation for having shown an interest in philosophy. In mosques, state-sponsored preachers regularly attack liberals, non-Wahhabi Muslims, Christians, and Jews but do not criticize those carrying out terrorism within the country because they sympathize with the "criminals rather than the victims."[54]

What is needed, he believes, is a more open variety of Islam. For a start, Saudis must learn to "see ourselves the way the rest of the world sees us—a nation that spawns terrorists—and think about why that is and what it means." Disaster can be averted only through reforms that entailed reorganizing the country from the ground up.[55]

The official response, however, was that the priority must be put on a return to traditional methods, interpretations, and values. In August 2003 a special half-hour Saudi television show, "War on Terrorism," which stressed this point, began airing just before the main news program. Beginning with Quranic quotations, the program showed film of destructive terrorist attacks, including the ones on September 11. Leading royal family members explained that Islam meant peace, unity, and friendship among world nations. Terrorism was a deviation from proper Islam by "charging the society with disbelief, violating national unity, sowing sedition, and shedding blood." These were criminal acts, not jihad, and they had nothing to do with Saudi society.[56]

The show's host explained, "Our country's curricula did not graduate terrorists or call for hating and fighting others. . . . Many of the terrorists were influenced by the concept of violence imported from abroad." Rather than calling for major reforms, the program recommends that people be guided by mainstream Saudi clerics and the government. It also blames the problem on parents not raising their children properly.[57]

At the same time, though, the show was effective at demonstrating how much bin Laden and other radical Islamists had distorted normative Islam as previously interpreted and practiced. For example, the program cited the following verse from the Qur'an: "If a man kills a believer intentionally, his recompense is Hell, to abide therein (forever): And the wrath and the curse of God are upon him, and a dreadful penalty is prepared for him." An unidentified imam is shown giving a sermon in which he says, "Where is terrorism in a religion that places peace above war? 'And if they incline to peace, incline you also to it.' Where is terrorism in a religion that respects rights under the darkest of circumstances when fighting erupts? Accordingly, it prohibits killing women, elderly, children, and unarmed people, and prohibits interference in the worship of others." Young people should consult respected scholars, the program explains, rather than listen to extremists without proper credentials.[58]

This is the relatively moderate voice of traditional Islam as well as a pragmatic appeal to Saudi interests. The 2003 program claimed that the September 11 attacks hurt Muslims, making it harder for them to travel to Western countries or conduct missionary activity, establish publications, or build mosques there. A Saudi cleric asked whether any sensible person could consider as jihad acts that harmed the nation and encouraged foreign intervention in Muslim countries, much less to bring death and destruction there. "Is it jihad that the blood of Muslims is spilled in the homeland of Muslims deliberately, intentionally, and for no crime or reason?"[59]

Moreover, the regime tries to block the reformist message even when that group proposes to help the regime fight the radical Islamist threat. For instance, Mishari al-Zaidi, a terrorist-turned-liberal, remarked that clerics "want us to say that Saudi extremists are influenced by outside and not indigenous ideas, but that is not true." When a former judge, Abd al-Aziz al-Qassim, gave a newspaper interview complaining that extremists were misusing Wahhabi doctrine to justify violence against non-Muslims, the regime's highest religious figure, Grand Mufti Abd al-Aziz al-Sheik, demanded that portions be deleted. When Qassim refused, the interview was not published. Another reformed extremist, Abdallah Bijad al-Otaibi, published an article accusing some members of the religious establishment of spreading extremist views. Sheik complained, and the newspaper printed an apology to him.[60]

꧁꧂

An interesting case study of the positions taken in this debate is that of Jamal Khashoggi, a professional journalist who has both liberal tendencies and good establishment connections. Khashoggi, born in 1959 in Medina, earned a degree from Indiana State University. He rose to be managing editor of the *Arab News* as well as a correspondent for foreign Arab newspapers. In 2003 he became editor-in-chief of *Al-Watan* but was quickly fired after he published opinion pieces criticizing the religious police, supporting more rights for women, and blaming Wahhabi extremism for terrorism. Afterward, though, he landed a job in London as an adviser to a Saudi prince.[61]

Politically, Khashoggi was no iconoclast. He praised Crown Prince Abdallah as the leader of the reform movement in Saudi Arabia while ridiculing Bush's initiative for democratization. "Reform," he wrote, "should be homegrown for it to be convincing; it should spring from each country according to its own requirements. Abdallah listens to his people, wants to widen political participation, and ensure that the country is productively integrated into the world system." According to Khashoggi, the crown prince sees globalization as a "chance to be grasped, not an evil to be avoided."[62]

Moreover, the journalist praised the prince as wanting to turn Saudi Arabia into "a powerful nation, strong in its adherence to its Islamic and Arab identity, yet open to the world and integrated with it." A lover of peace and an enemy of aggression, the new Saudi Arabia would hold grudges against no other country.[63]

When it comes to the Arab-Israeli conflict, however, Khashoggi defines terrorism out of existence. The Arabs condemn terrorism, but the Palestinians never do such things. They are merely acting in a normal manner against occupation. If Arafat pays those who kill Israeli civilians, this is not terrorism, but a leader's duty toward his fellow liberation fighters. Indeed, his criticism of the Palestinian leadership is that it ever accepted the Oslo agreement in the first place and promised to end armed struggle. When it claims to oppose terrorism, the United States is really demanding that the Palestinians surrender and that Israel keep all the territory.[64] This is, of course, a misstatement of U.S. policy, running directly contrary to President Clinton's peace proposals and his successor's acceptance of a Palestinian state.

Yet this is the man whom, despite such views, the Saudi government considers too moderate to edit a newspaper. The attitude toward terrorism even among liberals, therefore, is very mixed. They offer themselves as the governments' allies in fighting extremists. But the regimes often prefer conservatives who they hope to persuade through appeasement—of which one element is cracking down on liberals—to support the government instead of Islamist revolutionaries. Indeed, in many cases the rulers view repressing liberals and appeasing conservatives as an element in their war on terrorism, whose importance equals the actual battle against the terrorists themselves.

One of the most creative ideas for fighting terrorism—and a demonstration of how big an impact a small group of people could have—originated with a Jordanian writer, Shaker al-Nabulsi, was further developed by the help of al-Afif al-Akhdar as well as former Iraqi planning minister Jawad Hashem, and was implemented by the two main liberal Arab Web sites, Elaph and Middle East Transparent. They created a manifesto signed by several thousand others offering to help the UN persecute those issuing fatwas that "clothe such terrorist acts with legitimacy as being one of the sacred tenets of Muslim faith." Providing specific examples of such fatwas, it proposed the establishment of an international tribunal to persecute such people. Significantly, the fatwas included called for killing Israelis and Americans as well as dissident Arabs. In traditional terms, siding with an international body against fellow Muslims could be considered a betrayal. But that was the point liberals were trying to make, showing how such concepts had to be challenged and redefined for the good of Muslims, Arabs, and the world at large.[65]

At times, it seems as if the liberals need to remind many in the Arab world of a point made by a Saudi researcher named Ahmad al-Ruba'i: "To fly a civilian airplane and crash into [the World Trade Center] is not a great deed. A great deed is to manufacture an airplane and build a trade center. . . . The Arabs must replace the mentality that glorifies destruction with a mentality that glorifies construction."[66]

9

The Iraq War: Aggression or Liberation?

O ne of the main purposes of the U.S. attack on Iraq in 2003 was to overthrow that country's dictatorship and replace it with a democracy, bringing about the outcome that Arab liberals favored but had no power to implement themselves. The Bush administration's innovative interpretation of Middle East politics was that only if Arab regimes changed could the region become stable and solve its problems.

Thus, the Iraq war was waged on grounds consistent with the Arab liberal worldview. Moreover, liberal Iraqi exiles played an important role encouraging the United States to pursue this policy, predicting Saddam's downfall would make Iraq a stable moderate system whose people would be full of gratitude to the United States, along with encouraging a stronger liberal movement and a more pro-American attitude throughout the Arab world.

Some liberals elsewhere echoed this point of view. Nabil Sharaf al-Din, an Egyptian journalist, declared, "These people are establishing the first democracy in the Middle East. This country will be a platform for liberties in the whole region. In Iraq, the days of a leader who remains on his throne until he dies are gone."[1] Saad Eddin Ibrahim declared, "Arab democrats recognize that U.S. success in Iraq would strengthen their own democratic efforts elsewhere in the region." Arrayed against them and hoping for American failure in Iraq is "an unholy alliance of anti-democratic groups: Arab tyrants, old leftists, Ba'thists and Nasserites." But these forces have no future if the United States succeeds in Iraq.[2]

Fouad Ajami, an Arab American analyst, suggested before the war that it could vitalize the liberal movement, offering Iraqis and Arabs an escape from despotism.[3] But the U.S. invasion of Iraq did not spark a marked upsurge in liberal activism—other than in the smaller Gulf Arab monarchies—while giving regimes and Islamist oppositions a rallying point for anti-reform agitation.

As Ajami, a strong supporter of the war, noted afterward, despite evidence of Saddam's brutality, few Arabs outside Iraq criticized the old regime or praised the foreign liberators.[4] Instead, a famous Egyptian singer performed a new hit, "Better Saddam's Hell Than America's Paradise." Hazem Saghiya found the Arab reaction to the event "catastrophic," a bigger problem than the war itself. The Arab nationalists and Islamists saw regime change—which was after all aimed at keeping them from power—as imperialism rather than liberation. Rami Khouri saw the war in Iraq as just one more event making Arabs feel themselves "treated as less than humans, almost as animals," which, in turn, led many to commit or support terrorism.[5]

It should be remembered that Iraq had long exclusively been portrayed in the Arab world—though this image changed in the Gulf monarchies after its 1990 seizure of Kuwait—as a good, proud state that was a patriotically pan-Arab, progressive fighter against the West and Israel as well as reactionary Arab forces. The discovery of mass graves, the clear evidence of repression, and the masses' hatred for the regime should have led to something like the trauma of foreign Communists learning of slave labor camps in the USSR. But many Arabs reacted as the most hard-line Stalinists had done—with denial.

The Egyptian journalist Sayed Nassar, for instance, defended Saddam's record as having turned Baghdad from a primitive village into the capital of a strong country with many universities and a powerful army with which he defended his country. As for Iraq's problems, these were really the people's fault since they deserved their leader.[6] Another Saddam defender, Mustafa Bakri, editor of the Egyptian weekly *Al-Usbu*, showed the real reason for the establishment's view of the war. First, criticizing the deeds of Saddam's regime would mean the same could be done with other governments, which also had many crimes to hide. Second, if the United States overthrew Saddam, it could do likewise to all Arab governments. Faced with this threat, all the beneficiaries of those regimes should hang together in opposing change rather than losing power and being hung separately.[7]

Finally, he made the ultimate Arab nationalist case: whatever we think of Saddam, Bakri explained, he refused to surrender to the United States or make peace with Israel, and that is all that counts.[8] All the other factors by which governments are usually judged were of no importance.

In interview after interview throughout the Arab world, average people echoed these sentiments, explaining, in effect, that they didn't care how many Iraqis were killed or tortured by Saddam Hussein or how much money he stole as long as he followed the proper political line. They believed, in the words of Usama al-Ghazali Harb, that Arabs and Muslims "must always support" one of their own against foreigners "regardless of how wrong or even sinful" he was.[9] Accepting what they had heard in the media, they dismissed contrary views as American propaganda and lies, in the words of one young Egyptian merchant. It was the people, he thought, who should be ashamed for betraying him. Scornfully, he shook his head while watching Iraqis celebrate Saddam's arrest. "Yesterday they shouted 'with our soul and our blood, we will defend you, oh Saddam.'"[10]

The general opinion thus seemed to be that the masses should have fought harder to save their dictator, who was either a good leader or one infinitely better than his enemies. All Arabs and Muslims should stick together, disregarding any internal politics or problems. The war was merely an act of U.S. aggression against Arabs and Muslims intended to steal their oil, dominate their countries, and benefit Israel at their expense. In other words, rather than changing the mainstream Arab nationalist or Islamist positions, the event was merely interpreted through those prisms.

Regarding the new situation, then, the mainstream views called for more militant struggle rather than reform, to strengthen, not rebel against, the status quo. Syria's chief official intellectual, Ali Ukla Ursan, explained that the proper Arab response to the war was to unite so they could force the United States—"the center of evil"—to stop its aggression.[11] At the opposite end of the political spectrum, the head of Egypt's Al-Azhar Islamic university, a relative moderate, and one of the Arab world's most important Muslim clerics, Muhammad Tantawi, condemned the war as a crusade and urged Muslims to battle the "invaders."[12] Sheik

Yousef al-Qaradhawi compared the war to the Mongol king who piled up his Arab victims' skulls into a vast pyramid and destroyed entire cities.[13]

At the same time, however, Saddam's overthrow did alter the strategic situation and shake up Arab thinking to some extent. Rulers began to talk about reform and democracy, though usually as a rhetorical flourish unaccompanied by much action. Many Arab liberals supported the war or at least rejoiced at the results. Even those critical of it suggested that the main reason Arabs should make reforms themselves was to avoid having them imposed from outside.

Finally, there was always the hope that public attitudes had little or nothing to do with private sentiments, at least if conditions changed. This was a lesson taken from communism's collapse in Europe. Perhaps all the ideological or propagandistic statements meant nothing, given that once the evil system fell, people would speak up against it, expressing all the feelings they had to keep secret for years in order to avoid punishment.

Yet always there was a more powerful alternative viewpoint that dominated the scene, insisting that the actual situation of Iraq's people, the number of Iraqis tortured or murdered, was unimportant. The only relevant fact was that Saddam's government had an Arab nationalist ideology, supported the Palestinians, fought the United States, and was run by Muslims. If Iraqis wanted Saddam out of power, this was not an Arab liberation struggle anyone cared to support.

As Kanan Makiya, the most distinguished of the Iraqi émigré intellectuals, complained before the war, the Iraqi opposition was ostracized throughout the Arab world.[14] Makiya had produced a devastating critique of the Saddam regime and Arab intellectuals' willingness to apologize for dictatorial rulers and repression in his remarkable books, *The Republic of Fear* and *Cruelty and Silence*.[15] Because these ideas did not fit with the prevailing demand for a single-minded obsession with the Arab-Israeli conflict and the Western threat, his accounts were ignored or denounced in the Arab world.

Despairing of any other way of ousting the regime, and knowing that the Arab world would not lift a finger to help them, the exiled Iraqi opposition decided to break all the rules of Arab politics in supporting a war against their country's rulers by the United States. No wonder mainstream intellectuals and ruling regimes wanted to discredit them and prevent this message from reaching their own people. Iraqi exiles opposed to Saddam thus supported the war, and many advocated a democratic system thereafter. The regime's overthrow only reinforced their reformist worldview. This group, whether or not they personally returned to Iraq, constitutes an important addition to the Arab world's liberal forces.[16]

While largely indifferent to the actual fate of Iraq's people, other Arabs were very much concerned about how the successful implementation of Western liberation and democratization would affect their states.[17] Ahmad Chalabi, the movement's leader, expressed the Iraqi liberals' views clearly before the war began. This was not a war between Iraq and the United States, but an Iraqi war of national liberation in which the United States was helping. But Iraq's neighbors did not want this struggle to succeed because they feared democracy and any challenge to Arab nationalist ideology.[18]

No wonder, then, that it was considered unethical by mainstream Arab thought to oppose any Arab regime, no matter how repressive or incompetent. By allying with the United States, the opposition was perceived as traitorous. What the Iraq war did, however, was to challenge this prevailing doctrine. First, the Iraqi people's unwillingness to defend or mourn the regime showed that the dictator was not so beloved or benevolent. Second, a great deal of information emerged—including the mass graves of its victims—showing the regime's true and terrible nature. Third, the fact that the United States had been the agent of liberation in Iraq and wanted to promote democracy subverted the demonization of the United States that had been at the heart of the Arab world's ideological and political system. Finally, whatever its shortcomings, post-Saddam Iraq—with U.S. help—held free elections aimed at establishing a pluralist, democratic society.

These factors were key elements in the liberals' counterattack on the dominant ideology and its explanation of the war. Harb called Saddam's overthrow a "special moment" and the most important event in recent Arab history. It threw into relief these competing Arab worldviews.[19] Ironically, those most willing to accept the new liberal approach and reject Arab nationalism were the Gulf monarchies' intellectuals and in some cases rulers who, for their own strategic interests, were happy to see Saddam gone.

Saudi liberals were also excited. Abd al-Rahman al-Rashed, editor of *Al-Sharq al-Awsat*, enjoyed some support in the royal family. The newspaper had been the Arab media outlet most changed by the September 11 events, carrying a larger portion of liberal Arab writings than anywhere else. In a January 2003 article entitled "Why the Baghdad Regime Does Not Deserve to Be Defended," Rashed noted that no one should mourn a government that "has been the biggest source of unrest in the region."[20] When any Arab made such a statement, he knew that mainstream critics would rail against him for not putting primacy on the U.S. and Israeli threat.

Undaunted, Rashed recalled Iraq's long history of quarreling with all its neighbors and waging war on its own minorities. He reminded readers of Iraq's war against Iran, "the only justification for which was greed to gain more land and oil," and of its use of poison gas against its own people. This was followed by Iraq's occupation of Kuwait, its "threatening the whole region under flimsy pretexts," and continuing to be hostile and highly armed even after this defeat.[21]

Once Saddam's regime was gone, Rashed predicted, the Arab world would be better able to achieve stability and reform. He cited as a harbinger of liberal change Saudi Crown Prince Abdallah's January 2003 vague "reform program." The prince had been the country's de facto ruler since 1995, and his relatives owned *Al-Sharq al-Awsat*. The newspaper had also published an open letter from 104 Saudi public figures—former ministers, teachers, and writers—to the country's leaders calling for comprehensive reform, the release of political prisoners, an end to corruption, and a "directly elected advisory council that will represent all the country's citizens."[22]

There were numerous Kuwaiti advocates of regime change in Iraq since their country, as the victim of Iraqi aggression in 1990, had seen firsthand that regime's brutality. Ahmad al-Jarallah expressed his hope that Saddam's fate "will awaken the Arabs and make them see the real truth behind the patriotic slogans raised by this type of leaders."[23] Kuwait's minister of commerce, Abdullah Abdurahman al-Taweel, could not contain his enthusiasm about how Iraq's becoming a liberal democracy with a functioning civil society would change the region. The Syrians, he happily claimed, are "scared witless."[24]

Especially outspoken in this regard was Shafiq Ghabra, who argued that a democratic Iraq would serve as a catalyst for liberalization in the Arab world. "Iraq's transition to a democratic government," he wrote, "could mark the start of the fall of the 'Arab Wall,' the invisible barrier of authoritarianism and rigidity that isolates the region from the world." For tens of millions of Arabs, the toppling of Saddam was the fulfillment of their dreams.[25] Iraq's transformation could make it a sponsor of liberalism rather than radicalism, an inspiration of democratic forces even in Iran, and an encouragement to the more moderate Saudi princes to reform their own country.[26]

Perhaps the most systematic liberal Arab analysis of the war and the battle over its interpretation was made by Rashed.[27] The regimes' persuasive efforts were largely channeled through the media they controlled, and in this respect, Rashed complained, little had changed between 1967 and 2004. The partisanship, propaganda, and wishful thinking characterizing Arab thought, debate, and institutions had remained consistent. If anything, things were worse because the media now reached into every Arab home. In reporting, as in all other aspects of life in the Arab world, fairness and telling the truth "is akin to suicide." The only choice was to take a nationalist position or be accused of treason. Lying for the sake of the cause, the majority insists, is moral and honorable. One's duty is to conceal defeats and problems. This meant pretending that the Arabs would defeat Israel in 1967 and that Iraq would defeat the United States in 1991 or 2003. It also meant boycotting the Iraq opposition, covering up Saddam's crimes, and distorting what the United States said or did.[28]

The political line of both Arab nationalists and Islamists, which enjoyed a virtual monopoly from every institution, was that the U.S. sought to destroy Iraq, occupy it permanently, and steal its oil. The statements and actions of Iraqis who supported the U.S. effort were usually ignored. Television stations blacked out the Iraqi welcome for coalition troops and instead claimed that the Americans were savage in their treatment of civilians as well as deliberately killing Arab journalists to prevent them from revealing America's crimes. So powerful was this propaganda barrage, Rashed notes, that even supporters of democracy "started to rally behind a dictator and religious people started to congregate for prayer behind the leader of the [secular] Baath Party." The result was to make it harder for the Arabs to cope with the actual situation, which thus weakened them even further. Rashed asked the propagandists and demagogues, "How are you going to convince those minds that have been stuffed with rejection, to deal with reality?"[29]

But the war of words could not stem the advance of the coalition forces in Iraq. When coalition forces took Baghdad, Rashed wrote—in an optimistic assessment immediately following the allied victory—that not just Saddam fell but also the mentality that had backed him and other Arab dictators. "The Iraqi people themselves rejected that lie by their rejoicing. Arabs were shocked to discover that they had thought themselves to be "defending the Iraqi people, when they really were defending Saddam."[30]

Did everyone really wonder whether someday similar scenes might take place in other Arab capitals? That was the liberals' great hope and the big fear of the regimes, along with their supportive intellectual establishments and Islamist opponents as well. Rashed claimed this to be the war's most important outcome, the "challenge to the accepted political and cultural values . . . for the first time being examined live on air with proof they were failing. . . . This picture that showed the joy of Baghdad's people with the fall of the Iraqi regime ridiculed the Arabic political, cultural and media systems that falsely claimed to be fighting in the name of the people."[31]

The Iraq war divided the Arabs into two groups: "The rulers who claim that it was a war against the Arabs" and those, especially Iraqis, who knew it was a war of liberation "from a corrupt and murderous regime." All previous Arab wars had been fought against Israel or waged on behalf of the regimes, but this was the first war "against the deplorable Arabic state of affairs."[32]

Rashed was not the only one who drew these conclusions. Others voiced similar views, pleased that the dictatorship was gone and that events showed the people did not support it. A writer in the London-based *Al-Hayat* cheered that this was not merely the end of a regime but of a whole era in Arab history.[33] In Saudi Arabia, *Al-Watan* editorialized that "of course the masses did not support the Saddam regime because it had never done anything for them."[34] Another Saudi newspaper, *Al-Yom*, noted that any dictator who murdered and mistreated his people would end up being overthrown and humiliated.[35] In fact it had been U.S.

intervention and not Arab social processes that had produced this result in a single, exceptional, case.

Wahid Abd al-Majeed, assistant director of the Al-Ahram Center for Political and Strategic Studies in Cairo, found a new way to argue for reform as being in Egypt's interest. Because Egypt feared that a new Iraqi regime would become the model for the Arab world, the country should undertake its own domestic reforms as a way of competing.[36]

Some even went so far as to suggest that events in Iraq had discredited the whole half-century-long Arab nationalist vision. If, for example, the constitutional monarchy ruling Iraq from the 1930s to 1958 now seemed more successful than the Arab nationalist regimes of the succeeding four decades, the entire revolutionary movement had been a mistake. Yet the monarchy, noted the writer Najdat Fathi Safwat, had brought more unity, less sectarian strife, a better government and economy, greater freedom of speech and other rights, and less corruption than the Arab nationalists. Promising liberation and rapid progress, the nationalists had turned Iraq into a big prison.[37]

Such a sweeping reevaluation remained rare, however, certainly compared to the post-Communist rethinking in the former Soviet Union. Most of the Arab media, governments, and opposition parties ignored the old regime's misdeeds or distorted the facts to their own liking even after Saddam's statues had been pulled down in Baghdad. A meeting of Arab parliamentarians in Beirut refused to pass a resolution condemning Iraqi government human rights abuses despite the discovery of mass graves for the Arab Muslims it had murdered. Rashed called such behavior "a mark of shame." If members of parliaments would not speak up for the people against oppressive rulers, he asked, who would do so? They were interested only in condemning Zionists or the West "and have purposefully forgotten the crimes committed under our noses." How could these people face "an Iraqi woman sitting at the grave of her murdered children?"[38]

Abd al-Hamid al-Ansari spoke in similar terms, criticizing Arab analysts and journalists for understating the Iraqi regime's crimes and overstating its popularity. Misguided fatwas calling for jihad against coalition forces in Iraq had led to the death of those foolish enough to believe them. Why, he asked, do Arabs blindly back bad leaders and fail to learn from their mistakes while other nations like Germany and Japan rebounded from defeat so quickly and totally by changing their views?[39]

What seemed obvious to Ansari was the hypocrisy of the Arab media, which pretended it was siding with Iraq's people but actually aligned itself with the Iraqi regime. Ansari quoted a poor Iraqi as remarking that since the Arabs did nothing to help Iraqis, "Why are they attacking the coalition which wants to liberate us?" He could not understand why Arab leaders who call for jihad "have no comprehension that they are seeking violent revenge, which will hurt Iraq's people, for actions undertaken to help them."[40]

In trying to answer this question, Ansari quoted an Arab satellite television director as saying that the Arab masses can be won only—though it is not clear whether he means as viewers, political followers, or both— "by stirring them up emotionally" and encouraging "dreams of a great Arab victory and a great American defeat." But the media also acted on behalf of their educators, sponsors, and masters—the regimes, which planted in their heads so many "imaginary ideas, fables, and superstitions."[41]

While many Iraqis, including intellectuals, expressed joy at Saddam's downfall and appreciation to the United States, this phenomenon received far more attention in the Western, than in the Arab, media. A good example was a *Wall Street Journal* article by Awad Nasir, an Iraqi exile poet in London. He described the downfall of Saddam—whom he called "The Vampire"—as the fulfillment of his dreams, describing the moment when his sister told him over the phone from Baghdad, "The nightmare is over. We are free!"[42]

Who, he asked, had achieved this great feat? Not the Arab League "and its corrupt member regimes but the Americans." In his optimistic assessment, "Those who died to liberate our country are heroes." For this sacrifice the people of Iraq as well as most Arabs and Muslims are grateful.[43] In contrast, those lamenting Saddam were merely "a few isolated figures espousing the bankrupt ideologies of pan-Arabism and Islamism." But was that indeed true?

In fact, many continued to applaud and defend Saddam's regime, noted Ahmad al-Rab'i in *Al-Sharq al-Awsat*, "because they considered this regime to [be] nationalistic and an enemy of Zionism." Even after it was graphically shown how he had mistreated and murdered his own people, none of Saddam's defenders were ready "to apologize to the Iraqis, admit his mistakes, and face the truth."[44]

Yet the system's defenders did not have to extol Saddam, as they had a whole new set of symbols and heroes to cheer: the Iraqi "resistance," which used terrorism against its own people. As for Saddam himself, he was condemned not for how he treated his people but because he surrendered rather than martyring himself, as if his main sin was not his past behavior but that he did not cling firmly enough to his beliefs. There were those, however, who were true warriors of Arabism and Islam, not hypocrites. In the Arab world, the insurgent violence that followed the ruler's downfall trumped the rejoicing; the battle against occupation trumped the battle against dictatorship; America's crimes trumped Saddam's crimes, and the new terrorist upsurge became the real war of liberation in Iraq. All these transformations fit into the mainstream pattern of politics and ideology. Rather than undermine the ruling value system, the war in Iraq reinforced it, or at least was balanced by its renewal.

How could liberals compete with the appeal of this very effective system, which serves the interests of so many powerful people and institutions? The popularity of their dissenting views was exaggerated in the West precisely because such ideas were thought to be so obviously true and inevitably triumphant. Moreover, these were the kinds of Arab views Westerners were usually exposed to in articles and op-ed pieces. "The United States doesn't need to invade any more countries," said Iman Hamdi of the American University in Cairo in one such typical interview. "We've got the message."[45]

The simple fact, though, was that this liberal perspective was not broadcast very widely within the Arab world. Hosni Mubarak, for example, suggested that "imposing democracy by force" in Iraq was an attempt to Westernize the Arab world, implying that it was imperialistic, anti-Arab, and anti-Muslim.[46] This line was taken up throughout the Egyptian political, media, religious, and educational structure.

Thus, the idea was widely accepted that there was nothing to learn from Saddam's reign of terror and nothing had to be changed elsewhere, either in ideology or in practice. Rajah al-Khouri, writing in *Al-Nahar*, noted, "There is still no sign that [any] Arab regime has grasped the heavy weight of Saddam Hussein's horrifying crime." They ignored the fact that his regime's crimes showed how "contemporary Arabism includes tremendous measures of hatred and barbarism." They were blind to the fact that Iraq's rulers had murdered and tortured their people using nationalist, progressive, and Arabist slogans to justify the barbarism of a system whose horrors, according to Khouri, had surpassed Nazism and Stalinism.[47]

As Salem Mashkur wrote in *Al-Nahar*, to avoid repeating Iraq's tragedy would require a real understanding of the implications of the Iraqi experience. Yet is the Arab world going to carry out such an effort? After Mashkur presented his views in a meeting at the American University of Beirut, a Lebanese politician criticized them as "more Iraqi whining." Instead of talking about the crimes of Saddam's regime, the man complained, everyone should focus on the danger to the Arab nations posed by America's "oppressive conquest" of Iraq. He added that the mass graves should not excite any special horror because "these exist in any Arab country and are not unique to Iraq."[48]

Outraged at this effort to excuse the regime's massacres, Mashkur voiced his anger that while the dictatorship "slaughtered its own people for decades," these "'Jihad warriors'" and "Arab 'fighters'" said nothing. Some welcomed the killings; others justified their silence by claiming that the alleged atrocities were really just a foreign conspiracy. Such arguments, he stated, merely reflect the broad Arab belief that the individual is nothing, without any right to liberty or dignity.[49]

Thurayya al-Urayyid, writing in *Al-Hayat*, pointed out that the apologists for Saddam and cheerleaders of the new anti-Western war were merely recycling all the old, often-used slogans: Islam is in danger, U.S. policy is biased against the Arabs, and a united front is needed to fight a Western invasion. The real issue, Urayyid complained, was the existence of "a tyrant embodying the utmost of sadism and inhumanity" who had tortured and killed his people for three decades. Most Arabs simply labeled this "an internal Iraqi matter" and were indifferent to it.[50]

The great hope for the Arabs, Urayyid explained, was that the change in Iraq, by exposing "the inadequacy of our theorizing and slogans, will remove the blinkers" from Arab vision and thought so that many more would understand that the nation could survive only by joining the rest of the world in progress.[51]

The liberal perspective on the Iraq war of 2003 and its aftermath was thus composed of a number of elements in an effort to convince Arabs to make a very different interpretation of these events. First, they challenged the notion that Arabs or Muslims owed the past Iraqi regime any respect or support. Exiled Iraqi dissidents were at this campaign's forefront. Hamid Ali Alkifaey related that the Iraqi people were happy at Saddam's downfall and they thank President George Bush and Prime Minister Tony Blair for getting rid of him. He concluded, "I have yet to meet an Iraqi who is not thankful for the removal of Saddam."[52]

Thus, too, Kamel al-Sa'doun bitterly noted the sharp contrast between the prevailing Arab conception and the reality of Iraqi life under the old regime. Arab journalists, intellectuals, politicians, and poets came to "sing with their trilling voices" in support of Saddam and have their pictures taken with his gang while hundreds of their colleagues were being murdered.[53] One cannot help but be reminded of the Western experience with Stalinist communism. But there were also contrasts between the two cases. In the West, most countries were democratic; in the Arab world all were somewhat similar with virtually identical ideologies. In the West, the majority did not accept Moscow's doctrine, but in the Arab world, almost all shared the worldview dominant in Baghdad.

Second, Saddam was not an Arab hero but an Arab catastrophe. As Sa'doun put it, "Saddam Hussein's war was not against the Americans. Saddam's war was first and foremost against the Iraqis."[54]

Third, Saddam was no more than a typical dictator, comparable to Hitler, Stalin, or Idi Amin. Rashed called him "the devil of Iraq and one of the most criminal and evil creatures in the history of mankind."[55] Alkifaey said he was a terrorist who spent Iraq's wealth to buy weapons for use against his own people.[56]

Fourth, liberals challenged the view that by overthrowing and arresting Saddam, the West was acting in an anti-Arab or anti-Muslim manner. This presupposed, said Harb from Egypt, that Saddam truly reflected the aspirations of Iraq and the Arab world. "This cannot be further from the truth. Saddam never had any real legitimacy—his decisions and policies were in flat contradiction to Iraqi, Arab, and Islamic interests."[57]

In fact, the real humiliation for Arabs, explained Harb, was that they accepted a doctrine that justified Saddam, kept him in power, and let his catastrophic policies turn a richly endowed country into a poor one. Intellectuals who were "supposedly the representatives of our nations' consciences and the defenders of their liberty and dignity . . . supported him." Arabs failed to overthrow him "in defense of their own dignity and their own true interests."[58]

Ahmad al-Jarallah in Kuwait agreed. The coalition forces discovered not only mass graves but also "millions of people who never tasted freedom or enjoyed any rights in their life. Are these not worse and more dangerous than weapons of mass destruction? . . . Need we say anymore to prove this war was legitimate, one hundred percent?"[59]

The Saudi Muhammad Talal al-Rasheed pointed to the jubilation of Iraq's people as proving that whatever the reason for U.S. intervention, the end result couldn't have been happier for the Iraqis or more full of hope for other Arabs.[60] The Kuwaiti Muhammad al-Rumaihi insisted that the regime's overthrow benefited Iraqis, and "every new uncovered atrocity of the old regime [showed] more and more that the Iraqis have returned from hell literally."[61] Harb pointed out that because the Iraqis could not rid themselves of this terrible tyrant, he could only have been thrown out by an Anglo-American invasion.[62]

These were powerful arguments, but the number of people who made them was not large. The same applied to justifying the U.S. presence and condemning the insurgents' violence. If Saddam was unworthy of Arab support, his overthrow a good thing, and the United States was helping the Iraqi people, the liberal argument continued, the new battle was not a patriotic struggle to be supported but rather destructive terrorism to be reviled. Where, asked Rashed, were "the 'freedom fighters,' 'resistance,' and 'strugglers for the freedom of Iraq'" when Saddam was running amok?[63]

The uprising, scoffed Jarallah, was merely a terrorist campaign operating under the cover of patriotism, which merely wanted "to strip Iraqis of their new-found freedom and force them back into prison."[64] Harb pointed out that these operations sabotage progress toward reconstruction and extend the duration of the very U.S.-British occupation of Iraq they claim to be ejecting.[65]

Khaled al-Kishtainy, himself an Iraqi, asked by what right did radical Arabs living abroad or broadcasting on Al-Jazeera "encourage the terrorists, thieves, and murderers in Iraq" to carry out more crimes. Who gave them the right to ignore the great majority of the Iraqi people who wanted to rebuild their land, live in security, preserve the country's unity, and avoid social disintegration or civil war with the help of the United States, the only power capable of helping them do so?[66]

In this context, the coalition occupation of Iraq, as long as it was temporary, was justified. "America, for this brief moment at least," Rashed proclaimed, was a liberator.[67] "The notion that foreign occupiers are more brutal than local rulers," Rumaihi wrote, "has been proven wrong, after the atrocities of Saddam Hussein." When a government fails to provide its people with justice and security, and instead resorts to oppression, "foreign intervention thus becomes a must."[68]

Iraqi intellectuals argued, in total contrast to the mainstream Arab view, that the weakness of moderate Iraqi forces meant U.S. help was indispensable in order to achieve real reform. The Iraqi people want friendship with the Americans to ensure that radical Islamists or nationalists never return Iraq to the kind of rule that had destroyed it in the past. Who else would help Iraq if the coalition forces left and civil war broke out? asked Kamel Sa'doun. Arafat? The Arab League? "Gentlemen, not one of you [will do it, so] keep your distance. We have [already] had experience with you."[69]

What Iraqis did want was U.S. help to create an opportunity for openness and change as happened in Germany, South Korea, and other nations that the United States liberated.[70] U.S. forces were in Iraq, said Kishtainy, with the support "of the overwhelming majority" of Iraqis, engaged in "a noble and blessed" mission: "To sow the seeds of legitimacy of rule and of law, to establish a democratic government, to liberate women from the slavery and backwardness to which they are subject, to spread transparency in [public] administration, and to spread rationality and the spirit of science in education and in defending human rights."[71]

In short, they were carrying out the Arab liberal program, and so, suggested Rashed, "shouldn't we now be wise enough to give [the Americans] at least a chance, if not a real helping hand?"[72] The bottom line was that all Arabs of goodwill should join the liberals, despite tremendous pressure to do otherwise. Kishtainy issued an invitation to this effect, asking his readers in Al-Sharq al-Awsat: "Why not join me in condemning the Arab intellectuals who still support Saddam and await his return and in expressing thanks to the countries that sacrificed their sons in order to topple his regime? [Why not join me] in condemning the attacks aimed at preventing Iraq's revival and at restoring Saddam to his evil rule?"[73]

Liberals hoped that Iraq would become a beacon lighting the way toward freedom for the whole region. In the end, Iraqis would determine their country's fate, said Harb, but the line was drawn between those who hoped that violence would increase to drive out the foreign presence and those "praying that Iraq under the Americans will turn into the paradise of the Middle East, that it will flourish politically and economically."[74]

Liberals favored a democracy based on Iraqi nation-state nationalism rather than an Arab nationalist or Islamist dictatorship. They were aware of the difficulties in achieving that goal, for reasons ranging from the dictatorship's long brutalization to sectarian strife.[75] They knew also that whether other Arab people and countries saw democracy as attractive would depend on success in Iraq.[76]

At least, as Jarallah noted, Saddam's fate "must have come as a shock to other evil regimes which follow in his footsteps and make the same political miscalculations." The outcome was a warning to those who "massacre their people, bury them in mass graves, detain them in dungeons, invade their neighbors, and loot others' properties" that they must change their ways or suffer the same fate. Among their greatest sins, Jarallah said, was calling their reform-minded critics "traitors, betrayers, supporters of Zionists, imperialists."[77]

How Arab regimes would react to Iraq and what kind of role model that country would be were indeed among the most critical questions for the Arab world. Doubtless, these outcomes would also be key factors determining the fate of the liberal cause everywhere in the region.

The signs were not promising, however. For the liberals, the post-Saddam violence in Iraq is literally insane and they desperately want to convince their countrymen of what seems to be so obvious. What do the insurgents want? Jarallah asked. "To return Saddam to power and have more mass graves; to blame the country which liberated Iraq from the hold of a sadist dictator?" Such people were not patriots but terrorists trying to kill Iraqis and destabilize the country.[78] The West, added Hamid al-Hamoud, a Kuwaiti journalist, could protect itself from the extremists, but who would defend the other Arabs from them?[79]

The situation's ridiculousness was best exposed by Ghassan Charbel. What right did non-Iraqi politicians have to insist that Iraqi moderates are traitors, the Americans must be totally defeated, and that Iraq must be turned into a great battlefield? They had no interest in what the Iraqis themselves wanted. Why wouldn't these people let Iraqis choose their own government through elections? Why did they want to provoke ethnic conflict, the rule of militias, turning Iraq into a land of explosions and kidnappings? Wasn't it clear that such behavior would bring yet one more catastrophe for the Arab world? Wouldn't the occupation be ended much faster by letting Iraqis run their own country so they could ask the foreigners to leave?[80] Yet, much to their frustration, it was the liberals who were treated as the fools, troublemakers, and pariahs. Liberals pointed out that the establishment intellectuals and journalists were wrong in predicting that the Arabs would revolt against an American invasion of Iraq, that the Iraqi people would fight to keep Saddam in power, that the United States would try to turn Iraq into a colony, that elections there would be a failure, and that the insurgents would defeat the U.S. forces.[81] The liberals hoped that the successful creation of a democratic Iraq would give them the last laugh.

10

Women's Rights:
A Test Case for Reform

In many ways, the issue of equality for women should be one of the easiest problems for Arab liberals. After all, outside the conservative Gulf Arab kingdoms this idea is supposedly accepted in principle by radical Arab nationalists who have always posed as modernizers with a leftist social agenda. It is also important for Arab regimes to give lip service to formal political equality for women to ensure a good image in the West.[1]

Nevertheless, in practice, this doctrine is less accepted and seldom implemented. Although women have gained higher levels of education and entered the workforce in countries like Iraq and Syria, Arab nationalists have often been quite conservative in such matters or at least became more so in order to appease a growing Islamist trend. Formal legal equality did not translate into extensive opportunities for full participation in society or public life. As for the Gulf monarchies, even basic rights are still explicitly denied women today, justified by an interpretation of Islam that enshrines such practices as God's will.

But the problem goes even deeper because the treatment of women in some way sets the pace for broader social and psychological attitudes. The lower status of women is deeply ingrained culturally and psychologically in Arab society. Though this was generally true throughout the world until recent times, these attitudes have dramatically shifted elsewhere and seem to be doing so at an accelerated place.

The acceptance and practice of equality for women has long been associated with a high level of development. Moreover, any society that at the outset discards fifty percent of its human assets is inevitably going to be held back. If women are classified as inferior and treated in an authoritarian manner, it sets a pattern that also holds for other social relationships and the ideas that govern them. That is why Hisham Sharabi, a professor at Georgetown University, said that without gender equality the Arab world would remain like "a car mired in mud whose tires [spin] continuously, but stays in place."[2]

As in politics and ideology more generally, the overthrow of incipient Arab liberalism by nationalism in the 1950s destroyed a gradual process toward change regarding women. In the 1920s, for instance, many elite women in the more advanced Arab countries abandoned the veil. Traditionalist society was openly condemned by Arab intellectuals and politicians as bad or backward, inferior to Europe, which was the model to be imitated. There were figures like Hoda Sha'rawi, who played a leading role in the Egyptian national struggle, headed the Wafd party's women's commission, and established the Intellectual League of Egyptian Women.

Nasira Zein al-Din, a Lebanese woman, gave the classic reformist view during the pre-Arab nationalist liberal age, when Western-style modernization had tremendous legitimacy for the intellectual and political elite. The nations that have given up the veil, but not those that have kept it, she wrote, "have advanced in intellectual and material life," discovered through research the secrets of nature, and learned to control them. Meanwhile, "the veiled nations" sleep in stagnation, preferring to "only sing the songs of a glorious past and ancient tradition."[3]

Yet maintaining a system of inequality regarding women's status is also an integral part of the ruling system in the Arab world, even aside from the Islamist position, for the regime's survival is partly based on preserving a traditional, conservative, and undemocratic social system. Thus, both the earlier liberal age's democratic-oriented idea of borrowing from the West and the nationalist phase's militantly secular concept of imitating the Soviet bloc were both brought to a dead stop as political rigidity engendered, and benefited from, social rigidity. To make matters worse, as conservative and radical Islam revived and organized, women's status in many places actually declined. Bold social experiments were abandoned, and Islam was more tightly interpreted—or even reinterpreted—to keep women in their place.

❦

If the Arab world is engaged in a life-and-death struggle against imperialist and subversive forces, the battle to maintain gender roles becomes part of the battle to avoid becoming like the West while, by the same token, the idea of women's equality is part of the enemy's assault. The Muslim man had to fight on two fronts in the battle to save Arab-Muslim society, wrote the Moroccan sociologist Fatima Mernissi—in the political trenches and at home. The enemy "seduces one's wife, veiled or not, entering through the skylight of television . . . advertising messages, teenage songs, everyday technical information, courses for earning diplomas, languages and [social] codes to master."[4]

There are many hints and predictions of dramatic progress today, but in practice for women little change seems to occur. A good case study involves the issue of voting rights for women in Kuwait. After Kuwait was freed from Iraqi occupation in 1991, the emir, Jaber al-Ahmad al-Sabah, promised women more rights in appreciation for their patriotic role in the crisis. Consequently, in May 1999—the length of time elapsed is itself a sign of the slow pace of change in the region—he issued a decree giving women the right to vote and to run for office in the next Kuwaiti elections.[5] But parliament had to approve this decree before it would go into effect.

While Kuwait is the Gulf's—and maybe even the Arab world's—most democratic country, voting rights are strictly limited. Of two million people living there, only 800,000 are Kuwaiti citizens, and of these just 112,000 males are registered to vote. Because women outnumber men, after finally being given the franchise in 2005 they constitute a majority of voters in the future. They were also maybe even more conservative than the men. One indication of this was that the Muslim Brotherhood always dominated the national student organization even though 70 percent of its potential voters were women. Ironically, this reality suggests that if women could vote they would cast their ballots for parties opposing their right to do so.[6]

Even without women voting, the July 1999 parliamentary elections brought to office many who opposed the emir's decree. Although liberals did relatively well in the elections, they still only held sixteen of the fifty seats. Some of them rejected the decree to enfranchise women in principle as an action initiated without parliamentary approval, a constitutional right of the monarch they rejected as undemocratic. Most opponents were Islamists and traditionalist tribal representatives.

"Those women who are calling for political rights have reached meno-
pause and need someone to remind them of God," said one Islamist
member of parliament, Hussein al-Mutairi. He claimed few Kuwaiti
women wanted the vote. "How can a husband or a brother allow his wife
or sister to run in elections and meet voters, which often also involves
private one-to-one sessions?"[7] The head of Kuwait's Muslim Brotherhood, Abdallah al-Mutawa, labeled the advocates of women's suffrage "a
handful of brazen and painted women."[8]

Nevertheless, Kuwaiti advocates of women's suffrage and Western reporters alike spoke confidently of the reform's certain approval by parliament. The United States urged the legislature to pass the law as well.[9]
At the opening of the new session, Crown Prince and Prime Minister
Sa'ad al-Abdallah al-Sabah described the plan for women's suffrage as a
"courageous, liberating, civilized" step that would enhance the nation's
development.[10]

Instead, in November 1999, parliament first rejected the decree giving
women political rights by a 41-to-22 vote, then turned down a new version sponsored by five liberal members by a 32-to-30 margin. Given the
fact that 15 cabinet ministers appointed by the emir supported the bill,
among elected members the vote was a whopping 32 to 15 opposing it.[11]
One of those voting against was the liberal speaker of parliament because he needed to shore up his personal political support from the Islamist members. Others reported tremendous pressure from constituents to
reject the measure.[12]

As the results were announced, hundreds of men in the public gallery
applauded, and one Islamist cheered, "Kuwaiti people don't want women's
rights. Why do you want to force it on them?" Nearby, women in orange
shirts bearing the slogan "Vote in 2003" were disappointed. One activist
mourned, "This is tragic. We have scored a first in history. A parliament
votes to limit democracy."[13]

Fahmi Huweidi, an Islamic scholar who supported women's suffrage,
expressed his "shock and sadness" at both the decision and the scene
where young Islamists laughed and screamed for joy at the bill's defeat
as if they had heard that the Muslims had won some great victory over
Israel or the superpowers.[14] Ali al-Baghli, a former oil minister, condemned what he called "the fanatic mentality" of Islamist and tribalist
legislators. "I wish to convey to my colleagues," he intoned sarcastically,
"that all Western women do not work in strip clubs and bars."[15]

Supposedly, though, this was only to be a temporary setback. The government suggested it would resubmit the bill in 2000.[16] Muhammad al-Saqer, one of the liberal lawmakers who sponsored the bill, said, "One thing I know for sure, in 2003, women will have their political rights."[17] He was off by two years. In May 2005, Kuwaiti women received from parliament the right to vote and run for office, with a face-saving provision that women candidates had to do so in the context of Islamic law. Thus, while some progress has been made, advancement has proven to be neither quick nor irreversible.

Still, numerous instances of change could be cited, though any real social transformation was only just beginning. The government has given Kuwaiti women more opportunities in the armed forces.[18] A female civil servant at the higher education ministry—herself a member of the ruling family—was given some ministerial duties by the liberal education minister.[19] Kuwaiti women comprised 70 percent of Kuwait University graduates and 30 percent of the workforce.[20]

In other countries, too, there were new "firsts," mainly in the Maghreb— where even the Islamists found it hard to shake off French influence and a traditionally more tolerant interpretation of Islam—and in the non-Saudi Gulf states, where almost any gain for women constituted progress. Morocco, for example, chose its first female ambassador in three decades, approved legislation reserving 10 percent of seats in parliament for women, and passed a reformed family law. Both Algeria and Tunisia informally accepted quotas for women legislators.[21]

Especially significant was the Moroccan government's January 2004 Family Law, strongly backed by the king and lobbied for by women's groups. Among its provisions were that the wife is no longer legally obliged to obey her husband or be the ward of a male family member. The minimum age of marriage was set at eighteen years old, divorce was to be by mutual consent (a privilege Islam gives only to the man), and polygamy so regulated as to make its practice virtually impossible. On these and other issues, not only Islamists but mainstream religious conservatives could argue that the legislation violated religious law.[22]

As for the Gulf, the sultan of Oman appointed the first women to the cabinet, as an ambassador (as did Bahrain), to the consultative council, and to other posts. In Qatar women were in 1999 allowed to vote and run in elections. In the UAE a niece of the ruler was named minister for economy and planning in 2004.[23] Women were allowed onto the police force to perform traffic duties. The wife of the UAE's president, who headed the country's Women's Association, suggested that women should serve as cabinet ministers also. Women constituted two-thirds of the Internet users in Saudi Arabia. In Bahrain, women's participation in the commercial sector reached 30 percent, equivalent to that in the West.[24]

Yet all these developments still constitute relatively minor advances. The use of the veil was increasing, and in Egypt women's legal rights actually declined due to more Islamic-oriented legislation.[25] These trends were due directly to both the rising Islamist movements and the regimes' desire to appease or co-opt their supporters. Change has not proven to be a one-way street, with more alterations being made to please Islamists in several countries by freezing or even reversing progress than to satisfy liberals or women's rights advocates. After the Iranian revolution and a small 1979 uprising in Saudi Arabia, for example, religious education was stepped up and controls limiting women's rights were tightened to avoid any accusations of laxness.

One liberal strategy has been to argue, based on respected Islamic sources, that women's treatment in Arab states is based not on Islam but on local customs that deviate from a proper Muslim approach. For example, there are Islamic sources that can be used to argue that there was no separation of genders and that women played an important public role in Islam's early era.[26] Someday such ideas may be the basis for massive change, but at present they are accepted only by those who are already liberal reformists in their worldview.

Moreover, it should by no means be assumed that all women support liberal change or that women's rights activists hold liberal views. Many women are members of radical Islamist groups while, for example, the elder stateswoman of Egyptian feminism, Nawal al-Sa'adwai, holds radical Arab nationalist and anti-American positions extreme by even mainstream standards. Thus, too, one liberal woman argued that, ironically, an appropriate hatred of the United States would be the main inspiration for the liberal struggle against their own dictators. The people, she wrote, would be inspired by the battle against a U.S. dictatorship imposed on Iraq in which "Iraqis are fighting for themselves, not for a bloodthirsty [Saddam Hussein]."[27]

The Jordanian feminist Toujan Faisal, the only woman elected to her country's parliament, used her television program as early as 1988 to discuss wife battering, polygamy, and women's rights. When she first unsuccessfully ran for parliament in 1989, Islamists went to court trying to dissolve her marriage and have her children taken away from her. But Faisal is also an admirer of Saddam Hussein who explicitly applauded a Jordanian soldier's cold-blooded murder of Israeli schoolgirls.[28]

In addition, it is true that women can be equal without democracy—that is, having the same limited rights as male counterparts—or unequal with it. An example of the former situation is the successful lobbying by women's groups to win changes in Egypt's personal status law. A revised text passed in 2000 grants women the right to divorce without their husband's consent if they give up some of their financial rights. This provision was made possible because of a possible interpretation of Islamic law. There was also a new family court system, a fund to provide child support for impoverished families, a provision allowing the government to deduct wages of fathers who did not make alimony and child support payments, and other changes.[29]

In other ways, women can choose a situation that keeps them basically unequal, for example, by supporting Islamist parties. About three hundred women belong to Jordan's Islamic Action Front (IAF), and six even sit on its advisory council, though none on its ruling Executive Bureau. The party platform accepts women's voting rights and ability to participate in public life, though some members oppose that stand. At the same time, though, the IAF discourages women from running for office. It also is against Jordan's electoral quota system, which reserves a minimum of 6 out of 110 seats for women. In 2003, however, the IAF let one woman, Hayat Musimi, run on its slate because she was thought to be a good vote-getter, even though some members objected. She did relatively well but got into parliament only thanks to the quota system.[30]

Precisely because women's rights are a key element of the liberal program, opponents want to show that women themselves reject this stance, or at least its more controversial aspects. Equally, many women want to vindicate their demand for public participation by proving that they are as patriotic—or pious—as male counterparts and hold thoroughly mainstream, anti-liberal beliefs.

Thus, Maya al-Rahbi, a Syrian dissident, penned an acerbic "Letter from an Arab Woman" to Colin Powell, denouncing the U.S. prodemocracy effort. Those women who did support it were unrepresentative of true Arab opinion, she insisted: "The Arab women, Mr. Powell, are not stupid enough to believe your promises that you want to liberate them. Even if they truly need it, let it not be your way. . . . No Arab woman with any common sense would be tempted [to adopt] the democracy to which you claim to adhere and want to export to us, when your history is terrifyingly rife with racism and discrimination."[31]

In addition, as the example of voting in Kuwait and advances in other Gulf monarchies showed, reform on women's issues often came from the top, and submitting these questions to a democratic process is more likely to stop, than to encourage, change. The reform of family law in Morocco also came from the regime. Similarly, in Jordan the king tried to change Article 340 of the Jordanian Penal Code, which basically excuses the murder of a wife or relative to protect "family honor." Polls showed that 62 percent of the public opposed any change; Islamists passionately rejected the proposal, and the amendment could not get through parliament.[32]

Even in U.S.-occupied Iraq, the pattern was hard to break. Only three of twenty-five U.S.-appointed members of the governing council were women, one of whom was quickly assassinated by terrorists. On the Baghdad City Advisory Council only six out of thirty-seven were women. "Only by making certain that they are allowed to participate," wrote the two women members of the governing council, "can the United States and Iraqi Governing Council plant seeds of inclusion that will foster security, democracy and stability."[33] The governing council proposed making Islamic law the basis for provisions regulating the family, a step that would have repealed rights that women had enjoyed under the previous regime. When the provisional Iraqi constitution was adopted in March 2004, though, it explicitly endorsed equality for women and defined Islamic law as only one source of national law. Women also participated in large numbers—and were encouraged to do so by Shia clerics who wanted their votes—in the January 2005 Iraqi election.[34]

Saudi Arabia provides an interesting example of the fate of women's rights. Of course, that kingdom starts from a point far behind other Arab states on the issue. By that same standard, however, the smallest, most basic advances there would be hailed as major breakthroughs. While liberals speak up more on these questions and there are some promises from the top about change—especially directed at Western audiences—literally nothing has actually happened.

Consider, for example, the prohibition of women's driving in Saudi Arabia. Until 1990, this restriction was taken so much for granted it was not even put into law. Inspired by American female soldiers who drove vehicles in Saudi Arabia during the 1991 campaign to free Kuwait, however, about fifty Saudi women staged a protest by taking over from their chauffeurs and driving around Riyadh for a half hour. They were detained by police but had to be released because they had committed no crime. The interior minister quickly remedied that problem by issuing a ban, and the regime's chief mufti produced a fatwa calling female driving a source of depravity. Some of the driving protesters, punished by being fired from their jobs, were professors at a female college whose own students protested that they did not want to be taught by such infidels.[35]

Fourteen years later, much publicity was given to a statement by Prince Walid bin Talal calling for an end to the ban on women driving, but his more powerful uncle, interior minister Prince Nayef bin Abd al-Aziz, made it clear this would not happen.[36] One prominent cleric, Sheikh Ayed al-Qarni, spoke out against the prohibition, pointing out there was no major religious text against women driving, a position also taken by clerics in every other Muslim country in the world.[37] But women in Saudi Arabia are still not permitted to drive, and the idea of changing the law is not even under serious discussion.

In 1999 much attention was paid to a statement by Muhammad bin Jubeir, head of the country's ninety-member consultative council, that this relatively powerless legislative body might benefit by consulting women on some issues and that women might even attend meetings if they kept to their proper role. Some women did visit to watch sessions from a balcony. Jubeir also made it clear, however, that this did not mean they would be other than "guests and observers." They would certainly not be permitted to be members or take part in discussions. Public matters, he stressed, were the exclusive responsibility of men.[38] No change took place on this front, either.

One of the few small reforms made was permission for Saudi women to have their own identity cards for the first time rather than be listed on their husband's card. To obtain the card, however, they needed to have a legally registered guardian—either their husband or a male member of their family—go to the relevant government office, give consent, and fill out the form. Again, this treatment of women is contrary to accepted Islamic practice everywhere else, but Saudi clerics argued that the separate card violated religious principles. Even some women opposed the idea. And even those women who had the card found it refused at some government offices and banks despite the government's own regulation validating it.[39]

The depth of the problem was tragically revealed in the controversy over a March 2002 fire in the Thirty-first Girls' Middle School in Mecca. Fifteen girls died, and fifty more were injured while trying to escape the building. Casualties were higher than they might have been because the religious police blocked would-be rescuers from entering the building or students from leaving on grounds that in the scramble to escape the girls were not wearing their proper modest clothing. "When will we ever be ashamed of our attitude towards women?" Al-Riyadh's editor asked his readers. "We ascribe all of society's ills to them." He asked whether the religious police—the Committee for the Promotion of Virtue and the Prevention of Vice—"care about our wives, sisters, mothers and daughters more than we do?" Rather than reforming the system, the interior minister merely ordered that all critical media coverage of the event be ended. A government official stated the fire had been "God's will" and gave each reporter at his press conference an expensive lambskin briefcase.[40]

Another issue that set off a controversy was the talk given by Saudi businesswoman Lubna Olayan to the January 2004 Jedda Economic Forum. For the first time in a public setting, women were allowed to be in the same room as men, separated only by a screen. During her talk on "The Saudi Perception Regarding Growth," her veil repeatedly slipped, though she tried to readjust it. The combination of gender mixing, absence of a proper covering, and publication of her picture in several newspapers stirred the country's grand mufti to denounce this as an outrage to proper Islamic behavior.[41]

In contrast, Olayan spoke of her vision of Saudi Arabia as a prosperous, diversified economy in which everyone, "irrespective of gender . . . can find a job in the field for which he or she is best qualified." People would have a high living standard and evince mutual respect to all living there.[42] Such changes were imperative, she insisted, for the country's success: "If we want progress in Saudi Arabia, there is no substitute for reform."[43]

Liberals cheered her speech and expressed optimism. Nahed Taher, an economist working in a bank, remarked, "We women have been isolated within our homes because of discrimination, but today there is the political will to accept us in daily life."[44] Nasser Al-Sarami wrote in *Al-Riyadh*, "This is very important progress for [Saudi Arabia's] economic and social problems. With such people, change will surely come."[45] In neighboring Kuwait, a journalist insisted, "There is no doubt that the Saudi crown prince, Abdallah Ibn Abd al-'Aziz, who led the extensive reform in his kingdom, followed the events at the Jeddah forum and was proud of the women who participated."[46] The crown prince, however, did not express such sentiments himself.

In contrast, Abd al-Rahman Rashed expressed amazement that some were thrilled by the presence of ten Saudi women at one international conference. "It is not worth describing this as even a quarter of a step forward," he insisted. That same week, the regime rejected a proposal to establish technical education facilities for women.[47] At the same time, also, an officially sanctioned study was published arguing that women should focus even more on their traditional roles of wife and mother. Too many foreign, non-Muslim workers were being hired to do these domestic jobs, it explained, while Saudi women lived a life of slothful luxury.[48]

"There is no doubt that women will gain rights within . . . a few years," Prince Talal bin Abd al-Aziz, a brother to King Fahd, said in 1999.[49] Four years later Talal, who headed the Arab Gulf program for the UN development organization, was kidnapped from Switzerland because of his criticisms of regime policies, and brought back to Saudi Arabia to live under house arrest. The Saudi government held a dialogue to discuss women's rights—with male and female participants in separate rooms connected by closed-circuit television—but the recommendations mirrored the preferences of conservative traditionalists, and even then, no actual changes were made.[50]

Saudi Arabia is, of course, not typical of the Arab world's treatment of women. Yet while it deals with these issues in a medieval way, the rest of the Arab states are at roughly Victorian or pre-Victorian levels in this matter. For whatever may be formally on the law books, a woman would be hard put to walk unaccompanied into a local café in most of the Arab world and order a cup of coffee.

There was a time, perhaps, when conservatives—and certainly regimes—might have easily accepted remedies to many aspects of inequality. But this is much harder now that every detail of social, legal, or political behavior is seen by them in the context of Westernization, secularism, and reform. The fact that Islamists are ready to denounce steps toward equality—and use such developments to condemn the existing regimes—makes the situation even more difficult. Thus, making concessions on this question of women's rights is seen increasingly as being just as dangerous as other sorts of economic or political change. For example, extremist conservatives do not want women teachers who are going to influence their students to demand a more open, liberal society, even as these same forces demand that education be in the hands of people who think like them, or worse, in a way similar to bin Laden.[51]

In surveying the status of women in the Gulf, one researcher concluded that the governing elite there—at least outside of Saudi Arabia—"generally supports women's political rights, but strong social sentiment against women's participation in politics persists, as does economic and social discrimination."[52] Elsewhere in the region, except perhaps in Morocco and Jordan, the elites' support for women's rights is much less, while the widespread opposition is probably stronger.

It is tempting, drawing on historical Western experience, to conclude that there is a natural progression toward greater openness and reform in Arab societies. Taking their own societies and trends as inevitable, many Western observers assume that women will gain equality fairly rapidly in the Arab world. Yet this has been demonstrably untrue and—whatever one's faith in the long run—does not seem to be happening even at a gradual pace at present.

This was Rashed's conclusion, and his analysis extends far beyond Saudi Arabia alone. Westerners are wrong, he mused, to conclude that women's status is something arising from government policy. Rather, the situation reflects the real preferences and reality of Arab society. "I do not know how long this way of life will persist, because ever since the

1960s there were predictions that it would not stay for long in its present form."[53] Among liberal women activists, there seems to be more pessimism than optimism regarding the prospects for a revolution in women's rights and status. A Saudi woman writer, Wajiha al-Huweidar, sighs, "All Arab countries, without exception, harbor covert animosity and open discrimination against women. To this day, all official bodies reject any scientific discussion of a solution to women's problems," even as they endlessly insist that women are highly respected in Arab and Muslim societies. Especially notable, she adds, is how women's issues are still treated in a religious context. Only rarely does the state's legislation make things better, because it continues to accept a view of women defined by a reactionary reading of Islamic law.[54] Yet Huweidar can easily show the existence of equally valid alternative interpretations.[55]

Munjiyah Al-Sawaihi, a lecturer in Islamic Studies at al-Zaytouna religious university in Tunisia, extolled the situation in her country but declared, "Ignorant clerics are to this day controlling and dominating [public] thought in order to sanctify women's inferiority through their chauvinistic interpretations of religious texts." An Islamic satellite television channel marked International Women's Day in March 2005 with a discussion on the permissible level of wife-beating, even though there are important Islamic traditions forbidding this practice, not to mention international conventions signed by Arab governments that forbid discrimination against women. "I see nothing but the tightening of the noose around the woman," she concludes.[56]

"I feel terror, really," said Ghada Dassouky, a Syrian woman who hosts weekly women-only meetings to discuss liberal interpretations of Islam, "because we are worrying about whether or not a woman can show her toes and the Americans are researching deep space."[57]

11

A Thousand and One
Difficulties

T he West," remarked Fahmi Huweidi, an Egyptian with Islamist sym-
pathies, "took more than 100 years to reach a decent level of democracy. Why then do they expect us to attain democracy overnight?"[1] This
is a reasonable question. Though liberals respond that the level of war,
violence, and crisis, along with the threat of radical Islamism and the
specter of global terror, means that time is short, historical processes do
not necessarily respond to the demands made upon them.

Certainly, there is a degree of open discontent in the Arab world that
might be called unprecedented. At the same time, while the chorus calling for reform is relatively louder, so is the counterattack. Perhaps a better way to put the central question for the Arab societies is to ask how
this dissatisfaction will be channeled in the early twenty-first century:
through the present system's reinforcement, through revolutionary
Islamism, or through liberalism.

There can be no sharper disagreement about the nature of Arab liberalism than that between two analysts in Washington think tanks, Jon
Alterman and Tamara Cofman Wittes. Alterman says that Arab liberals
are increasingly isolated and losing ground to radical forces that appeal
more to young people. Compared to the Islamists who run social services and take over professional organizations, "All too often, Arab liberals' activity ends when they deliver copy to their editors."[2] Wittes argues
that while the liberal movement is young and weak, it is increasingly
vocal and visible.[3] In a real sense, both views are accurate.

Yet with all the liberals' weaknesses and shortcomings, there is also no
denying the underlying, pervasive anger and frustration in the Arab

world that might stoke the locomotive of democratic change. The point is illustrated by a small incident. In November 2003, the distant country of Georgia had a peaceful revolution. Faced with corruption, mismanagement, and a rigged election, the masses took to the streets and forced the government's resignation. Such an event was obviously a dream for liberal Arabs, but it also highlighted the wide gap between the Arabs' situation and the rest of the world.

A writer in the United Arab Emirates was inspired by this event to ask:

> Why aren't Arab societies experiencing [similar] revolutions? Why are they comatose while all the peoples of the world—including those of Africa—have since 1989 been dancing to the rhythm of a single genuine and universal revolution sweeping [the world] towards . . . democracy? Why has the Arab region still not sprouted democratic and liberal movements offering the Arab peoples an alternative to the existing variety of despotism and authoritarian regimes? . . . [Why] . . . for over a century . . . has the nationalist option in the Arab world been given precedence over the democratic option? . . . Sixty years of tyranny in the name of rosy dreams of liberation, unity, and independence have led to the exploitation of the Arab world's civil societies, and have dried up their sources of renewal, innovation, and creativity.[4]

In Lebanon, a columnist expressed his envy at the Georgians' political situation: "It was . . . as if they and we Arabs lived on different planets, and on our planet none know the meaning of the will of the peoples. . . . The crises and shortcomings have been piling up for years. . . . Everyone is apparently helpless to initiate [anything]. . . . The citizens gaze at [what is being done] in despair or indifference."[5]

A Jordanian counterpart had a virtually identical reaction: "We belong to peoples grown accustomed to humiliation and repression." The only attribute in which Arabs led the world was corruption.[6] Things looked the same from Saudi Arabia, where a writer pointed out that what happened in Georgia—the overthrow of a dictator without bloodshed or terrorism—was impossible among the Arabs, who "believe only in killing to solve problems." Why is it that others can bring change without violence, "while among us suicide [bombers] grow thick as weeds in spring?"[7]

While these writers were voicing disgust with the existing system, they were simultaneously acknowledging the tremendous difficulty of changing it. At least the concepts of "reform" and "democracy"—in no small part due to the much-maligned U.S. sponsorship of these notions—have become commonplace in Arab discussions. In 2005, though, a massive series of demonstrations did take place in Lebanon, successfully demanding the withdrawal of Syrian troops from the country, which Damascus had agreed to a decade earlier.

Yet these same buzzwords are also manipulated and emptied of content by the same regimes that, like the Islamists, derided this program. For example, after the fall of Iraq's Baath party government, its Syrian counterpart reorganized hard-line forces there into a new pro-Damascus group trying to reestablish an Arab nationalist dictatorship in Baghdad. The sheeplike name in which they chose to clothe this extremist wolf was the Reform party.[8]

In Syria itself, whose dictator Bashar al-Assad sometimes styled himself a reform leader, the editor of the regime's newspaper, Mahdi Dakhlallah, explained that democratic change would be conducted under the ruling party's leadership because it represented all the people. He claimed that the existing system was open and encouraged dialogue. Rather than blocking development and reform, it was the motive force for achieving it.[9]

Similarly, in Egypt, Ibrahim Nafi, editor of *Al-Ahram* and voice of the establishment, wrote that the government was already carrying out reform.[10] Hosni Mubarak explained, "We are the state that enjoys democracy in this part of the world."[11] He promised in a speech to his party's convention to "spread the culture of democracy." "One-party rule is over," proclaimed his son Gamal. Meanwhile, though, the government's reform program has actually tightened up political restrictions. The regime's idea of reform is to improve governance rather than institute democracy, to follow the "Chinese model" in creating economic liberalization and greater efficiency without political change.[12] It is unlikely to implement even this type of program.

Morocco's king also promised much and delivered—albeit a bit more than others—very little. As one liberal journalist put it, "Slowing, one could even say halting, progress toward openness."[13] In Tunisia, the regime maintained a good international image by being secular, moderate in foreign policy, and carrying out economic reform while still maintaining all the apparatus of a dictatorship at home. In October 2004 the president allowed himself to receive only 94.5 percent of the vote compared to the 99 percent he obtained in the three previous elections.[14]

Not to be outdone by other Arab states, Jordan's foreign minister Marwan Muasher, in a January 2004 lecture, called on the Arab world "to adopt a new political order" to keep up with global change and the need for economic progress. If reforms were not made quickly, they might have to be done so later "at a higher price." He also noted that anyone calling for political reforms and more freedom in the Arab world was condemned as an American agent. As if to prove his point, the first questioner from the audience claimed Jordan was basing its proposed educational reform on Israel's system, immediately equating reform with a treasonous subservience to Zionism. "The opponents of reform and change," Muasher snorted, "operate by labeling."[15]

In contrast, liberal Arabs are correct in labeling the regimes' new fondness for talking about reform as merely cosmetic and propagandistic. A good example is the staging of frequent officially sponsored conferences that speak of change as a substitute for it. One such meeting took place in Yemen in January 2004. The keynote speaker, Yemeni president Ali Abdallah Saleh, hailed democracy as "the choice of the modern age for all people of the world and the rescue ship for political regimes."[16] According to the conference's final declaration: "Democracy and human rights, application of the rule of law, which are compatible with all faiths and cultures, are interdependent and inseparable, and human rights must underpin any meaningful conception of democracy in order to strengthen the foundations and its ability to promote and protect human rights."[17]

Yet as a prominent opposition leader accurately explained, "When everyone goes back home, little action will follow." He recalled that a similar meeting in the same place a year earlier had produced a "wonderful declaration . . . still locked in a drawer awaiting implementation."[18] Another participant, Ahmad al-Rab'i, expressed the frustration of civil society activists as they watched Arab government officials dominate the opening session. "Each one described his land as Paradise on Earth," a country encouraging civil society, giving full rights to women, and so on.[19]

If indeed things were already so democratic, what need was there for a conference? But, Rab'i continued, both speakers and audience knew these words were mere "idle chatter spoken to cover up the tremendous deficiencies from which these countries suffer in the areas of human rights and individual freedoms." In contrast, reform activists spoke of "the grim state of affairs" in most Arab countries, in which free institutions are harassed, civil rights violated, thinkers prevented from writing, and the press restricted, and women face severe discrimination. There is, he noted correctly, a "deep abyss" between these two versions of Arab reality.[20]

What is most justified by the facts was the deep cynicism of those, including many liberals, who feared that nothing was changing in the Arab world. In Lebanon, the New TV channel was shut down for two days after it broke the broadcasting law by criticizing Lebanese and Syrian officials by name.[21] In Jordan the Symposium for Arab Thought expelled a member who spoke of the U.S. troops in Iraq as "liberation forces."[22] In Egypt three men were arrested and brought up on criminal charges of damaging the country's reputation for distributing a humorous bumper sticker that made fun of Cairo drivers as tending to run red lights.[23] In Morocco a journalist was sentenced to prison for "insulting" the king in satirical articles.[24]

While Jordan held elections, it barred Toujan Faisal from running as a candidate because she had been convicted for "insulting the dignity of the state" by accusing an official of corruption.[25] The fact remained that there is still no real liberal party in any Arab country except Kuwait, virtually no liberal newspaper being published on Arab-ruled soil, and no charismatic liberal leader who had a national following anywhere.

What then did the liberal impulse amount to in reality?

- For regimes that gave it lip service, reform is mainly a gimmick to answer a U.S. prodemocracy policy that had already brought about the overthrow of Iraq's regime. To ward off U.S. pressure or a possible liberal upsurge, rulers try to portray themselves as the real reformers.

- In Gulf Arab monarchies, notably Saudi Arabia, talk—but no real action—about reform is part of the regime strategy to fight a growing internal terrorism problem fed by the system of anti-American, anti-Israel indoctrination intended to preserve the regime and traditional structures of society. The rulers recognize that there is a need to tone down some of the deliberately fostered religious extremism lest it turn against themselves.

- To some extent there is also recognition from the top that Arab political systems really are outmoded and inefficient. Limited change is thus acceptable in theory, particularly economic and educational reforms, though in practice even these are often whittled down to nothing.

- In several countries—Jordan and Morocco are two examples—the elite is more Westernized than the masses. They know about Western political philosophy and are affected by what the rest of the world thinks about them. Such people do accept something akin to the liberal idea that Westernization is a good thing and that a more "modern" society is a point of pride. A few decades ago, this made them the target of attack by radical nationalists for being Western agents. Today they must be careful not to provoke the same kind of attack by Islamists. But even if they genuinely want reforms, can they persuade their people while not inflaming the radicals?

Given all these factors, one can expect relatively little to change. The current situation is dismal and stagnant, yet those in control today would rather be running the swamp than sitting in a democratic regime's prison.

Aside from the simple fact of self-interest—those in power seek to continue enjoying their privileges—there are other good reasons for the tremendous difficulty in fixing what is wrong with the Arab world. While the lesson of Saddam's overthrow had some effect on regimes in terms of talking a lot, and thinking a little, about reform, they also bear in mind other dramatic events as urging them toward caution. These include:

1. In the USSR and the Soviet bloc in Eastern Europe, Mikhail Gorbachev's reforms created a chain reaction ending with communism's complete collapse. The revolution in Romania, where the dictator faced a firing squad, is an especially frightening example for these people.

2. In Iran, the shah's efforts at modernization and reform made for social upheaval that helped spark an Islamist revolution that overthrew him.

3. In Yugoslavia, greater openness led to bloody ethnic civil strife, resulting in the country's disintegration.

4. In Algeria, the prospect of free and fair elections was about to bring to power an Islamist regime, which was prevented only by a military coup and a bloody civil war that continues to this day.

5. The violent post-Saddam instability in Iraq raises the question of whether the people there are really better off. A state ruled by a dictatorship may be considered better than a terrible state of anarchy.

6. The post-Saddam ethnic strife in Iraq is a warning for other regimes that might face Sunni-Shia, Muslim-Coptic, Muslim-Christian, Muslim-Alawite, Arab-Berber, or Arab-Kurdish strife.

In this context, there are several ironic paradoxes facing reform or reformers, especially because these factors dominate the thinking of the ruling elites and the most influential thinkers in those societies:

- The current system, with all its problems, does keep incumbent regimes in power. If they avoid the kind of extreme adventurism practiced by Saddam Hussein, they are unlikely to meet his fate.

- Dictatorships can neutralize foreign criticism through changes in rhetoric or policy that do not reduce their overwhelming domestic control. Even the Libyan dictator Mu'ammar al-Qadhafi, no exemplar of brilliant realism, has well understood this fact. By confessing his secret efforts to get nuclear weapons and offering compensation for past terror attacks against a Western target or two, he has bought immunity from U.S. retaliation and international sanctions.

- The rulers know that change is more likely to undermine them and eventually bring them down than to make them beloved reformers or successful democratic politicians. They know exactly what the liberal Arabs really want to achieve. At the same time, they attribute similar subversive intent to the United States. They are deaf to reform not because of U.S. policies but simply because the U.S.-backed program is completely against their most basic interests.

- Any opening in the political system may help radical Islamist forces create more instability and make things worse. Advocates of reform deride this claim by saying that the masses really favor democracy, but even many potential liberals do not seem to believe this assertion. As a result, they support the regime, fearing that something worse might happen if it falls.

- Popular opinion has opposed liberal reform and sided with the Islamists on many occasions. The failed attempt by regimes to give women the vote in Kuwait in 1999—reversed in 2005 only due to support from parliament members appointed by the emir—or to change laws unfair to women in Egypt and Jordan provide examples.

- Many people, including those in leading positions, believe their own propaganda. Their worldview is shaped by radical Arab nationalist thinking with a strong dash of Islamist (or at least the reactionary-traditionalist version of Islamic) thinking. They are certain of vast conspiracies against them, the total evil of Israel and the United States, the threat of the West, the decadence of democracy, and the horrors of modernism.

- Using a Western language, addressing a Western or at least English-speaking audience, or living in the West are all factors conducive to developing a different, liberal, point of view. The vast majority of Arabs, of course, are not subject to these influences. On the contrary, the mainstream position is continually reinforced in their minds, with few exceptions.

- There is no doubt that Arab liberals face a harder struggle than their counterparts in other countries and past centuries. Relatively few living in the Arab world dare challenge outright the basic premises of the mainstream world view—Heggy, Salem, Ghabra, and Ibrahim are a few examples—because such open, total negation of the hegemonic ideology is difficult and dangerous.

- Accepting—or pretending to believe—some of their opponents' premises seems easier and safer but also reinforces the status quo without necessarily persuading anyone. Liberals can insist that they have the best strategy for defeating the Islamists, bringing victory over Israel or the United States, and saving the regimes, yet is this strategy really going to catapult them to influence or power?

The result is that it is going to take the Arab world a long time to get out of its current mess, and the prospects for democracy seem quite distant. This will be even more true if things go badly in Baghdad, but the situation is bad enough, even given a best-case outcome for post-Saddam Iraq.

There is nothing mystical and exotic about the Arab state of affairs or even much that is unique, except for its timing. In general, there are strong parallels between the Arab world's situation and what has happened elsewhere in the world during the last century or two. The problem is that the Arab world is the globe's last holdout against modernization and does not seem to be in a hurry to end that condition.

Similarly, there is nothing exceptional about Islam as a religion in its effect on society except that it has remained stronger and more inflexible to a later point in history than its counterparts. There are many examples from the history of the Christian churches opposing social change, democracy, and freedom of thought, but those battles are over, many of them long ago. By the late 1700s, European intellectuals were writing critically about religion and politics in a way that today is still impossible in the Arab world. Whereas the reactionary side was defeated after a struggle lasting decades in Europe and Latin America, such forces are still in power in Arab states.[26]

To make matters worse, the reactionaries include not only religious conservatives but also the nationalist left. In the Arab world, in contrast to history elsewhere, the forces supporting dictatorship and the status quo have doubled, while their liberal opponents are left with few supporters or even people willing to listen to them.

This does not mean that change is impossible, only that it is very hard and will take a full historical era. It does not mean that there are not some signs of change, usually those that regimes accept as necessary for self-preservation. An educational and religious system that manufactures extremist Islamist revolutionaries ready to overthrow them by force is not in the rulers' interests. The actual or discussed revision of school curricula in places like Kuwait, Saudi Arabia, and Jordan is intended to curtail such extremism.[27]

There also seems to be a growing sector among young people, intellectuals, professionals, and businesspeople—among other groups—that could form a future constituency for liberal reform.[28] In Morocco, there is a lively civil society and strong women's groups.[29] A greater dynamism at the bottom and flexibility at the top seem evident in the "reactionary" monarchies of the Gulf and in Morocco, compared to the "progressive"

Arab nationalist regimes that increasingly resemble the Soviet Union in its most dinosaurlike period.

The way things could be was illustrated by an event in tiny Bahrain in January 2004. Bahrain's elected parliament held a special televised session to denounce alleged government corruption in managing the country's pension funds. Members, including Islamists, demanded that accused cabinet members resign for making bad investments that benefited themselves, and that they change the system and return the lost money. One liberal member declared that the special session showed the people that parliament was not a "rubber stamp" for the regime.[30]

The government denied the accusations and presented its defense to the legislators, but a high official proclaimed himself "happy" to be part of "this historic day" on which Bahrain's democracy showed itself so well. "The government supports the Parliament's eagerness to exercise its monitoring role," he added. "I am really proud of the work done by the special committee." In turn, parliamentarians praised the ruler's democratic reforms and the government for its cooperation.[31]

Such events, normal not only in Western terms but for most of the world—and even up to a point in Iran, where a big reformist movement developed and won relatively free elections, though in the end failed to make any change—remained very rare in the Arab world. The gap between talk and action was perhaps clearest in Saudi Arabia.

Edward Walker, head of the U.S.-based Middle East Institute, made the strongest case for the idea that Saudi Arabia was entering a reform era. The process was necessarily cautious given the tremendous opposition to change as well as the differences of opinion in the royal family. In a speech to Islamic clerics, King Fahd urged them to "highlight the dangers" posed by extremism to Islam, to battle against "deviant thinking," and annul fatwas legitimizing radical acts. The government claimed to have fired more than two thousand imams who had advocated extremism—although there seems to be no documentation for this—and it was certainly fighting in its own interest against al-Qa'ida terrorists.[32]

Yet, indeed, some things went noticeably backward. "Censorship of books is more rigid now than forty years back," according to one newspaper columnist.[33] Asked what role the media could play in the struggle for reform, Jamal Khashoggi responded, "I don't see a single paper calling for reform."[34]

A group of Saudi professional men openly expressed their concerns to a sympathetic visitor. "We were educated in America, and I see the world going against everything I have built," said Dr. Mujahid al-Sawwaf, a lawyer in Jeddah and a former professor at Umm al-Qura University in Mecca. "We were always for liberalism, but some of the terrorists were my students."[35]

"My daughter is for bin Laden," another man admitted. Her walls were covered with pictures of Palestinian girl martyrs. "If we go into her room at night, she'll be listening to Britney Spears, but as soon as we close the door she's listening to martyr songs." Others agreed. Their children derided them for not fighting against Israel in past wars. A dentist said, "One of the children said to me, 'Uncle, is it true that when you went to the West you became a puppet like our leadership?' Our kids don't want to study in America, as we did. Bin Laden changed our life. He proved that mighty America is vulnerable. . . . We're afraid of our future, but the youth think America is on the verge of collapsing and it's time for us to fight it."[36]

Such attitudes are not mere extensions of traditional views but part of the Arab world's new era, revitalizing old concepts and infusing them with a new mixture of Islamism and jihad. This kind of thinking was most concentrated in Saudi Arabia, but it was often in evidence elsewhere, too.

Some observers suggested that behind the scenes in Saudi Arabia there was real hope of change from above. A reform-minded faction of the royal family, headed by Crown Prince Abdallah, the country's de facto ruler, was said to be contending with an antichange group led by Prince Nayef. Some members of the ruling family clearly favored change.[37] Prince Bandar bin Khalid al-Faisal, chairman of the board of the liberal *Al-Watan*, predicted the system would become less centralized and give more people a bigger say in governing. He accepted the idea that only reform would ensure stability.[38] Given the lack of information on the royal family's inner workings, it was hard to prove or disprove any particular analysis of its alignments.

At any rate, though, there was certainly more grassroots activity. On September 24, 2003, a petition entitled "In Defense of the Nation" and signed by 306 Saudis from many walks of life, was presented to the king and crown prince. It warned that reforms and "popular participation in decision making" were necessary to avert a major crisis. The signers wanted an elected parliament with real power, an independent judiciary, and freedom to organize civil society groups.[39] The petition's contents, however, were not even published in any Saudi newspaper.

Each apparent step forward—often merely a promise of progress—was met by an equal, often material, backward pace. Crown Prince Abdallah established a forum for national dialogue and invited a wide variety of people to attend, but the recommendations arising from the discussions, held in a beautiful building created solely to house the meetings, were very conservative and, at any rate, had no effect. In the media, *Al-Watan* ran more liberal articles, but then its editor, Jamal Khashoggi, was fired by the regime shortly after criticizing some clerics for supporting Islamist terrorists. Hussein Shobokshi was allowed to publish an article describing a liberal future Saudi Arabia in an English-language paper but not in Arabic, and then lost his column as a result.

Prince Sultan bin Abd al-Aziz made liberal pronouncements, then was reportedly lured by Saudi officials to a meeting in Geneva, drugged, and forcibly returned to house arrest in Riyadh.[40] In March 2004, the Saudi government approved the establishment of an official human rights association, whose members flew off to London to explain how the kingdom was moving toward liberalization. A few days later, thirteen prominent independent liberals, genuine reformers, were taken into police custody and charged with endangering national unity.[41] Those promising not to petition for reform or talk to reporters were quickly released. One reformer remarked, "This will make people lose trust in the government and their promises. It contradicts 100 percent what they have been promising." In May 2005, the only three arrested dissidents who had not promised to stop their activities were sentenced to six, seven, and nine years in prison.[42]

One gimmick used by regimes is to create their own human rights or civil society groups, which can then be guaranteed not to cause any problems for the government. In the Saudi case, a leading prince explained that dissidents were those rebelling "against their fathers and their country" and thus could not expect support from the state-backed human rights body. "I urge you not to think that the national human rights association was founded to assist offenders" against the law, he said. The new chairman of this National Organization for Human Rights, Abdallah Bin Saleh al-Ubeid, explained that "there are those who consider certain issues a violation of human rights, while we consider them a safeguard to human rights. For example, executions, amputating the hand of a thief, or flogging an adulterer."[43] Several of these proregime "human rights" apologists were later appointed to high government posts.

In Egypt the state-backed National Council for Human Rights remains quite vague in its discussion of issues, which includes nothing that would offend the government; indeed, the council avoids any serious discussion of the country at all.[44] The regime even sponsored a major journal on democracy, producing more copies in English than in Arabic and publishing little about the Arab world and almost nothing about Egypt in its pages.

Similarly, there were promises in many countries of reforming education to make it more tolerance-oriented, but these were accompanied by little action or even high-level denials that any change would indeed be made.[45] In Saudi Arabia no government action was taken against 160 clerics, many of them government employees, who accused liberals of being traitors loyal to infidels, and the government denounced educational reform as a plot by "the Zionist-Crusader government in Washington . . . to convert the Muslims to another religion."[46]

As for women's rights, the Saudi mufti reinforced prohibitions against men and women mixing professionally or socially after the speech by Lubna Olayan at an international economic forum. Raid Qusti, a liberal academic, complained, "Since 1990 we've been saying the same thing—that reform is essential but that we are not ready. When are we going to be ready then?"[47]

It could also be argued that the lack of democracy not only holds up economic development but becomes dangerous in a highly technological society. Hussein Shobokshi, a U.S.-educated wealthy building contractor, warned that Riyadh's sewage disposal system was built improperly by a corrupt government official who went unpunished because of his connections with the royal family. The inferior work spread disease and might lead to a massive flood in the event of an earthquake.[48]

In Saudi Arabia's case it would take considerable change to make it even equivalent to a "normal" Arab country. After all, in most such states there are elections, parliaments that can nominally pass laws, rights supposedly guaranteed under constitutions, and the ability to form unions and civil society groups. Saudi Arabia could thus undergo major reforms and be a more pleasant place to live for its people without being any more democratic than Egypt, Jordan, or Syria.

Some Saudi liberals expressed visions of what a truly better future for Saudi Arabia would be like. In an August 2003 article in *Okaz,* Shobokshi related a bedtime story he told his seven-year-old daughter about a country where she would be able to drive and be a lawyer; where there are elections, human rights conferences, and female cabinet ministers; where Indian immigrants can become citizens; and where mosques hold educational classes that discuss religion freely. In response, he received both praise and death threats. But perhaps the most significant factor is that as a result of the article—and despite Shobokshi's being a major stockholder in both newspapers—*Okaz* and the *Arab News* permanently canceled his column.[49]

Another vision was expressed by Lubna Olayan in her speech at the January 2004 Jeddah Economic Forum. "If Saudi Arabia wants to progress," she told the audience, it has to embrace change. Such reforms "will strengthen us and make us more competitive," while at the same time they will be adapted "in a way that preserves our core Islamic values and related traditions."[50]

But many—perhaps most—Saudis interpreted their core Islamic values and traditions as being inconsistent with her attending the meeting or giving a speech in the first place. The main response to her talk was a fatwa from the country's mufti denouncing her for speaking in front of an audience that included men and for her failure to keep her veil in place.

No one knows better than the Arab liberals themselves about the extent of the challenges they face. It is within this context that they must find solutions both to their tactical difficulties and to the Arab world's wider problems. In general, they have a clear idea of the results needed, though getting there strategically is the problem.

A more minimal reformist strategy is outlined by Abd al-Mun'im Sa'id, a member of the Egyptian establishment with liberal views. He supports a combination of change and stability within the existing system. The Egyptian state, he argues, can make such a transformation. The judiciary is fairly independent, though there are limits; the media is vibrant; and interest groups already exist. The state is not merely a dictatorship but has a strong institutional structure. Gamal Mubarak, the president's son, is on the liberals' side. Why then, Sa'id says, should the country take too many risks by making major changes, especially when Egyptians are naturally conservative and prize legitimacy?[51]

Yet Sa'id, too, believes that the country's bureaucrats urge slower progress as an excuse for doing little or nothing. He acknowledges that the extensive talk about even a mere economic reform never leads anywhere. Egypt, he explains, is like a "D" student who never actually fails but barely gets along.[52]

In contrast, Tarek Heggy, his fellow Egyptian, suggests that a more thoroughgoing transformation is needed, with the alternative to the existing system requiring "a concerted effort that combines scientific knowledge; modern management techniques; a serious program for reform and development; an educational revolution [to institute a modern school system] based on creativity not memory tests; expanding the scope of general freedoms and allowing for wider popular participation in public affairs."[53]

According to Shafiq Ghabra, the main goals for reformists include "good governance, open economies, privatization, and elements of liberalism and democracy." He foresees this system as somehow absorbing Islamism and Arab nationalism rather than defeating them.[54] This view is the product of a dilemma forcing liberals to scale back their demands and expectations: the fact that Arabs have been forced into an unpalatable choice between incumbent dictatorships and extremist opposition, with no middle ground. Ghabra explains this problem clearly:

> Choose the present authoritarian governments with all their shortcomings, bad economic policies and limited . . . social and personal freedom. Or choose upheaval and the extremists whose theocracy would be draped in strict codes of behavior governing such things as dress, social interaction and the role of women in public life. Faced with these alternatives during the past two decades, the Middle East opted for stagnation. . . . Just about the only ideology the region hasn't tried is liberal capitalist democracy of one form or another.[55]

Even Ghabra, one of the boldest and most outspoken reformers, must trim his sails to cope with this problem. Reform, he concludes, will happen only when the Arab world feels that it is "a route that can be taken without jeopardizing the Islamic, Arab and national components of its identity."[56] He also suggests that either too much or too little reform will bring radical Islamists to power. Too much, by alienating the mainstream of society, destabilizing countries, and being exploited by the Islamists who are "the only organized force." Too little, by paralyzing economic development, creating unemployment, and radicalizing the young. Thus, he concludes, the "push for change needs to be steady, but gradual," requiring a great deal of time and discussion.[57]

As a result, the reformists—unlike their counterparts in the rest of the world—do not have the luxury of concentrating their efforts against the existing dictatorial regimes.[58] They must "defend certain elements of the status quo as if the extremists were on the verge of taking power while seeking reform and democracy as if the radicals were not there threatening to fill the vacuum."[59]

Yet while their response is understandable, liberals also face the same tempting traps as mainstream intellectuals, especially as the regime offers them lucrative jobs and positions of honor. It is, as Ahmed Abdallah states when talking about the Egyptian intelligentsia, "a problem of intellectual integrity [that] befalls them as they sometimes negate or turn around what they know is true, as they confess in their private talk." Starting by defending the regime in part or compromising with it— inspired by their political weakness and wish to form an alliance against the greater Islamist threat—could they end up inviting the accusation "that they are mere muwazzafeen (state employees) who just take orders to tailor their writings to official requirements?"[60]

One factor militating against such an unfortunate result is their knowledge that, as Ghabra states, "Arab autocrats," no matter what they say, "won't do anything unless they're nudged and pushed."[61] But pushed by whom? There are clear limits to what either the United States or the liberals can do, and in both cases the efforts entail a backlash that might be equal to or stronger than the constructive effect.

The very forces built into the system—its repressive and violent power; orchestrated xenophobia; labeling dissidents as enemy agents who are against Islam; and so on—remain quite powerful. This rests on a foundation of what Fouad Ajami has called a "righteous sense of Arab victimhood—which overlooks what Arab rulers do to others while lamenting its own condition." It seeks to "reject the message of reform by dwelling on the sins of the American messenger. . . . It can call up the fury of the Israeli-Palestinian violence and use it as an alibi for yet more self-pity and rage. It can shout down its own would-be reformers, write them off as accomplices of a foreign assault. It can throw up its defenses and wait for the United States to weary of its expedition."[62]

Many specific examples illustrate this point. In a meeting between Egyptian president Hosni Mubarak and Saudi Arabia's rulers in early 2004, these leaders' joint statement affirmed, of course, that they want to "proceed on the path of development, modernization and reform in keeping with their people's interests and values," but only if it is compatible with "their specificities and Arab identity."[63]

This stance would, of course, be quite understandable if it were not a complete and total lie. It is not hard to understand why the leaders of dictatorial regimes in which power and wealth are monopolized by a small group do not want to give up their privileges. This is the way dictatorships have always worked throughout the world.

These are not, however, the rationales used by the regimes and their supporting bureaucrats, intellectuals, or media to justify their refusal to fight corruption, permit civil liberties, allow free speech, stop repressing moderate dissidents, and the many other ways they stay in power. In the Middle East, a great deal of sand is thrown into the air which succeeds in obscuring these simple facts. Precisely because they are able to persuade many of their people on these points—partly through endless repetition of their arguments and partly through discrediting or silencing alternative viewpoints—the Middle East has remained a zone of dictatorships while other regions have proved far more flexible toward change.

What are the main excuses used to reject all serious efforts to bring about reform? These are the four horsemen of the Middle Eastern apocalypse that help explain the region's chronic failures:

The Arab-Israeli conflict paradox. The regimes and their supporters say that nothing can change unless this issue is resolved, and then Arab states act to ensure that it will not be solved by refusing compromise, backing terrorism, and inciting their people toward militancy. Thus, even the moderate Egyptian intellectual Muhammad Sid-Ahmed said in *Al-Ahram* that U.S. proposals for democratization were unacceptable because they would ensure that "the Palestinian cause would lose its specific character and central position." Yet what possible real connection does this issue really have with a better educational system, fair elections, freer speech, and less corruption in the Arab world?

America and state-sponsored xenophobia. The pretense here is that the United States wants to impose a detailed program of specific changes on the Arab world. This is rejected as unwarranted (read "imperialistic") interference in sovereign states by a country with a record that makes it unworthy as a sponsor for democracy.

The Egyptian academic and editor Usama al-Ghazali Harb, who takes some liberal positions, protests that the United States long supported traditionalists against reformers in order to further U.S. interests, using the rationale that stability was more important than democracy and offering the excuse of "deference to the 'traditions and local traits' of traditional societies."[64]

But which is it? Is the problem that the United States supports the regimes, which makes it an imperialist boss, or that it challenges them, which makes it an imperialist aggressor?

The former Arab League secretary-general Esmat Abd al-Meguid asked the United States, "How can you speak about democracy when you have these things that are happening in Palestine and in Iraq?"[65] The implication is that Arab regimes are doing the United States a favor if they consider treating their own people better. At the same time, they misstate U.S. policy. Then secretary of state Colin Powell said in response to Arab criticisms, "I agree with the Egyptians and the Saudis: [reform] can't be imposed from outside. It has to be accepted from the inside."[66]

Arab and Islamic "specificity." When it suits them, mainstream Arab intellectuals and journalists rage that the West talks about them as if they are "different" from itself. At other times, the nationalists and Islamists claim that the requirements of Arab identity and Islamic religion require a different system of government and society. Yet if the Japanese, Indians, or many others can so successfully blend modern society and democracy with their cultures, why cannot Arabs do so?

Iraq. The Saudi-Egyptian statement rejecting reform for their own societies also demanded the withdrawal of U.S.-led occupation forces in Iraq. Again, though, is this an issue that should delay any change or even serious examination of the well-known shortcomings of Arab states and societies? By enacting reforms, are Arab countries doing the United States a favor for which some price should be exacted?

Yet the most serious critique of liberalism's more immediate prospects came from Mansour al-Nogaidan, one of the most energetic and courageous Saudis in their ranks. He quotes an Arab philosopher as saying, "If you bring Queen Elizabeth to rule in Yemen, she will rule like Imam Ahmad, one of the most radical religious leaders there. And if you bring Imam Ahmad to England, he will rule like Queen Elizabeth."[67] This means that institutions and historical experiences are not so easily transferred.

It is easy for liberals to dismiss the reservations and fears of their critics as self-interested deceit, and indeed there is much truth in this complaint. Yet the stakes are very high, and if the liberals are wrong—as optimistic reformers have often been in history—they could end by bringing massive instability and even more suffering to their part of the world. Usama al-Baz, President Mubarak's main adviser, warned that "if we introduce lots of changes in a short period of time, the people cannot digest it." He used the following analogy: "Suppose that somebody has a fever, and he has to take some antibiotics. He is told to take it every six or eight hours. Should he take 48 tablets at once to feel better?"[68]

Saad Eddin Ibrahim views such statements as merely ways "to scare the West" that reform will lead to an Islamist takeover. "None of these fears, in my opinion, is warranted."[69] But what if his opinion is in error? There have been many such cases in history: those who said that anything was better than the czar and wound up with Stalin; the collapse of the weak, imperfect Weimar Republic in Germany; or the impetus to reform in Iran that turned into an Islamist revolution. Good intentions can become wishful thinking that, in turn, leads to a deadly outcome.

The reform movement has a secret weapon of which the liberals themselves have been almost completely unaware: the attractiveness of democracy for ethnic and communal groups. It is no accident that liberals have overlooked this issue because it has been one of the most dangerous arguments against them.

Liberals have always emphasized their desire to unite their countries, appealing to citizens across the board with the hope of reducing—rather than increasing—the likelihood of ethnic strife. Their enemies have warned that democracy will lead to national disintegration. Particularly for minority ruling groups—notably the Alawites in Syria and the Sunnis in Iraq—this is a terrifying prospect, carrying with it the possibility of not only a loss of power but even massacres and potential genocide.

But events in Lebanon and Iraq during 2005—indeed, the two most important developments that seemed to mark an upsurge for the liberal cause—both pointed to this factor as critical. On February 14, 2005, former Lebanese prime minister Rafiq al-Hariri, who had challenged Syria's continued domination of Lebanon, was assassinated by a bomb in downtown Beirut, probably by Syria. Massive protests erupted in Lebanon demanding the withdrawal of troops, which Syria had promised in 1989. Under international pressure, Syria pulled out its troops.

His regime and its Lebanese supporters used the old argument that those calling for change were merely following the Western line against the Arabs. The pro-Syrian Lebanese labor minister, Assem Qanso, for example, charged that those demanding Syria's withdrawal wanted to destroy the country's Arabism and help "American and Israeli tanks" occupy the country.[70] Yet these claims did not deter most Lebanese. As a result of this movement and international pressure from both Europe and the United States, Syria pulled its army out of the country and the puppet government in Beirut resigned.

Lebanon is the only Arab state where these groups have always been legitimate political actors. Paradoxically, it is also the sole Arab country where local patriotism has openly existed. Among other things, Lebanon was loved because it let these groups flourish rather than subordinating them to a powerful central government.

Lebanon thus represented freedom and pluralism, something worth protecting from subordination to a Sunni Muslim–dominated regional empire operating in the name of Arab nationalism. Of course, there were always those, intoxicated on ideology or seeking their own advantage—historically, Sunni Muslims—who were ready to align with the outsiders. In the end, though, the outsider who took over was Syria.

At that point Lebanese patriotism was reborn on a broad basis, bring-ing together three communities—Christians, Druze, and Sunni Mus-lims—against a Syrian domination that was seen as benefiting none of them. Hezbollah, the most important single Shia Muslim group (but not the only one), is a Syrian client and pushed its community to support a continuing Syrian presence. But even among the Shia, there are elements of Lebanese patriotism as well.

After getting rid of Syria, but still too traumatized by a long, bloody civil war to let disputes get out of hand, Lebanon was beginning to get back to "normal," which means that politics will probably revolve around communal parties making deals to share power and resources. Going back to the period before the civil war broke out in the mid-1970s was actually a step forward for Lebanon. At the same time, though, it was not a bold breakthrough to an unprecedented level of democracy.[71]

Politicians from the country's long-powerful political families stepped back into leadership positions. No better symbol of this reality can be found than the important role played in the insurgency by Walid Jum-blatt, the Druze warlord whose father had been assassinated by Syria in 1976. Jumblatt had a long record as an extremist. Suddenly he was pro-claiming sentiments like those of the most passionate liberal. Jumblatt confessed that he had been cynical about the attempt to transform Iraq, but when he saw the success of that country's January 2005 elections, he thought "it was the start of a new Arab world." Seemingly overcome with enthusiasm for democratic revolt, he proclaimed enthusiastically, "The Syrian people, the Egyptian people, all say that something is chang-ing. The Berlin Wall has fallen. We can see it."[72]

Quickly, however, the demonstrations in Lebanon faded away, and Jumblatt appeared to lose his prodemocratic passion. As liberalism, democracy, and reform seemed to become powerful popular forces, all sorts of hard-liners and charlatans suddenly began portraying them-selves—at least in interviews with Western reporters—as courageous dissidents.

Still, if people saw democracy as the wave of the present or the future, such a development might very much improve its prospects. The Iraqi election did impress people throughout the Arab world. And there, as in Lebanon, ethnic factors seemed to defy expectations in contributing to the creation of a stable democratic system. In the January 2005 election, almost 80 percent of parliamentary seats were won by communal parties—and it would have been more if the Sunni Muslims had not virtually boycotted the vote. The elections succeeded not so much because of any devotion to liberal democracy but because the Kurdish and Shia leaders—including the Muslim clerics among them—ordered their people to vote. And they did so because they knew they would win.

This is not a democracy based on individual preferences, national loyalties, or liberal values, but on communal ties. There is no strong liberal party that can appeal to national patriotism, transcending communal loyalties and winning support on the basis of issues. Yet in a sense, this situation makes democracy more secure. First, it builds an Iraqi patriotism because only a sovereign Iraq can preserve this deal. Second, given the demographics, the Kurds and Shia know they will go on winning every election in the future. This gives them a tremendous incentive to support future elections. And third, when these two communities made a deal to establish a government, it marked the beginning of pluralism. These groups also made clear their readiness to bring the Sunni Muslims into such a coalition, which would greatly strengthen the system. The bloody Sunni insurgency was inspired in part by fears that this group had lost its status as the country's rulers. But if the Sunnis fail to make a deal with the other two communities based on an understanding of the value of democratic pluralism, they will be far worse off.

While the intellectual advocates of democracy are individual liberals, the fruits of an electoral-based system are likely to be reaped by large communal-based parties and Islamist movements, which are much more capable of organizing large groups of people. The outcome will vary according to the specific situation. In some places, like Lebanon and Iraq, the results may be good. In others, the existing regimes will have far more appeal as people fear the potential for civil war or an Islamist takeover.

Still, those likely to support democracy in the Arab world are the ones convinced that they can win fair elections. Large groups holding such ideas are most likely to emerge from existing ethnic religious communities rather than from diverse parties built up gradually from individuals' conversion to a liberal worldview.

In this context too, though, Islamists might end up as the big winners. Within Lebanon, the largest single community, the Shia Muslims, was led by Hezbollah. Almost half the seats in the January 2005 Iraqi election were won by an Islamist-led coalition of Shia Muslims. These events inspired other Islamists—particularly in Egypt and Syria as well as among the Palestinians—to conclude that electoral democracy might be in their interests.

Yousef al-Qaradhawi, the Qatar-based Egyptian cleric who is the leading spiritual guide to the Muslim Brotherhood movements in various countries, explained that only a small minority of Arabs are pro-Western or secularist. If truly fair elections were to be held, he insisted, Islamists would win by landslides. His argument was partly subverted by his use of Iran as an example.[73] True, in the early days of the Iranian revolution, large majorities had supported an Islamic state. Two decades later, however, the voters had turned against the regime. Still, the Islamists had remained in power in Tehran, and even the popular shift against them had taken almost two decades. Qaradhawi's threat must be taken seriously.

Both the good news and the bad news is that once the status quo in the Arab world is breached, anything can happen.

Clearly, a long-term plan is required, or else a democratic endeavor could end tragically with a takeover by the most extreme Islamist elements. As Nogaidan puts it: "Culture and society will dictate the way you rule. . . . Democracy needs a liberal culture. In the beginning we need freedom, we need different parties to have their rights and a culture that allows people to be represented."[74]

One way of developing a strategy in this context was revealed in various statements, including the Saudi petition "In Defense of the Nation" presented to the king and crown prince in 2003. The title reveals the underlying concept—the liberals are rallying to defend the country and help the government against the real threat, that of radical Islamism. The proposal has three basic points:[75]

1. The country is in dire threat of violence and revolution. Both the government and the liberals want to stop this crisis.

2. The people and government "are partners in protecting the stability, security and unity of the nation" against the radical threat.

3. The best—and only—way to stave off instability, violence, and a nightmarish revolution is to implement major reforms.

If the regime waits too long to do so, the radical Islamists will win
and terrorism will spread throughout the society.

The list of proposed reforms includes turning the consultative council
into a real elected parliament, creating an independent judiciary, re-
specting human rights, legalizing civil society groups, accepting diversity, and creating a culture of tolerance. This also requires rooting out
governmental corruption, diversifying the economy, distributing resources
fairly, ending poverty and unemployment, improving health and hous-
ing, and raising the status of women.[76]

This may be the best strategy the liberals can come up with, but it has
two major weaknesses. First, regimes may well not be convinced that liberals are their best allies. Appeasing radicals, and certainly traditionalist
conservatives, may be an attractive alternative. The rulers and their supporters know that making concessions to liberals may actually inflame
the Islamists and push traditionalists into the revolutionary camp.

Second, regimes may well be convinced that liberals are simply competing with the radical Islamists over the right to bury them. After all, if
they carry out the reforms that liberals want, the regime's power will be
severely undermined and the individuals now in control of the system—
and benefiting from it—will be thrown out.

In the final analysis, it is very hard for the liberals to come up with any
impressive strategy or a political line that will win over the masses, at
least in the short run.

In spite of all these doubts the simple bottom line, most liberals
argue, is this: No matter how great the difficulties, no matter how long
the struggle, there is no substitute for waging the battle. "There are a
thousand and one difficulties facing us as we work to institute democracy," writes Ibrahim. "And yet what choice do we have except to try?"
Only democratic government, respect for human rights, and the rule of
law can "protect our countries, our region and the world against the
threats of terrorism and of crises that compel outsiders to come and use
military force on our shores."[77]

By merely cataloguing all the reasons why democracy won't work, he
continues, one arrives at a "paralysis by analysis."[78] The Arab world's sad

state and the failure of alternatives already tried are the best argument for taking a different approach. As one Arab writer argues: "The notion that strength resides in large standing armies and up-to-date weapons of destruction has proved bankrupt. Real strength is always internal, in the creative, cultural, and wealth producing capabilities of a people. It is found in civil society, not in the army or in the state."[79]

If the liberal movement is going to make a breakthrough, it might come from an unexpected and dramatic event, like the Egyptian coup of 1952, which put Arab nationalism as the hegemonic force in the region, or the 1979 Iranian revolution, which brought Islamism to center stage. The Arab liberals are advocates of a third revolution whose main features include democracy, moderation, human rights and civil liberties, a market economy, friendship with the West, peace with Israel, a reformed Islam, and other features.

This "third revolution" might emerge from the complex situation in Iraq or the boiling up of resistance in other Arab states. Or the transition might be a long drawn-out process encompassing decades. Ibrahim suggested that liberals someday might resort to civil strife, a category in which he included the Egyptian national uprising of 1919, the non-violent movement in India led by Mahatma Gandhi, and allegedly the first (but not the second) Palestinian intifada. Ultimately, the advocates of political reform might not merely be confined to asking the "despotic regimes" to heed their demands. But such a new stage seems a long way off.[80]

Another liberal cautions that a great deal of work has to be done prior to that point. "The decay of Arab society has reached such an extent that 'regime change' would certainly be far from enough. Change has to come from the bottom (building of civil society) which means it has to be gradual."[81] This standpoint takes seriously the regimes' warning—and the public's fear—that major change could unravel societies altogether, threatening communal civil war and general anarchy as well as the possibility of an Islamist takeover.

There are, as a 2004 Cairo conference on reform put it, four main potential paths to transforming their societies. The imposition of change from abroad, as in Iraq, is seen as an exceptional case. Revolution, given the absence of a mass democratic movement or one that can mobilize a coup on its behalf, is unlikely. A third possibility is gradual reform from above, a model somewhat in evidence in Morocco and some Gulf monarchies. Finally, the most likely road to success is building a civil society that combines a network of organizations, education, and influencing ruling elites to support reform.[82]

But that last, most probable, scenario is a very long-term one. It can be diverted by clever ruling elites or derailed entirely by Islamist rivals. Still, if a large group in the Arab world—whether a majority or sizable minority—will someday speak and struggle for democracy, the views then expressed could confound all the public statements made in the last half-century about what people in Arab societies think. Ali Salem puts it this way, "We in the Arab world love freedom and want the chance at a decent life. We are not different from you, as it sometimes seems. We may be just temporarily backward."[83] Fawaz Gerges concludes that "people in the Middle East want democracy. Thousands of courageous Muslims have paid dearly for speaking out against state oppression and religious fanaticism and for demanding political enfranchisement. These democrats hold the key to the Arab world's future and deserve America's support."[84]

Perhaps Ghabra's words of hope present the best-case analysis of a growing power for Arab liberalism:

> People respect courage and decency, and are in search of principled leaders and representatives. Only by speaking out can one reach out to the silent majority of Arabs and Muslims. I have learned that many people in my society and the broader Arab world are fed up with extremism, and are looking for reason and modernity, for a third path that is neither too far to the right or to the left. And many people are willing to defend their beliefs, take risks and stand up for what is right.[85]

Even so, Ghabra concluded, such a transition would be long, violent, and complex, taking at least a decade.[86] Recalling the fall of dictatorships in Portugal, Spain, Greece, the Philippines, South Korea, and Latin America, Ibrahim suggested that only a few weeks earlier those countries' citizens would have said such a change was impossible because their rulers were too strong. The lesson, he suggests, is that "we should not underestimate what the will of determined people can do. . . . All of history is the result of the work of few people in every culture, in every society, who had a mission and who believed what they were doing."[87]

The Arab liberals are such people. This does not mean that they will win, at least not quickly or easily, but for the good of their own societies and the world as a whole, it is far better if they do.

NOTES

1: HEARTBREAK AND HOPE

1. The 1980–1988 Iran-Iraq war, the 1991 war over Kuwait, and the 2003 war to overthrow Saddam Hussein.

2. Beirut *Daily Star*, August 31, 2004.

3. Letter to the author, March 3, 2005.

4. *Democracy Digest*, July 23, 2004.

5. On the existing system in the region, see the author's *The Tragedy of the Middle East* (Cambridge: Cambridge University Press, 2002). This book is based on that analysis but focuses on the Arab liberal critique of that situation and the prospects for change.

6. Saad Eddin Ibrahim, "A Dissident Asks: Can Bush Turn Words into Action?" *Washington Post*, November 24, 2003.

7. Rami Khouri, "A View from the Arab World," *Jordan Times*, February 19, 2003.

8. Saad Eddin Ibrahim, "Broaden the Road Map," *Washington Post*, May 12, 2003.

9. It is part of the paradox of development that many decades after Ataturk's death, Turkey is on the verge of full membership in Europe at the same time as its government is ruled by Islamists, albeit moderate ones.

10. Tarek Heggy, "Our Need for a Culture of Compromise," *Al-Ahram*, September 29, 2002.

11. Ibid.

12. *Al-Ahram*, May 25, 2001.

13. Tarek Heggy, "The Required Change in Egypt," *Watani*, December 22 and 29, 2002.

14. Tawfiq al-Hakim, *The Return of Consciousness* (New York: New York University Press, 1985).

15. For a discussion of the conflict's effect on contemporary Arab politics, see the author's *The Arab States and the Palestine Conflict* (Syracuse, NY: Syracuse University Press, 1982).

16. Zuheir Abdallah, "Why Do Arabs Hate the West, Especially the U.S.?" *Al-Hayat*, August 8, 2003.

17. This and following material is taken from the obituary of Abdel Rahman Badawi by Adel Darwish, *The Independent*, August 7, 2002.

18. Saeed Okasha, "Remembering Egypt's Cassandra," *Cairo Times*, January 3–9, 2002.

19. Barry Rubin, *Islamic Fundamentalism in Egyptian Politics*, rev. ed. (New York: Palgrave Macmillan, 2002).

20. *Al-Ahali*, June 14, 1989.

21. *Cairo Times*, January 3–9, 2002.

22. Ibid.

23. Nathan Brown, *The Rule of Law in the Arab World: Courts in Egypt and the Gulf* (Cambridge: Cambridge University Press, 1997), 114.

24. www.metransparent.com/texts/arab_liberals_appeal_to_un_for_int_court_against_terror_fatwas.htm, October 24, 2004; www.elaph.com/elaphweb/ElaphWriter/2004/10/18190.htm, October 24, 2004.

25. Hani Shukrallah, *Al-Ahram Weekly*, March 8–14, 2001.

26. Fawaz A. Gerges, "The Tragedy of Arab-American Relations," *Christian Science Monitor*, September 18, 2001.

27. Rami Khouri, *Jordan Times*, June 30, 1998.

28. Hazem Saghia, *Al-Hayat*, February 28, 2001, translation by MEMRI, no. 198, March 27, 2001.

29. There is even an organization of Arab reformers living in European exile, the Project for Democracy Studies in Arab Countries. See Mai Yamani, "Arab Blues at Oxford," *International Herald Tribune*, September 2, 2004.

30. Hume Horan, "Those Young Arab Muslims and Us," *Middle East Quarterly*, Fall 2002.

31. Translated in MEMRI, no. 198, March 27, 2001.

32. Tarek Heggy, "Two Misconceptions Concerning Egyptians," *Al-Ahram*, January 25, 2003.

33. Ibid.

34. Lafif Lakhdar [sic], "Why the Reversion to Islamic Archaism?" *Against War and Terrorism*, March 2002. Downloaded from www.struggle.ws/pdf/war/warterrorpam2.html. This article was first published in *Khamsin* (1981).

35. Ibid., 16.

36. Malu Halasa, "Funny Precarious," *Guardian*, July 27, 2002.

37. Ibid.

38. Ibid.

39. Interview with Shafiq Ghabra, "The Pace of Change," *Arabies*, January 2004. Downloaded from www.arabialink.com/Archive/GWPersp/GWP2004/GWP_2004_01_23.htm, January 23, 2004.

40. BBC, July 6, 2003; AP, July 6, 2003.

41. Agence France-Presse, July 4, 1999.

42. Klaus Schwab et al. Arab World Competitiveness Report 2002–2003; *The Arab Human Development Report 2002* and *The Arab Human Development Report 2003*.

43. Ibid.

44. *Al-Ahram Weekly*, July 11–17, 2002.

45. *Al-Watan*, July 3, 2002.

46. Shafiq Ghabra, "The Decline—and Rebirth—of Arab Moderation," *The National Interest*, January 8, 2003. Ghabra was also a columnist for the Kuwaiti *Al-Ra'y al-A'am*, the Lebanese *Al-Nahar*, and the UAE newspaper *Al-Bayan*.

47. Ghabra, *Arabies*. It should be noted that contact with the West and the United States—even the same area that influenced Ghabra—has had a radicalizing effect on other Arabs who went there as students. See, for example, the story of Sayyid Qutb in Barry Rubin and Judith Colp Rubin, *Hating America: A History* (New York: Oxford University Press, 2004), 162–164.

48. Ibid.

49. Lecture at the University of Utah, February 19, 2004. Text at www.hum.utah.edu/mec/Lectures/2004%20lecture%20pages/ibrahim.html.

50. Ghabra, *Arabies*.

51. Ibid.

52. Ibid.

53. Text, White House Office of the Press Secretary, Remarks by the President in Commencement Address at the University of South Carolina, May 9, 2003.

54. Ibid.

55. Ibid.

56. Ibid.

57. Tarek Heggy, "The Required Change in Egypt," *Watani*, December 22 and 29, 2002.

2: "BETTER SADDAM'S HELL THAN AMERICA'S PARADISE"

1. Mustafa Kamel El-Sayid, a Cairo University political science professor, *Al-Ahram Weekly*, February 25, 2004.

2. Including the Democratic Front for the Liberation of Palestine, the Popular Front for the Liberation of Palestine, and the Popular Front for the Liberation of the Occupied Arab Gulf, the Arab Nationalist Movement, or the South Yemen National Liberation Front.

3. Text of bin Laden statement, *Washington Post*, November 1, 2004.

4. It can be argued that Western television programming—music and entertainment mostly—is available on Arab-language television, radio, CDs, cassettes, and books, in both imported versions and local imitations. This material is a cultural influence but presents ideas only indirectly and offers images of the United States and Europe that are not the best that the West has to offer. On this cultural battle, see Jihad N. Fakhreddine, Beirut *Daily Star*, September 9, 2004.

5. June 15, 2004, Al-Jazeera television, translation by MEMRI, no. 759, August 6, 2004, www.memri.org/bin/articles.cgi?Page=archives&Area=sd&ID=SP7590.

6. Rami Khouri, *Jordan Times*, June 30, 1998.

7. *Akhbar al-Youm*, November 3, 2001. Translation by MEMRI, no. 302, November 20, 2001, www.memri.org/bin/articles.cgi?Page=archives&Area=sd&ID=SP30201.

8. *Al-Hayat*, July 29, 2001, translation by MEMRI, no. 257, August 17, 2001, www.memri.org/bin/articles.cgi?Page=archives&Area=sd&ID=SP25701.

9. Tarek Heggy, *Critique of the Arab Mind* (Cairo, 1998). See also Tarek Heggy, *Essays on Egypt's Cultural Dilemma*, www.heggy.org/books/egypt/8.htm, pp. 249–272.

10. Ibid.

11. Ibn Khaldun Center newsletter, May 1998.

12. Ibid.

13. Abd al-Mun'im Sa'id, head of the Al-Ahram Center for Political and Strategic Studies in Cairo, also participated.

14. Shafiq Ghabra, *Philadelphia Inquirer*, February 15, 2002.

15. Ibid.

16. Ibid.

17. *Al-Watani*, July 7, 2002.

18. Ibid.

19. *Philadelphia Inquirer*, February 13, 2002.

20. Ibid.

21. Robert Rabil, *Daily Star*, June 9, 2003.

22. *Akhbar al-Sharq*, June 1, 2003. See also www.reformsyria.com/documents/Intellectuals%20appeal%20for%20Syria%20reforms.pdf. The basic line of argument is strikingly similar to that of the Saudi democracy petition of the same year.

23. Tueni, born in 1926, was the publisher of *Al-Nahar* newspaper. A former member of parliament, a cabinet minister, and ambassador to the UN, he spoke out for free speech and Lebanon's independence from Syrian control. See www.annahar.com.lb/NAboutUs/pg3.htm

and www.npr.org/programs/morning/transcripts/2003/jan/030106.seelye.html, January 3, 2003.

24. Ayed al-Manaa, *Al-Watan*, September 15, 2002.

25. *Al-Rai al-Aam*, September 30, 2002.

26. Naji Sadeq Sharrab, "Interview with an Arab Leader, *Al-Quds*, May 5, 2003, translation by MEMRI, no. 524, June 19, 2003, www.memri.org/bin/articles.cgi?Page=archives &Area=sd&ID=SP52403.

27. Ibid.

28. Muhammad Moussa, *Al-Ahram Weekly*, May 28–June 3, 2003.

29. Text of Arab Summit final resolution, May 23, 2004. See www.albawaba.com/ headlines/TheNews.php3?sid=277498&dir=news&lang=e.

30. Tarek Heggy, "We . . . and the Reality Around Us," *Al-Ahram*, May 11, 2003.

31. Muhammad Jaber al-Ansari, *Al-Hayat*, June 8, 2003.

32. Hossam Itani, *Al-Safir*, June 20, 2003.

33. Ibid.

34. Mustafa al-Feki, *Al-Khaleej*, June 17, 2003.

35. Yousef al-Qaradhawi, Qatar Television, June 13, 2003, downloaded from www .qaradawi.net.

36. Ghassan al-Atiyyah, *Daily Star*, July 13, 2002.

37. Ibid.

38. Taufiq Abu Bakr, "The Arab Liberal Trend and Its Moment of Opportunity," *Al-Ayyam*, May 28, 2003.

3: THE COURAGE OF THEIR CONVICTIONS

1. *Al-Watani*, July 7, 2002.

2. Saad Eddin Ibrahim, "The Sick Man of the World," *Washington Post*, March 28, 2004.

3. Nawaf Obaid, "Al Qaeda's Bomb Backfire," *Washington Post*, May 18, 2003.

4. Ahmad Bishara, "Fighting Terror? Start Here," *Arab Times*, September 28, 2001.

5. *Al-Hayat*, July 29, 2001, translation by MEMRI, no. 257, August 17, 2001, www.memri .org/bin/articles.cgi?Page=archives&Area=sd&ID=SP25701.

6. Claudi Rosett, "Save Fathi Eljahmi," *Wall Street Journal*, September 8, 2004.

7. Ibid.

8. *Cairo Times*, December 21, 2000–January 3, 2001. On book-banning by Al-Azhar, see also *Cairo Times*, September 4, 1997. In Lebanon, a well-known singer was accused but later acquitted of blasphemy for using Qur'anic verses in a song. See *Middle East Intelligence Bulletin*, vol. 1, no. 10, October 1999.

9. Ibn Khaldun Center newsletter, January 2000.

10. Lecture at the University of Utah, February 19, 2004. Text at www.hum.utah.edu/mec/ Lectures/2004%20lecture%20pages/ibrahim.html.

11. Associated Press, November 9, 2002.

12. Ibn Khaldun Center newsletter, September 1999.

13. Daniel Swift, "Said Eddin Ibrahim: Through the Arab Looking Glass," *Open Democracy*, November 4, 2003.

14. *Al-Ahram*, May 25, 2001; *Al-Akhbar*, May 27, 2001.

15. *Al-Quds Al-Arabiyya*, October 15, 2002.

16. Ibid.

17. Ibid.

18. *Al-Ahram*, May 25, 2001; *Al-Akhbar*, May 27, 2001.

19. *Al-Usbu*, October 7, 2002, translation in MEMRI, no. 429, October 15, 2002, www .memri.org/bin/articles.cgi?Page=archives&Area=sd&ID=SP42902.

20. *Cairo Times*, May 31–June 6, 2001.

21. Associated Press, March 18, 2003.

22. Saad Eddin Ibrahim, "The Sick Man of the World," *Washington Post*, March 28, 2004.

23. Ayman Nour, "Letter from Prison: 'Did I Take Democracy Too Seriously?'" *Newsweek*, March 14, 2005.

24. Al Jazeera television, May 23, 2001, translation by MEMRI, no. 245, July 23, 2001, www.memri.org/bin/articles.cgi?Page=archives&Area=sd&ID=SP24501.

25. *Cairo Times*, September 4, 1997.

26. Ali Salem, "My Drive to Israel," *Middle East Quarterly*, vol. 9, no. 1, Winter 2002.

27. Eyal Zisser, "Syria's Assad, the Approach of a Fifth Term of Office," Washington Institute for Near East Policy, *Policywatch* no. 366, February 5, 1999.

28. *New York Times*, January 27, 2000. See also Roula Khalaf, "Syria's Golden Opportunity," *Financial Times*, October 13, 1999.

29. Hazem Saghiya, "The Speech That Bashar al-Asad Will Never Make," *Al-Hayat*, June 25, 2000, translation in MEMRI, no. 112, July 6, 2000, www.memri.org/bin/articles.cgi?Page=archives&Area=sd&ID=SP11200.

30. Ibid.

31. *New York Times*, January 27, 2000.

32. *Al-Safir*, July 16, 2001, translation in MEMRI, no. 244, July 20, 2001, www.memri .org/bin/articles.cgi?Page=archives&Area=sd&ID=SP24401.

33. *New York Times*, December 2, 2003.

34. *Al-Quds Al-Arabi*, February 20, 2001.

35. Syrian Press Agency, July 17, 2000.

36. *Al-Hayat*, January 15, 2001; *Al-Sharq al-Awsat*, February 8, 2001.

37. The document was published in *Al-Hayat*, September 27, 2000. Sections are translated in MEMRI, no. 131, September 29, 2000, www.memri.org/bin/articles.cgi?Page=archives&Area=sd&ID=SP13100.

38. *Al-Hayat*, January 16, 2001.

39. *Al-Quds Al-Arabi*, February 2, 2001. See also *Al-Safir*, January 24, 2001.

40. *Al-Hayat*, January 13, 2001, translation in MEMRI, no. 47, February 9, 2001, www .memri.org/bin/articles.cgi?Page=archives&Area=ia&ID=IA4701.

41. Ibid.

42. Ibid.

43. *Al-Sharq al-Awsat*, February 8, 2001.

44. *Al-Ba'th*, February 1, 2001.

45. *Al-Usbu' al-Adabi*, December 16, 2000.

46. *Al-Sharq al-Awsat*, February 18, 2001.

47. *Al-Sharq al-Awsat*, February 17, 2001.

48. *Al-Nahar*, February 19, 2001.

49. See, for example, Khaddam's statement quoted in *Al-Sharq al-Awsat*, February 18, 2001.

50. *Al-Hayat* , January 21, 2001.

51. *New York Times*, March 12, 2001.

52. *Al-Sharq al-Awsat*, February 8, 2001, translation in MEMRI, no. 49, February 16, 2001, www.memri.org/bin/articles.cgi?Page=archives&Area=ia&ID=IA4901.

53. Gary Gambill, "Dark Days Ahead for Syria's Liberal Reformers," *Middle East Intelligence Bulletin*, vol. 3, no. 2, February 2001.

54. *Al-Sharq al-Awsat*, February 8, 2001, translation in MEMRI, no. 49, February 16, 2001, www.memri.org/bin/articles.cgi?Page=archives&Area=ia&ID=IA4901.

55. *Al-Quds al-Arabi*, February 19, 2001.

56. Robert Rabil, *Daily Star*, June 9, 2003. On the repression in Syria, see Syrian Human Rights Committee, *Annual Report 2003* (London, 2003).

57. BBC, March 20, 2002.

58. *Democracy Digest*, July 29, 2004, vol. 1, no. 13.

59. The group's leader, Aktham Naisse, a lawyer from Latakia, had spent seven years in jail for founding a human rights group in 1991. Associated Press, March 8 and 10, 2004; text of petition, *Al-Nahar*, February 10, 2004.

60. *Al-Watan*, April 30, 2003, translation in MEMRI, no. 504, May 13, 2003, www.memri .org/bin/opener_latest.cgi?ID=SD50403.

61. Associated Press, May 28, 2003.

62. Lawrence Wright, "The Kingdom of Silence," *New Yorker*, January 5, 2004.

63. His full name was Ahmad ibn Abd al-Halim ibn Abd Allah ibn Abi al-Qasim ibn Taymiyya, Taqi al-Din Abu al-Abbas ibn Shihab al-Din ibn Majd al-Din al-Harrani al-Dimashqi al-Hanbali. He lived between 661 and 728.

64. *Al-Watan*, March 14, 15, 17, and 19, 2003.

65. Wright, *New Yorker*.

66. Ibid.

67. *New York Times*, June 13, 2003.

68. Associated Press, May 28, 2003.

69. Statement of November 6, 2004, downloaded from www.hesbah.com/news.asp.

70. Agence France-Presse, May 13, 2003.

71. *Los Angeles Times*, May 8, 2004.

72. *New York Times*, April 30, 2003.

73. Economist Intelligence Unit, UAE, pp. 14–15; *Daily Telegraph*, June 15, 2003.

74. *Gulf News* and *Jordan Times*, December 12, 2003.

75. Economist Intelligence Unit, *Country Report: Qatar*, April 2003, pp. 15–18; Inter Press News Services, April 30, 2003; Agence France-Presse, May 8, 2003; CNN report, April 27, 2003.

76. Economist Intelligence Unit, *Bahrain Country Profile* (London, 2003), pp. 6–7.

77. *Gulf News*, October 5, 2004; Beirut *Daily Star*, November 23, 2004. On liberalism in Bahrain, see also Beirut *Daily Star*, September 7, 2004.

78. Marwan Muasher, "A Path to Arab Democracy," *New York Times*, April 28, 2003.

79. Toujan Faisal and Ian Urbina, "Jordan's Troubling Detour," *Los Angeles Times*, July 6, 2003.

80. *Al-Ahram Weekly*, November 20–26, 2003.

81. Quoted in Ziad K. Abdelnour, "Democratization of Capital in the Arab World," *Middle East Intelligence Bulletin*, vol. 5, no. 5, May 2003.

4: WHAT'S WRONG WITH ARAB SOCIETY?

1. Reported on Al-Jazeera television, October 18, 2002, cited in MEMRI, no. 439, November 13, 2002, www.memri.org/bin/articles.cgi?Page=archives&Area=sd&ID=SP43902.

2. Al-Afif al-Akhdar, "What Did the Missiles Falling on Baghdad Tell Me?" www.elaph .com.:9090/elaph/arabic/frontendProcess.jsp?SCREENID=PRINTaRTICLE, translation in MEMRI, no. 499, May 4, 2003, www.memri.org/bin/opener_latest.cgi?ID=SD49903.

3. Al-Afif al-Akhdar, "How Our Narcissistic Wound and Religious Narcissism Combine to Destroy Our Future"; "Why Religious Narcissism Is the Golden Collar [Obstructing] Our Assimilation into the Modern Age"; and "Irrational Religious Education Is the Obstacle to

the [Arabs'] Joining the Modern Age," in www.elaph.com.:9090/elaph/arabic, June 15, 16, and 23, 2003, translation in MEMRI, no. 576, September 21, 2003, www.memri.org/bin/articles.cgi?Page=archives&Area=sd&ID=SP57603.

4. Ibid.

5. Ibid.

6. Ibid.

7. Ibid.

8. Radwan al-Sayyed, *al-Mustaqbal,* June 13, 2003.

9. Abu Ahmad Mustafa, "When Will the Arabs Learn the Lesson, Just Once," *Al-Sharq al-Awsat,* October 27, 2002, translation in MEMRI, no. 540, July 22, 2003, www.memri.org/bin/articles.cgi?Page=archives&Area=sd&ID=SP54003#_ednref6.

10. Ibid.

11. Tarek Heggy, "We . . . and the Reality Around Us," *Al-Ahram,* May 11, 2003.

12. Tarek Heggy, "Our Need for a 'Culture of Compromise,'" *Al-Ahram,* September 29, 2002.

13. Ibid.

14. Ibid.

15. Tarek Heggy, "The Future: Should We Wait for It . . . or Create It?" *Al-Ahram,* August 10, 2002.

16. Ibid.

17. Tarek Heggy, "Comments on the Required Change in Egypt," *Watani,* December 22 and 29, 2002.

18. Shafiq Ghabra, *Al-Rai al-Aam,* June 11, 2003.

19. Usama al-Ghazali Harb, "The Moment of Truth," *Al-Ahram Weekly,* April 24–30, 2003; and *Al-Siyassa al-Dawliya,* January 2004, translation in MEMRI, no. 663, February 16, 2004, www.memri.org/bin/opener_latest.cgi?ID=SD66304.

20. "A Big Lie Stuffed with Little Lies," *Roz al-Yousef,* December 27, 2003, translation in MEMRI, no. 645, January 16, 2004, www.memri.org/bin/articles.cgi?Page=archives&Area=sd&ID=SP64504#_edn1.

21. Abd al-Mun'im Sa'id, *Al-Ahram Weekly,* October 6, 2002.

22. Abdallah Rashid, "Long Live Dictatorship," *Al-Itihad,* June 29, 2003, translation in MEMRI, no. 536, July 10, 2003, www.memri.org/bin/articles.cgi?Page=archives&Area=sd&ID=SP53603.

23. Ibid.

24. Cited in Zvi Bar'el, "Syria: Where Time Stood Still Since 1963," *Haaretz,* September 25, 2003.

25. See, for example, Othman al-Rawath, a member of the Saudi Shura Council and professor of political science at King Saud University, in *Al-Sharq al-Awsat,* July 7, 2003.

26. *Al-Quds,* September 30, 2002.

27. Abd Al-Raouf Haddad, *Akhbar al-Sharq,* June 20, 2002.

28. Mahmoud Al-Mahamid, *Akhbar al-Sharq,* June 20, 2002.

29. Ali Salem, "My Drive to Israel," *Middle East Quarterly,* vol. 9, no. 1, Winter 2002.

30. Ibid.

31. "Arab Statesmanship's Fatal Flaw: Backward Political Decision-Making," *Al-Quds al-Arabi,* May 18, 2003, translation in MEMRI, no. 518, June 5, 2003, www.memri.org/bin/opener_latest.cgi?ID=SD51803. See also www.elaph.com.:9090/elaph/ arabic/frontendProcess.jsp, May 17, 2003.

32. Ibid.

33. Ibid. On the Saddam story he cites Sa'ad al-Bazaz, *The Generals Are the Last to Learn,* p. 101.

34. Ibid.

35. Ibid.

36. *Al-Rai al-Aam*, June 8, 2003.

37. Radwan al-Sayyed, professor of Islamic Philosophy at Lebanon University, *Al-Mustaqbal*, June 13, 2003.

38. Ibid.

39. Urfan Nizamuddin, *Al-Hayat*, June 16, 2003.

40. Muhammad al-Ansari, *Al-Hayat*, June 16, 2003.

41. Fouad Ajami, "What the Muslim World Is Watching," *New York Times Magazine*, November 18, 2001.

42. Abu Ahmad Mustafa (pseudonym), "When Will the Arabs Learn the Lesson, Just Once," *Al-Sharq al-Awsat*, October 27, 2002, translation in MEMRI, no. 540, July 22, 2003, www.memri.org/bin/opener_latest.cgi?ID=SD54003.

43. Interview with Abd al-Hamid al-Ansari, *Al-Ray*, January 6, 2002, translation in MEMRI, no. 337, January 29, 2002, www.memri.org/bin/articles.cgi?Page=archives&Area=sd&ID=SP33702.

44. Ibid. For a non-Arab Muslim example of the same phenomenon see the interview with Pakistani leader Pervez Musharraf, *Washington Post*, September 26, 2004. When asked if he thought al-Qa'ida wanted to overthrow the Egyptian and Saudi governments and install radical Islamist regimes, he responded only—and incorrectly—that both bin Laden's organization and the September 11 attacks had their origins in the Palestinian struggle.

45. *Al-Rajah*, April 20, 2003.

46. *Al-Ahram Weekly*, October 6, 2002.

47. Ibid.

48. Muhammad Ahmad Al-Hassani, *Okaz*, May 14, 2003, translation in MEMRI, no. 505, May 15, 2003, www.memri.org/bin/articles.cgi?Page=archives&Area=sd&ID=SP50503.

49. Arab Human Development Report, United Nations Development Program, 2002.

50. Ziad K. Abdelnour, "Democratization of Capital in the Arab World," *Middle East Intelligence Bulletin*, vol. 5, no. 5, May 2003.

51. Ibid.

52. Ibid.

53. Cited in Zvi Bar'el, "Syria: Where Time Stood Still Since 1963," *Haaretz*, September 25, 2003.

54. *Al-Ahram Weekly*, April 26–May 2, 2001; Menas Associates newsletter, "Sainsbury's Scales Back Local Presence," December 2000, vol. 10, no. 11, www.menas.co.uk/Egfa0004.html.

55. Tarek Heggy, "Why Do I Write?" downloaded from www.heggy.org/why.htm. The following list uses his basic points while expanding them and briefly discussing some of their implications.

56. Ibid.

57. Ibid.

58. Ibid.

59. Ibid.

60. *Al-Hayat*, December 12, 2001, translation in MEMRI, no. 314, December 14, 2001, www.memri.org/bin/articles.cgi?Page=archives&Area=sd&ID=SP31401.

61. Tarek Heggy, www.heggy.org/why.htm.

62. The text of the Alexandria Declaration can be found in *Democracy Digest*, vol. 1, no. 1, May 6, 2004, and at www.al-bab.com/arab/docs/reform/alex2004.htm; arabreformforum.com; and MEMRI, no. 179, June 11, 2004, at www.memri.org/bin/latestnews.cgi?ID=IA17904.

63. For the text, see *Democracy Digest*, vol. 1, no. 18, October 19, 2004.

64. *Daily Star*, January 8, 2004.

5: WHOSE ISLAM?

1. *Philadelphia Inquirer*, February 13, 2002.

2. www.metransparent.com/texts/sayyed_qimni_who_is_the_crook.htm, November 24, 2004, translation in MEMRI, no. 847, January 14, 2005.

3. Transcript, conversation between Kuwaiti liberals and *New York Times* columnist Nicholas Kristof, October 15, 2004.

4. "The Arabs and History," *Al-Sharq al-Awsat*, October 27, 2002, translation in MEMRI, no. 540, July 22, 2003, www.memri.org/bin/articles.cgi?Page=archives&Area=sd&ID=SP54003.

5. For discussions of liberal Islam, see Charles Kurzman, *Modernist Islam, 1840–1940: A Sourcebook* (New York: Oxford University Press, 2002), and *Liberal Islam: A Sourcebook* (New York: Oxford University Press, 1998). See also his articles, "Pro-U.S. Fatwas," *Middle East Policy*, vol. 10, no. 3 (Fall 2003): 155–166 and "Liberalism," in John L. Esposito, ed., *The Oxford Dictionary of Islam* (New York: Oxford University Press, 2003), 180–181. What is especially striking about these and other discussions of liberal Muslims is how few of them involve Arabs, especially Arabs living in the Middle East.

6. www.metransparent.com/texts/sayyed_qimni_who_is_the_crook.htm, November 24, 2004, translation in MEMRI, no. 847, January 14, 2005.

7. *Democracy Digest*, June 11, 2004.

8. Prince Hassan bin Talal, "The View of a Modern Arab Intellectual: The Modern Islamic State," *Al-Hayat*, August 27, 2002, translation in MEMRI, September 13, 2002, www.memri .de/uebersetzungen_analysen/laender/syrien_libanon_jordanien/jordanien_kronprinz_13 _09_02.pdf.

9. Ibid.

10. Ibid.

11. Tarek Heggy, "Islam Between Copying and Thinking," www.heggy.org/egyptian_islam .htm.

12. Lafif Lakhdar [*sic*], "Why the Reversion to Islamic Archaism?" *Against War and Terrorism*, March 2002, p. 13, www.struggle.ws/pdf/war/warterrorpam2.html.

13. Al-Afif al-Akhdar, posted on www.elaph.com in June 2003, translation in MEMRI, no. 576, September 21, 2003, www.memri.org/bin/articles.cgi?Page=archives&Area=sd&ID =SP57603.

14. Heggy, "Islam Between Copying and Thinking," www.heggy.org/egyptian_islam.htm.

15. On the reformist effort, see, for example, Mansoor Moaddel and Kamran Talattof, *Modernist and Fundamentalist Debates in Islam: A Reader* (New York: Palgrave Macmillan, 2002).

16. Another technique is to attribute radical Islamist ideas and movements to non-Arab Muslims. See Zvi Bar'el, "The Language of Islam," *Ha'aretz*, December 9, 2002.

17. *Roz al-Yousef*, May 17, 24, and 31, 2003, translation in MEMRI, no. 526, June 20, 2003, www.memri.org/bin/articles.cgi?Page=countries&Area=saudiarabia&ID=SP52603. See also *Al-Quds al-Arabi*, May 19, 2003.

18. On the internal roots of Egyptian Islamism, see, for example, Barry Rubin, *Islamic Fundamentalism in Egyptian Politics* (New York: Palgrave Macmillan, 1991).

19. *Al-Sharq al-Awsat*, September 16, 2002, translation in MEMRI, no. 436, November 3, 2002, www.memri.org/bin/articles.cgi?Page=archives&Area=sd&ID=SP43602.

20. *Al-Ahram*, March 27, 2002.

21. The text of the Alexandria Declaration can be found in *Democracy Digest*, May 6, 2004, and at www.al-bab.com/arab/docs/reform/alex2004.htm; arabreformforum.com; and MEMRI, no. 179, June 11, 2004, at www.memri.org/bin/latestnews.cgi?ID=IA17904.

22. *Al-Ahram*, March 6, 2002.

23. Ahmad Bishara, "After Afghanistan: Liberating Islam," *Arab Times* (Kuwait), September 17, 2001.

24. Ibid.

25. This is the critique of Radwan al-Sayyed, professor of Islamic Studies at Lebanon University, who earned doctorates at Al-Azhar and in Germany. He argues that those who want to reform Islam, with whom he has sympathy, play into the Islamists' hands by undermining the establishment's authority. Omayma Abdel-Latif, "The Muslim Condition," *Al-Ahram Weekly*, November 4–10, 2004.

26. *Al-Hayat*, January 13, 2002, translation in MEMRI, no. 333, January 18, 2002, www.memri.org/bin/articles.cgi?Page=archives&Area=sd&ID=SP33302.

27. *Al-Watan*, May 22, 2003.

28. Ibid.

29. Lawrence Wright, "The Kingdom of Silence, *New Yorker*, January 5, 2004.

30. On this issue in Kuwait, see Agence France-Presse, December 29, 2003; *Kuwait Times*, December 28, 2003.

31. Cited in Zvi Bar'el, *Ha'aretz*, January 7, 2004.

32. Ibn Khaldun Center newsletter, October 1998.

33. www.elaph.com.:9090/elaph/arabic/ June 23, 2003.

34. *Al-Raya*, January 6, 2002, translation in MEMRI, no. 337, January 29, 2002, www.memri.org/bin/articles.cgi?Page=archives&Area=sd&ID=SP33802.

35. Ibid.

36. *Al-Watan*, May 14, 2003.

37. Raid Qusti, *Arab News*, May 14, 2003.

38. *Al-Watan*, September 1, 2003, translation in MEMRI, no. 644, January 14, 2004, www.memri.org/bin/articles.cgi?Page=archives&Area=sd&ID=SP64404.

39. Ibid.

40. www.metransparent.com/texts/sayyed_qimni_who_is_the_crook.htm, November 24, 2004, translation in MEMRI, no. 847, January 14, 2005.

41. "Telling the Truth, Facing the Whip," *New York Times*, November 28, 2003.

42. Mohamed [*sic*] Charfi, "Reaching the Next Muslim Generation," *New York Times*, March 12, 2002.

43. Ibid.

44. Ibid.

45. This and the following material is taken from Latif Lakhdar, "Moving from Salafi to Rationalist Education," *MERIA Journal*, vol. 9, no. 1 (March 2005): 30–44, meria.idc.ac.il/journal/2005/issue1/lakhdar.pdf.

46. Ibid.

47. *Jordan Times*, November 27, 2001.

48. Al-Afif al-Akhdar, posted on www.elaph.com in June 2003, translation in MEMRI, no. 576, September 21, 2003, www.memri.org/bin/articles.cgi?Page=archives&Area=sd&ID=SP57603.

49. Neil MacFarquhar, "Syria, Long Ruthlessly Secular, Sees Fervent Islamic Resurgence," *New York Times*, October 20, 2003.

50. Ibid.

51. Shafiq N. Ghabra, "A Kuwaiti's Tale: My Debate with Israelis Brought Me Trouble at Home—and Then Hope," *Washington Post*, March 31, 2002.

52. This account is taken from *Index on Censorship*, April 1996.

53. "Telling the Truth, Facing the Whip," *New York Times*, November 28, 2003.

54. Neil MacFarquhar, "Under Pressure to Change, Saudis Debate Their Future," *New York Times*, November 23, 2003.

55. Abu Ahmad Mustafa, *Al-Sharq al-Awsat*, September 13, 2003, translation in MEMRI, no. 579, September 26, 2003, www.memri.org/bin/opener_latest.cgi?ID=SD57903.

56. *Arab Times* (Kuwait), April 15, 2004.

57. Ahmed al-Jarallah, "One Step Is Not Enough," *Arab Times*, December 2, 2003.

58. Abu Ahmad Mustafa, *Al-Sharq al-Awsat*, September 13, 2003, translation in MEMRI, no. 579, September 26, 2003, www.memri.org/bin/opener_latest.cgi?ID=SD57903.

59. *Jordan Times*, November 27, 2001.

60. Maha al-Azar, "U.S.-Based Professor Claims Jews Want to Control Arab World: 'Conspiracy' Involves Americans," *Daily Star*, November 20, 2002.

61. Interview with Abd al-Mun'im Sa'id, August 4, 2004.

62. www.islah300.org/vboard/showthread.php?t=120471, January 23, 2005.

63. Al-Jazeera television, February 6, 2005.

64. www.mengos.net/events/04newsevents/egypt/october/ibnkhaldun-English.htm.

65. Ibid.

66. *Al-Rai al-Aam*, October 6, 2004.

6: AMERICA: SATAN OR SAVIOR?

1. Talk by Hazem Saghiya, Washington Institute for Near East Policy, May 8, 2003.

2. Hazem Saghiyah, "Is There a Path to an Alternative Progressive Agenda?" Arab Media Internet Network, July 18, 2004. Downloaded from amin.org/eng/uncat/2004/jul/jul18 .html.

3. *Al-Hayat*, April 5, 2004.

4. Fouad Ajami, "Arabs Have Nobody to Blame but Themselves," *Wall Street Journal*, October 16, 2001.

5. On these issues, see Barry Rubin and Judith Colp Rubin, *Hating America: A History* (New York: Oxford University Press, 2004).

6. He was referring to Bush's November 6, 2003, speech at the National Endowment for Democracy. The text is available at www.ned.org/events/anniversary/oct1603-Bush.html.

7. The White House, "Remarks by the President at Whitehall Palace Royal Banqueting House—Whitehall Palace, London, England," November 2003.

8. Ibid.

9. Salameh Nematt, *Al-Hayat*, June 16, 2003.

10. See, for example, Glenn Frankel, "Egypt Muzzles Calls for Democracy Reformers Say Billions in U.S. Aid Prop Up Authoritarian Rule," *Washington Post*, January 6, 2004.

11. *Arab News*, October 29, 2002. See also *Ain al-Yaqeen*, November 22, 2002.

12. Associated Press, March 19, 2004.

13. There is, of course, an interesting example of another Middle Eastern country where the United States followed a different policy: Iran. In 1953, the United States sponsored a coup against a parliamentary government, thus revitalizing an autocratic system, something it never did in the Arab world. On later occasions, the United States pressed the regime for democratic reform. While the issue is a complex one, it is arguable that either aspect of this strategy—the backing of a traditional regime or the prodemocratic pressures—helped destabilize the shah, bring to power Khomeini, and set in motion events leading to massive wars and the rise of a powerful Islamist movement in the region. The Iran case is rarely discussed, however, in the Arab debate on this issue. For a discussion of this point and its ramifications, see the author's *Paved with Good Intentions: The American Experience and Iran* (New York: Viking Penguin, 1980) and "Regime Change in Iran: A Reassessment," *Meria Journal*, vol. 7, no. 2 (June 2003): 68–78.

14. Rami G. Khouri, "Anti-Americanism in the Arab World: Its Roots, Repercussions, and Remedies," February 12, 2003. Lecture at the University of Utah, Middle East Center's 2003 Iraq Crisis Lecture Series. www.hum.utah.edu/mec/Lectures/khouri.html.

15. Maha al-Azar, "U.S.-based Professor Claims Jews Want to Control Arab World: 'Conspiracy' Involves Americans," *Daily Star*, November 20, 2002.

16. *Al-Ahram*, September 20, 2002, translation in MEMRI, no. 423, October 1, 2002, www.memri.org/bin/articles.cgi?Page=archives&Area=sd&ID=SP42302.

17. *Al-Ahram*, September 24, 2002, as translated in ibid.

18. *Al-Usbu*, September 23, 2002, as translated in ibid.

19. Hume Horan, "Those Young Arab Muslims and Us," *Middle East Quarterly*, Fall 2002.

20. *Al-Musawwar*, January 10, 2003, translation in MEMRI, no. 465, February 5, 2003, www.memri.org/bin/articles.cgi?Page=archives&Area=sd&ID=SP46503.

21. *Al-Gumhouriyya*, November 12, 2003, translation in MEMRI, no. 615, November 25, 2003, www.memri.org/bin/articles.cgi?Page=subjects&Area=reform&ID=SP61503.

22. *Al-Ahram*, November 10, 2003, translation in MEMRI, no. 615, November 25, 2003, www.memri.org/bin/articles.cgi?Page=subjects&Area=reform&ID=SP61503.

23. *Al-Wafd*, November 11, 2003.

24. *Al-Watan*, December 17, 2002, translation in MEMRI, no. 117, January 3, 2003.

25. *Al-Sharq al-Awsat*, December 24, 2002, translation in MEMRI, no. 117, January 3, 2003, www.memri.org/bin/articles.cgi?Page=archives&Area=ia&ID=IA11703.

26. Sayyed al-Qimni, "Fahmi Huweidi's Hypocrisy," *Al-Ahram*, November 2, 2004.

27. Sayyed al-Qimni in *Middle East Transparent*, www.metransparent.com, translation in MEMRI, January 14, 2005, no. 847, www.memri.org/bin/opener_latest.cgi?ID=SD84705.

28. *'Okaz*, December 17, 2002, translation in MEMRI, no. 117, January 3, 2003, www.memri.org/bin/articles.cgi?Page=archives&Area=ia&ID=IA11703.

29. "Freedom for Who?" *Al-Ahram Weekly*, February 19–24, 2004.

30. *Al-Rai*, December 23, 2002, translation in MEMRI, no. 117, January 3, 2003, www.memri.org/bin/articles.cgi?Page=archives&Area=ia&ID=IA11703.

31. Mustafa el-Feki, "The Coming of Age," *Al-Ahram Weekly*, May 15–21, 2003.

32. *Al-Rai*, December 17, 2002, translation in MEMRI, no. 115, December 31, 2002, www.memri.org/bin/articles.cgi?Page=archives&Area=ia&ID=IA11502.

33. *Al-Hayat*, November 6, 2002.

34. *Al-Nahar*, October 11, 2003, translation in MEMRI, no. 599, October 30, 2003, www.memri.org/bin/opener_latest.cgi?ID=SD59903.

35. *Al-Ahram*, June 12, 2002. Harb received his Ph.D. in political science from Cairo University in 1985 and taught at several universities.

36. Usama al-Ghazali Harb, "The Moment of Truth," *Al-Ahram Weekly*, April 24–30, 2003.

37. Ibid.

38. Usama al-Ghazali Harb, "The Trouble with America," *Al-Siyassa al-Dawliyya*, January 2002.

39. Ibid.

40. Ibid.

41. *Al-Ahram Weekly*, May 15–21, 2003.

42. Ibid.

43. *Al-Rai*, December 17, 2002, translation in MEMRI, no. 116, January 1, 2003, www.memri.org/bin/opener_latest.cgi?ID=IA11603. Similar ideas came from Ibrahim al-Bahrawi, a professor at Ain Shams University, who urged Arab reformers to push harder for change from within because they best knew how to do so. *Al-Ahram*, December 18, 2002, translation in MEMRI, no. 116, January 1, 2003, www.memri.org/bin/opener_latest.cgi?ID =IA11603.

44. Nader Fergany, "Knowing Our Friends," *Al-Ahram Weekly*, December 26–January 1, 2002.

45. Ibid.

46. *Al-Raya*, January 6, 2002, translation in MEMRI, no. 337, January 29, 2002, www .memri.org/bin/articles.cgi?Page=archives&Area=sd&ID=SP33802.

47. Ibid.

48. Ibid.

49. *Al-Sharq al-Awsat*, February 4, 2004, translation in MEMRI, no. 660, February 10, 2004, www.memri.org/bin/opener_latest.cgi?ID=SD66004.

50. Ibid.

51. Ahmad Bishara, "A Story Worth Telling," *Arab Times*, December 11, 2001.

52. *Arab News*, May 14, 2003.

53. *Arab Times*, March 19, 2003.

54. *Al-Ayyam*, December 28, 2002, translation in MEMRI, no. 116, January 1, 2003, www.memri.org/bin/opener_latest.cgi?ID=IA11603.

55. Anas Zahid, "Face Yourselves," *Al-Sharq al-Awsat*, April 19, 2003.

56. Siyamend Othman, "The Day After: Planning for a Post-Saddam Iraq," www .iraqfoundation.org/studies/2002/cnov/4_dayafter.html, November 4, 2002.

57. Toujan Faisal and Ian Urbina, "Jordan's Troubling Detour," *Los Angeles Times*, July 6, 2003.

58. *Time*, January 21, 2003.

59. Associated Press, January 27, 2004.

60. Text, Rami G. Khouri, "A View from the Arab World," February 19, 2003 via Internet.

61. Ibid.

62. Cited in Jonathan Schanzer, "A Tale of Two Qatars," Washington Institute for Near East Policy *Policywatch*, no. 685, December 6, 2002.

63. Ibid.

64. Kamel Labidi, "The Wrong Man to Promote Democracy," *New York Times*, February 21, 2004. Labidi is a former Amnesty International official.

65. Ibid.

66. Kamel Labidi, "U.S. Policy Sets Back Arab Human Rights," Iraqi Crisis Report no. 10, April 2, 2003.

67. Rami G. Khouri, "Arabs and Americans—Guarding the Chicken," *Jordan Times*, May 14, 2003.

68. Ibid.

69. For a fuller evaluation on Arab anti-Americanism, see Rubin and Rubin, *Hating America*.

70. *Saudi Gazette*, November 30, 2003.

71. Mohammad al-Rumaihi, "The Arabs' National Interests," *Al-Hayat*, June 11, 2003.

72. *Al-Ahram Weekly*, December 5–11, 2002.

73. Ibid.

74. *Arab Times*, November 23, 2003.

75. Ahmed Abdallah, *Egypt before and after September 11, 2001: Problems of Political Transformation in a Complicated International Setting*," Deutsches Orient-Institut im Verbund Deutsches Übersee-Institut, *Focus* no. 9, March 2003.

76. Ibid.

77. Ibid.

78. Khouri, "Anti-Americanism in the Arab World: Its Roots, Repercussions, and Remedies."

79. Saad Eddin Ibrahim, "Broaden the Road Map," *Washington Post*, May 12, 2003.

80. Ahmad Bishara, "Other Victors in U.S. Elections," *Arab Times* (Kuwait), November 6, 2004. Several Arab liberals expressed such ideas in private communications with the author. For a similar view, see Ahmad Jarallah, *Al-Siyassah*, November 15, 2004.

81. Bishara, *Arab Times*.

82. Fouad Ajami, "Iraq and the Arabs' Future," *Foreign Affairs*, January/February 2003.

83. Text in *Democracy Digest*, vol. 1, no. 6, June 11, 2004.

84. *Al-Ahram Weekly*, April 1–7, 2004.

7: ISRAEL: THE GREAT EXCUSE

1. This chapter is not about the Arab-Israeli conflict as such and is not intended as a way to discuss the rights and wrongs, proposed solutions, or details of that conflict.

2. Tarek Heggy, "The Arab-Israeli Conflict: Where To?" *Akhbar Al-Youm*, November 20, 2004.

3. Tarek Heggy, "A Word in the Palestinian Ear," May 25, 2004, www.heggy.org/Palestinian_Ear.htm.

4. Abu Ahmad Mustafa, "When Will the Arabs Learn the Lesson, Just Once," *Al-Sharq al-Awsat*, October 27, 2002, translation in MEMRI, no. 540, July 22, 2003, www.memri.org/bin/opener_latest.cgi?ID=SD54003.

5. Transcript, "The Day After: Planning for a Post-Saddam Iraq," November 4, 2002, www.iraqfoundation.org/studies/2002/cnov/4_dayafter.html.

6. *Los Angeles Times*, March 28, 2004.

7. Saad Eddin Ibrahim, "The Sick Man of the World," *Washington Post*, March 28, 2004.

8. Ibid.

9. Text in *Democracy Digest*, June 11, 2004.

10. The English edition was published as Muhammad Sayyid Ahmad, *After the Guns Fall Silent* (New York: St. Martin's Press, 1977).

11. Ibn Khaldun Center newsletter, December 1996.

12. Ibid.; *Arab Times* (Kuwait), March 30, 2004.

13. Khaled Al-Qishtini, "Farewell, Arabism," *Al-Sharq al-Awsat*, July 20, 2003, translation in MEMRI, no. 545, July 31, 2003, www.memri.org/bin/articles.cgi?Page=archives&Area=sd&ID=SP54503.

14. By using the word *Nakbah*, defined in contemporary Palestinian rhetoric as their total defeat in 1948, Akhdar was warning that another defeat might drive the Palestinians off the land and end any hope of their ever getting a state or existing as a separate people.

15. Akhdar, *Al-Quds*, October 17, 2000, translation in MEMRI, no. 142, October 20, 2000, www.memri.org/bin/articles.cgi?Page=archives&Area=sd&ID=SP14200.

16. The book was published as *Rihla ila Isra'il* (Cairo: Akhbar al-Yawm, 1994). See also Salem's article in *Al-Hayat*, November 5, 2003.

17. See *Cairo Times*, May 31–June 6, 2001; *New York Times*, August 4, 2000.

18. *Al-Ahram Weekly*, May 31–June 6, 2001.

19. *Middle East Quarterly*, Winter 2002. The full text is available at www.meforum.org/article/130.

20. Ibid.

21. Ibid.

22. Ibid.

23. Ibid.

24. Ibid.

25. Ibid.

26. Agence France-Presse, October 14, 2003.

27. *Al-Ahram*, December 19, 2002, translation in MEMRI, no. 115, www.memri.org/bin/opener_latest.cgi?ID=IA11502.

28. *Al-Watan*, December 15, 2002, translation in ibid.

29. Agence France-Presse, February 25, 2004; Voice of America, February 22, 2004.

30. *Al-Ahram*, November 20–26, 2003.

31. United Nations Development Program Arab Fund for Economic and Social Development, *The Arab Human Development Report 2002: Creating Opportunities for Future Generations* (New York: United Nations Development Program, Regional Bureau for Arab States, 2002), p. 2.

32. Hassan Hafez, *Al-Wafd*, February 26, 2000.

33. For examples of this tendency see MEMRI, no. 62, "Egyptian Reactions to the Egypt-Air Crash Investigation," December 6, 1999, www.memri.org/bin/articles.cgi?Page=archives&Area=sd&ID=SP6299; and MEMRI, no. 79, "Anti-Semitism in the Egyptian Media Part III: 'International Jewish Conspiracies,'" March 20, 2000, www.memri.org/bin/articles.cgi?Page=archives&Area=sd&ID=SP7900.

34. *Al-Hayat*, December 6, 2000, translation in MEMRI, no. 169, December 29, 2000, www.memri.org/bin/articles.cgi?Page=archives&Area=sd&ID=SP16900.

35. Interview with Kul al-Arab, January 19, 2005, translation in MEMRI, no. 864, February 15, 2005, www.memri.org/bin/articles.cgi?Page=archives&Area=sd&ID=SP86405.

36. *Al-Hayat*, February 9, March 2, and March 21, 2000, translation in MEMRI, no. 84, April 6, 2000, www.memri.org/bin/articles.cgi?Page=archives&Area=sd&ID=SP8400.

37. *Al-Hayat*, February 9, 2000, translation in MEMRI, no. 84, April 6, 2000, www.memri.org/bin/articles.cgi?Page=archives&Area=sd&ID=SP8400.

38. *Al-Hayat*, March 21, 2000.

39. Ibid.

40. Editorial: "It's All Israel's Fault!" *Arab News*, April 26, 2003.

41. Ibid.

42. "An Opposing Direction" on Al-Jazeera television, hosted by Faisal al-Qasim, February 12, 2002.

43. Isma'il Dabaj, *Al-Hayat*, February 27, 2002, translation in MEMRI, no. 350, February 27, 2002, www.memri.org/bin/articles.cgi?Page=archives&Area=sd&ID=SP35002.

44. *Al-Watan*, April 8, 2002.

45. "Sharon Is a Terrorist—And You?" *Akhbar al-Yom*, November 3, 2001, translation in MEMRI, November 20, 2001, www.memri.de/uebersetzungen_analysen/themen/liberal_voices/ges_pol_culture_20_11_01.html.

46. Ibid.

47. Taufiq Abu Bakr, "The Arab Liberal Trend and Its Moment of Opportunity," *Al-Ayyam*, May 28, 2003, translation in MEMRI, no. 520, June 10, 2003, www.memri.org/bin/articles.cgi?Page=archives&Area=sd&ID=SP52003#_edn1.

48. Private discussions and correspondence.

49. Amin al-Mahdi, *Al-Hayat*, September 9, 2002, translation in MEMRI, no. 422, September 25, 2002, www.memri.org/bin/opener_latest.cgi?ID=SD42202.

50. Agence France-Presse, December 4, 2001.

51. *Al-Akhbar*, Dec. 16, 2001. English translation: Haim Malka, "Must Innocents Die? The Islamic Debate over Suicide Attacks," *Middle East Quarterly*, Spring 2003.

52. Ahmad Shawqi Iffat, *Al-Wafd*, February 12, 2003. On the ineffectiveness of Arab and Palestinian policy requiring a major change toward a more moderate strategy, see, for

example, Hazem Abd al-Rahman, *Al-Ahram*, October 6, 2004; Maged al-Kayalli, *Al-Hayat*, October 7, 2004.

53. Ibid.

54. *Al-Watan*, June 30, 2002, translation in MEMRI, no. 101, July 5, 2002; Agence France-Presse, December 4, 2002; www.memri.org/bin/articles.cgi?Page=archives&Area=ia&ID=IA10102; Qatari television, June 13, 2003, downloaded from www.qaradawi.net.

55. *Al-Nahar*, January 19, 2004, translation in MEMRI, no. 649, January 23, 2004, www.memri.org/bin/opener_latest.cgi?ID=SD64904.

56. *Al-Nahar*, October 11, 2003, translation in MEMRI, no. 599, October 30, 2003, www.memri.org/bin/opener_latest.cgi?ID=SD59903.

57. *Al-Ahram*, October 1, 2002, in *FBIS*.

58. Qishtini, *Al-Sharq al-Awsat*, July 20, 2003.

59. Ahmed al-Jarallah, "Playing into the Hands of Israel," *Arab Times*, September 12, 2003.

60. Salameh Nematt in *Al-Hayat*, June 10, 2003.

61. Abd al-Rahman al-Rashed, "The Palestinian Leadership Must Go," *Al-Sharq al-Awsat*, August 28, 2003, translation in MEMRI, no. 561, August 29, 2003, www.memri.org/bin/opener_latest.cgi?ID=SD56103.

62. Ibid.

63. Andrew Hammond, "The Fight Goes On," *Cairo Times*, May 30–June 5, 2002, www.cairotimes.com/content/archiv06/press.html.

64. *Al-Hayat*, July 14, 2002, translation in MEMRI, no. 401, July 21, 2002, www.memri.org/bin/articles.cgi?Page=archives&Area=sd&ID=SP40102.

65. Shafiq Ghabra, "A Kuwaiti's Tale: My Debate with Israelis Brought Me Trouble at Home and then Hope," *Washington Post*, March 31, 2002.

66. It is ironic to note, of course, that the radicals might draw an opposite conclusion from these two examples: armed struggle can defeat the enemy and force him out of existence. The French pulled out of Algeria with the departure of all the colonists, while South Vietnam was wiped off the map. Thus, negotiations may be justified not by their bringing about compromise but through their use as a tool to achieve total victory. This is similar to Arafat's philosophy on this point. See Barry Rubin and Judith Colp Rubin, *Yasir Arafat: A Political Biography* (New York: Oxford University Press, 2003).

67. *Al-Hayat*, July 14, 2002, translation in MEMRI, no. 401, July 21, 2002, www.memri.org/bin/articles.cgi?Page=archives&Area=sd&ID=SP40102.

68. See, for example, the editorial by Jubran Tweini in *Al-Nahar*, August 14, 2003, translation in MEMRI, no. 557, August 25, 2003, www.memri.org/bin/opener_latest.cgi?ID=SD55703.

69. Beirut *Daily Star*, November 13, 2002.

70. *Al-Hayat*, September 9, 2002, translation in MEMRI, no. 422, September 25, 2002, www.memri.org/bin/opener_latest.cgi?ID=SD42202.

71. Ibid.

72. Ibid.

73. Shafiq Ghabra, "The Arab Peace Initiative: The Necessities of Reviving the Initiative and the Risks of Stagnation," Common Ground News Service, November 13, 2003.

74. Ibid.

75. *Al-Ahram Weekly*, September 14–20, 2000.

76. *Al-Ahram Weekly*, April 24–30, 2003.

77. Qishtini, *Al-Sharq al-Awsat*, July 20, 2003.

78. Ghabra, "The Arab Peace Initiative."

79. This statement is based on a large number of private conversations.

80. For a discussion of this issue in the Palestinian context, which parallels that of the Arab states, see Barry Rubin, *The PLO—Between Anti-Zionism and Antisemitism* (Jerusalem: Hebrew University, 1995).

81. *Al-Hayat*, November 3, 2002, translation in MEMRI, no. 109, November 8, 2002, www.memri.org/bin/articles.cgi?Page=archives&Area=ia&ID=IA10902.

82. Ibrahim al-Arabi, *Al-Hayat*, November 1, 2002.

83. *Jerusalem Post*, November 19, 2002.

84. *Al-Hayat*, December 12, 2001, translation in MEMRI, no. 314, December 14, 2001, www.memri.org/bin/articles.cgi?Page=archives&Area=sd&ID=SP31401.

85. *Al-Hayat*, April 2 and 15, 2000.

86. *Al-Ahram*, November 6, 2002, translation in MEMRI, no. 113, November 20, 2002, www.memri.org/bin/articles.cgi?Page=archives&Area=ia&ID=IA11302.

87. *Al-Hayat*, March 13, 2001, translation in MEMRI, no. 135, April 23, 2003, www.memri.org/bin/articles.cgi?Page=archives&Area=ia&ID=IA13503.

88. Ibid.

89. *Le Monde*, March 16, 2001.

90. The original article appeared in *Al-Riyadh*, March 10, 2002, translation in MEMRI, no. 354, March 13, 2002, www.memri.org/bin/articles.cgi?Page+subjects&Area=antisemitism&ID=SP35402#_ednl. The apology appeared in *Al-Riyadh*, March 19, 2002, translation in MEMRI, no. 357, www.memri.org/bin/articles.cgi?Page=archives&Area=sd&ID =SP35702.

91. *Al-Ahram*, December 24, 2002, translation in MEMRI, no. 135, April 23, 2003, www.memri.org/bin/articles.cgi?Page=archives&Area=ia&ID=IA13503.

92. Ibid.

93. *Al-Ahram*, December 25, 2002, translation in ibid.

94. www.palestine-info/arabic/palestoday/readers/mashhoor/22_04_01.htm.

95. See Wiesenthal Center Report, March 25, 2003, www.wiesenthal.com/social/press/pr_print.cfm?ItemID=7378.

96. Quoted in "An Arab Liberal Looks at the Post-Saddam Middle East," *Policywatch*, no. 756, May 13, 2003, www.washingtoninstitute.org/watch/policywatch/policywatch2003/756.htm.

97. *Al-Watani*, July 7, 2002.

98. Heggy, "The Arab-Israeli Conflict: Between Reason and Hysteria," *Al-Watani*, July 7, 2002.

99. Ibid.

100. Ibid.

101. Ibid.

8: THE CHALLENGE OF TERRORISM

1. Tarek Heggy, "We . . . and the Reality Around Us," *Al-Ahram*, May 11, 2003.

2. Jordanian television, June 8, 2004, translation in MEMRI, no. 770, August 24, 2004, www.memri.org/bin/opener_latest.cgi?ID=SD77004.

3. Ahmad Bishara, "Averting Disaster in Saudi Arabia," *Arab Times* (Kuwait), June 6, 2004.

4. The reaction to the U.S.-led war on Iraq in 2003 is discussed in chapter 9. For Arab reactions to the September 11 attack, see Cameron Brown, "The Shot Seen around the World: The Middle East Reacts to September 11th," *MERIA Journal* (December 2001): 69–89, meria.idc.ac.il/journal/2001/issue4/jv5n4a4.htm.

5. *Al-Sharq al-Awsat*, October 9, 2004, translation in MEMRI, no. 796, October 11, 2004. www.memri.org/bin/opener_latest.cgi?ID=SD79604.

6. See, for example, Barry Rubin, *Islamic Fundamentalism in Egyptian Politics*, rev. ed. (New York: Palgrave Macmillan, 2002).

7. Ahmed Abdallah, *Egypt before and after September 11, 2001: Problems of Political Transformation in a Complicated International Setting*, Deutsches Orient-Institut Im Verbund Deutsches Obersee-Institut, no. 9, March 2003.

8. For example, Tareq Massarwa, *Al-Rai*, October 16, 2002.

9. Charles Kurzman, "Pro-U.S. Fatwas," *Middle East Policy*, vol. 10, no. 3 (Fall 2003), 159–160; Sheikh Yousef al-Qaradhawi, sermon of June 13, 2003, Qatar Television, June 13, 2003, translation in MEMRI, no. 531, June 27, 2003, www.memri.org/bin/articles.cgi?Page=archives&Area=sd&ID=SP53103. See also, "Reactions to Sheikh Al-Qaradhawi's Fatwa Calling for the Abduction and Killing of American Civilians in Iraq," MEMRI report no. 794, October 6, 2004, www.memri.org/bin/articles.cgi?Page=archives&Area=sd&ID=SP79404.

10. *Al-Raya*, January 6, 2002, translation in MEMRI, no. 338, January 30, 2002, www.memri.org/bin/articles.cgi?Page=archives&Area=sd&ID=SP33802.

11. Ali Salem, "An Apology from an Arab," *Time*, September 1, 2002.

12. Mohammad al Rumaihi, *Al-Hayat*, June 11, 2003.

13. Transcript, conversation with *New York Times* columnist Nicholas Kristof, Kuwait University Center for Strategic and Future Studies, October 15, 2002.

14. Ahmad Bishara, "Averting Disaster in Saudi Arabia," *Arab Times* (Kuwait), June 6, 2004. This is borne out by a government-sponsored study of Saudi schools' curricula. See the text at www.alwihdah.com/print.asp?cat=1&id=711, January 15, 2004, and also Aluma Dankowitz, "Saudi Study Offers Critical Analysis of the Kingdom's Religious Curricula," MEMRI, no. 195, November 9, 2004, www.memri.org/bin/opener_latest.cgi?ID=IA19504.

15. *Jordan Times*, October 7, 2001.

16. Ibid.

17. *Al-Safir*, September 13, 2004, translation in MEMRI, no. 787, September 22, 2004, www.memri.org/bin/articles.cgi?Page=archives&Area=sd&ID=SP78704.

18. *Arab News* (Saudi Arabia), May 18, 2003.

19. *Jordan Times*, May 18, 2003. For the official Egyptian line on terrorism, see the interior minister's interview with *Al-Musawwar*, December 28, 2001, and the analysis of it in Ahmed Abdallah, *Egypt before and after September 11, 2001: Problems of Political Transformation in a Complicated International Setting*.

20. Urfan Nizamuldine, "Terror Only Wrought Destruction," *Al-Hayat*, June 14, 2004.

21. Ahmad Bishara, *Arab Times* (Kuwait), October 10, 2001.

22. *Al-Sharq al-Awsat*, September 4, 2004; *Sunday Telegraph*, September 5, 2004. For a similar argument, see Raid Qusti, *Arab News* (Saudi Arabia), May 5, 2004.

23. Interview with Australian Broadcasting Company, October 9, 2001, www.abc.net.au/4corners/atta/interviews/ahmed.htm.

24. Ibn Khaldun Center Newsletter, September 1998.

25. *Arab Times (Kuwait)*, November 23, 2003.

26. *Al-Sharq al-Awsat*, October 25, 2001.

27. *Al-Raya*, January 6, 2002.

28. Aboubakr Jamal, "Morocco's Choice: Openness or Terror," *New York Times*, May 31, 2003.

29. Ibid.

30. Ahmad Bishara, "National Agenda for War on Terror," *Arab Times* (Kuwait), October 17, 2001.

31. Ibid.

32. *Arab Times* (Kuwait), November 23, 2003.

33. Ahmed al-Jarallah, "Saudi Wish," *Arab Times* (Kuwait), December 6, 2003.

34. Neil MacFarquhar, "Saudis Quietly Debate Intolerance by Muslims," *New York Times*, July 12, 2002.

35. Ahmad Bishara, "Averting Disaster in Saudi Arabia," *Arab Times* (Kuwait), June 6, 2004.

36. Ibid.

37. Khaled Hamed al-Suleiman, *'Okaz*, May 14, 2003, translation in MEMRI, no. 505, May 13, 2003, www.memri.org/bin/articles.cgi?Page=archives&Area=sd&ID=SP50503.

38. Joel Brinkley, "Saudis Blame U.S. and Its Role in Iraq for Rise of Terror," *New York Times*, October 14, 2004.

39. Raid Qusti, *Arab News* (Saudi Arabia), May 14, 2003.

40. *Al-Riyadh*, February 24, 2005.

41. Ahmad Bishara, "Averting Disaster in Saudi Arabia," *Arab Times* (Kuwait), June 6, 2004.

42. MacFarquhar, *New York Times*, July 12, 2002.

43. 'Abed Khazandar, *'Okaz*, May 14, 2003, translation in MEMRI, no. 505, May 13, 2003, www.memri.org/bin/aricles.cgi?Page=archives&Area=sd&ID=SP50503.

44. Al-Jowhara bint Muhammad al-Anqari, *'Okaz*, May 14, 2003, translation in ibid.

45. Associated Press, January 31, 2004.

46. Associated Press, January 20, 2005.

47. *Arab News* (Saudi Arabia), May 18, 2003.

48. Ibid.

49. *Arab News* (Saudi Arabia), May 14 and May 15, 2003.

50. Sulaiman al-Hattlan, "Homegrown Fanatics," *New York Times*, May 15, 2003.

51. Ibid.

52. Elizabeth Rubin, "The Jihadi Who Kept Asking Why," *New York Times Magazine*, March 7, 2004.

53. Mansour al-Nogaidan, "Telling the Truth, Facing the Whip," *New York Times*, November 28, 2003.

54. Ibid.

55. Ibid.

56. FBIS Report, "TV Begins Airing Daily Program on 'War on Terrorism,'" August 5, 2003.

57. Ibid.

58. FBIS Report, "Saudi TV Continues to Air Program on Terrorism, Reactions to Terrorist Acts," August 11, 2003.

59. Ibid.

60. Faiza Saleh Ambah, "Saudi Arabia's Reformers Feel Under Fire," Associated Press, August 4, 2003.

61. Transcript, interview with Jamal Khashoggi, "Saudi Arabia: Is Reform on the Way?" BBC Television, August 1, 2003, news.bbc.co.uk/2/hi/programmes/hardtalk/3117167.stm.

62. *Arab News* (Saudi Arabia), January 29, 2003.

63. Ibid.

64. *Arab News* (Saudi Arabia), April 12, 2003.

65. Text from www.elaph.com/elaphweb/Politics/2004/10/17789.htm, October 24, 2004, and www.metransparent.com/texts/arab_liberals_appeal_to_un_for_int_court_against_terror_fatwas.htm. On popular support for the petition, see www.elaph.com/elaphweb/ElaphWriter/2004/10/18190.htm, October 24, 2004.

66. Al-Arabiya TV (Dubai), 9/11/2004, www.memritv.org/search.asp?ACT=S9&P1=255.

9: THE IRAQ WAR: AGGRESSION OR LIBERATION?

1. Nabil Sharaf al-Din, Al-Jazeera television, November 23, 2004, Clip no. 386, www .memritv.org/Search.asp?ACT=S9&P1=386.

2. He was referring to Bush's November 6, 2003, speech at the National Endowment for Democracy. For the text, see www.ned.org/events/anniversary/oct1603-Bush.html.

3. Fouad Ajami, "Iraq and the Arabs' Future," *Foreign Affairs*, January/February 2003.

4. Ibid.

5. "An Arab Liberal Looks at the Post-Saddam Middle East," Washington Institute for Near East Policy, *Policywatch*, no. 756, May 13, 2003.

6. *Al-Sharq al-Awsat*, December 15, 2003.

7. Ibid.

8. Ibid.

9. Harb, "The Moment of Truth," *Al-Ahram Weekly*, April 24–30, 2003.

10. Agence France-Presse, December 14, 2003.

11. It tells something about the state of Arab politics that even Ursan admitted the regimes would do nothing more than issue statements of protest. *Kul al-Arab*, January 2, 2004, translation in MEMRI, no. 646, January 19, 2004, www.memri.org/bin/opener_latest .cgi?ID=SD64604.

12. Fouad Ajami, "A Journey Without Maps," *U.S. News & World Report*, May 26, 2003.

13. Sheikh Yousef al-Qaradhawi, sermon, June 13, 2003, Qatar television, June 13, 2003.

14. Transcript, "The Day After: Planning for a Post-Saddam Iraq," American Enterprise Institute Conference, October 3, 2004.

15. Kanan Makiya, *Republic of Fear* (Berkeley: University of California Press, 1989); Makiya, *Cruelty and Silence* (New York: Norton, 1994).

16. Robert G. Rabil, "The Iraqi Opposition's Evolution: From Conflict to Unity?" *Meria Journal*, vol. 6, no. 4 (December 2002): 1–17, meria.idc.ac.il/journal/2002/issue4/rabil.pdf.

17. Ibid.

18. Ibid.

19. Harb, "The Moment of Truth," *Al-Ahram Weekly*, April 24–30, 2003.

20. Abd al-Rahman al-Rashed, "Why the Baghdad Regime Does Not Deserve to Be Defended," *Al-Sharq al-Awsat*, January 28, 2003, translation in Foreign Broadcast Information Service (FBIS), U.S. Department of Commerce.

21. Ibid.

22. Ibid.

23. *Arab Times* (Kuwait), December 16, 2003.

24. *Wall Street Journal*, November 21, 2003.

25. Shafiq Ghabra, "It's Time to Tear Down the 'Arab Wall,'" *Washington Post*, November 23, 2003.

26. Shafiq Ghabra, "Impact of an Iraq Confrontation on Gulf States," Washington Institute for Near East Policy, *Policywatch*, no. 705, January 27, 2003. Arguably, though, the Iranian hard-liners' barring of reform candidates leading to the regime's victory in the March 2004 elections—in other words a major antireform campaign—was the actual immediate result for Iran of the Iraq war.

27. He resigned as editor in January 2004 for personal reasons but took an administrative post with the newspaper.

28. Abd al-Rahman al-Rashed, *Al-Sharq al-Awsat*, March 27, 2003, translation in MEMRI, no. 491, April 6, 2003, www.memri.org/bin/articles.cgi?Page=archives&Area=sd &ID=SP49103.

29. Abd al-Rahman al-Rashed, *Al-Sharq al-Awsat*, March 29, 2003, translation in ibid.

30. Abd al-Rahman al-Rashed, *Al-Sharq al Awsat*, April 15, 2003.

31. Ibid.

32. Ibid.

33. Ghassan Sharbal, *Al-Hayat*, April 10, 2003.

34. *Al-Watan*, April 10, 2003.

35. *Al-Yom*, April 10, 2003.

36. *Al-Hayat*, March 26, 2003.

37. Najdat Fathi Safwat, *Al-Hayat*, June 17, 2003.

38. *Arab View*, June 25, 2003.

39. Sheikh Abd al-Hamid al-Ansari, "Arab Media's Conduct During the War Is Indicative of a Deeper Malaise," *Arab News*, April 21, 2003.

40. *Al-Rayah*, April 20, 2003, translation in *Arab Press Review*, April 20, 2004.

41. Ansari, "Arab Media's Conduct During the War," *Arab News*, April 21, 2003.

42. Awad Nasir, "After the War, Thank You, An Iraqi Poet Celebrates the Dictator's Fall," *Wall Street Journal*, May 8, 2003. See also Hamid Ali Alkifaey, *Guardian*, May 16 and 21, and July 14, 2003.

43. Nasir, *Wall Street Journal*, May 8, 2003.

44. *Al-Sharq al-Awsat*, May 19, 2003, translation in MEMRI, no. 519, June 9, 2003, www.memri.org/bin/opener_latest.cgi?ID=SD51903.

45. Paul Geitner, "Iraq War's Impact Spreads in Arab World," Associated Press, May 3, 2003.

46. Ibid.

47. *Al-Nahar*, May 20, 2003.

48. *Al-Nahar*, May 21, 2003, translation in MEMRI, no. 419, June 9, 2003, www.memri.org/bin/articles.cgi?Page=archives&Area=sd&ID=SP51903.

49. Ibid.

50. Thurayya al-Urayyid, "The Pain of Being Arab," *Al-Hayat*, May 12, 2003; *The Age*, June 9, 2003.

51. Urayyid, *Al-Hayat*, May 12, 2003.

52. *Guardian*, May 21, 2003.

53. Kamel al-Sa'doun, "It Is Liberation, Even if the Whole World Says Otherwise," *Al-Sharq al-Awsat*, September 29, 2003, translation in MEMRI, no. 590, October 16, 2003, www.memri.org/bin/articles.cgi?Page=archives&Area=sd&ID=SP59003.

54. Ibid.

55. *Arab Times*, December 15, 2003.

56. *Guardian*, May 21, 2003.

57. *Al-Siyassa al-Dawliya*, January 2004, translation in MEMRI, no. 663, February 16, 2004, www.memri.org/bin/articles.cgi?Page=archives&Area=sd&ID=SP66304.

58. Ibid.

59. *Arab Times*, December 10, 2003.

60. *Arab News* (Saudi Arabia), December 18, 2003.

61. *Al-Hayat*, August 6, 2003.

62. *Al-Ahram*, April 23, 2003.

63. *Arab News* (Saudi Arabia), December 18, 2003.

64. *Arab Times* (Kuwait), December 10, 2003.

65. *Al-Siyassa al-Dawliya*, January 2004, translation in MEMRI, no. 663, February 16, 2004, www.memri.org/bin/articles.cgi?Page=archives&Area=sd&ID=SP66304.

66. *Al-Sharq al-Awsat*, July 20, 2003, translation in MEMRI, no. 545, July 31, 2003, www.memri.org/bin/opener_latest.cgi?ID=SD54503.

67. *Arab News* (Saudi Arabia), December 18, 2003.

68. Mohammad al-Rumaihi, "The Arabs' National Interests," *Al-Hayat*, June 11, 2003.

69. Kamel Sa'doun, "A Safe Iraqi Future under American Protection," *Al-Sharq al-Awsat*, January 9, 2003, translation in MEMRI, no. 590, October 16, 2003, www.memri.org/bin/articles .cgi?Page=archives&Area=sd&ID=SP59003.

70. Ibid.

71. *Al-Sharq al-Awsat*, July 20, 2003, translation in MEMRI, no. 545, July 31, 2003, www.memri.org/bin/opener_latest.cgi?ID=SD54503.

72. *Arab News* (Saudi Arabia), December 18, 2003.

73. *Al-Sharq al-Awsat*, July 20, 2003, translation in MEMRI, no. 545, July 31, 2003, www.memri.org/bin/opener_latest.cgi?ID=SD54503.

74. *Al-Ahram Weekly*, May 15-21, 2003.

75. Mohamad Bahr El Ouloum, "Fundamental Pillars for Iraq's Political Future," *Al-Hayat*, June 30, 2003.

76. Salama A Salama, "Democracy's prospects," *Al-Ahram Weekly*, May 1–7, 2003.

77. *Arab Times* (Saudi Arabia), December 15, 2003.

78. *Arab Times* (Kuwait), April 15, 2004.

79. Hamid al-Hmoud, *Al-Quds*, September 30, 2002.

80. *Al-Hayat*, June 25, 2004.

81. Amr Hamzawy, *Washington Post*, February 6, 2005.

10: WOMEN'S RIGHTS: A TEST CASE FOR REFORM

1. The basic theme of much literature on this subject is that promoting women's rights will inevitably encourage those involved and the society thus affected to support greater democratization. Among writings on this issue are Janet Afary, "The Human Rights of Middle Eastern and Muslim Women: A Project for the 21st Century," *Human Rights Quarterly*, vol. 26, no. 1 (February 2004): 106–125; Valentine M. Moghadam, *Modernizing Women: Gender and Social Change in the Middle East* (Boulder, Colo.: Lynne Rienner Publishers, 2003); Rania Salem, Barbara Ibrahim, and Martha Brady, "Negotiating Leadership Roles: Young Women's Experience in Rural Egypt," *Women's Studies Quarterly*, vol. 31, no. 3/4 (Fall 2003): 174–191; Eleanor Abdella Doumato and Marsha Pripstein Posusney, *Women and Globalization in the Arab Middle East: Gender, Economy, and Society* (Boulder, Colo.: Lynne Rienner Publishers, 2003).

2. Maha al-Azar, "U.S.-Based Professor Claims Jews Want to Control Arab World: 'Conspiracy' Involves Americans," *Daily Star*, November 20, 2002.

3. Nazira Zein-ed-Din, "Unveiling and Veiling: On the Liberation of the Woman and Social Renewal in the Islamic World," translated by Ali Badran and Margot Badran, in *Opening the Gates: A Century of Arab Feminist Writing*, ed. Margot Badran and Miriam Cooke (Bloomington: Indiana University Press, 1990), 272–276.

4. Fatema Mernissi, *The Veil and the Male Élite: A Feminist Interpretation of Women's Rights in Islam*, trans. Mary Jo Lakeland (Bloomington: Indiana University Press, 1987).

5. *Guardian*, December 1, 1999.

6. *The Independent*, November 14, 1999; Reuters, November 16, 1999; *Financial Times*, July 6, 1999. See also Haya Abdulrahman al-Mughni, "The Politics of Women's Suffrage in Kuwait," *Arab Reform Bulletin*, vol. 2, no. 7 (July 2004); Haya Abdulrahman al-Mughni, *Women in Kuwait: The Politics of Gender* (London: Saqi Books, 2000).

7. Ashraf Fouad, "Kuwait Delays Historic Women's Rights Vote," Reuters, November 9, 1999.

8. David Hirst, "Kuwait Stalls on Votes for Women," *Guardian*, November 24, 1999.

9. Reuters, November 23, 1999.

10. Reuters, July 20, 1999.

11. Reuters, November 30, 1999.

12. Reuters, November 23, 1999.

13. *The Independent*, November 24, 1999.

14. *Al-Hayat al-Jadida*, December 8, 1999.

15. Douglas Jehl, *New York Times*, December 12, 1999.

16. Associated Press, December 1, 1999.

17. Ibid.

18. Associated Press, July 7, 1999.

19. Reuters, December 7, 1999.

20. Agence France-Presse, July 1, 1999.

21. *The Economist*, October 1, 1999. See also Abderrahim Sabir, "New Liberties for Moroccan Women," *The Humanist*, vol. 64, no. 4 (July/August 2004): 35–36.

22. "Support Morocco's Effort to Reform the Civil Status Code and Grant Women Greater Rights," Women's Learning Partnership Alert, July 23, 2001, www.learningpartnership.org/events/newsalerts/morocco0701.phtml.

23. *Arab News* (Saudi Arabia), November 3, 2004.

24. For example, see Reuters, September 16 and 30, November 15, and December 2, 1999; *Gulf News*, April 3, 2003; *Akhbar al-Khaleej*, January 10, 2004. On women's representation in parliaments, see *Arab Reform Bulletin*, July 2003; Inter-Press Service, November 25, 1999.

25. For a detailed account of this point regarding Egypt, see Sherifa Zuhur, "The Mixed Impact of Feminist Struggles in Egypt in the 1990s," *MERIA Journal*, vol. 5, no. 1 (March 2001): 78–89. Available at meria.idc.ac.il/journal/2001/issue1/zuhur.pdf. See also *The Economist*, November 27, 1999.

26. *Arab News* (Saudi Arabia), May 12, 2004.

27. Mona Eltahawy, *IHT*, April 21, 2004. She writes for *Al-Sharq al-Awsat* and is managing editor of *Arab Women's eNews*.

28. On her acceptance of secret funding from Saddam Hussein, see Associated Press, January 27, 2004.

29. Diane Singerman, "Women and Strategies for Change: An Egyptian Model," *Arab Reform Bulletin*, vol. 2, no. 7 (July 2004).

30. Janine Clark, "Women in Islamist Parties: The Case of Jordan's Islamic Action Front," *Arab Reform Bulletin*, vol. 2, no. 7 (July 2004).

31. Dr. Maya Al-Rahbi, "A Letter from an Arab Woman to Colin Powell," *Akhbar al-Shar*, www.thisissyria.net/2002/12/23/articles.%20html#2, December 23, 2002, translation in MEMRI, no. 115, December 31, 2002, www.memri.org/bin/opener_latest.cgi?ID=IA11502.

32. Rana Husseini, "Poll Shows Widespread Opposition to Abolishing Article 340," *Jordan Times*, November 9, 1999.

33. *New York Times*, December 3, 2003.

34. Text of letter, December 18, 2003.

35. Lawrence Wright, "The Kingdom of Silence," *New Yorker*, January 5, 2004.

36. *New York Times*, December 12, 1999; Reuters, October 4, 1999.

37. *Arab News* (Saudi Arabia), January 11, 2004.

38. Associated Press, October 3 and 4, 1999.

39. *Arab News* (Saudi Arabia), November 22 and December 14, 2002.

40. Wright, "Kingdom of Silence."

41. Agence France-Presse, January 20, 2004; Al-Jazeera, January 21, 2004, translation in MEMRI, no. 670, March 1, 2004, www.memri.org/bin/articles.cgi?Page=archives&Area=sd&ID=SP67004.

42. Text of Lubna Olayan speech, January 17, 2004.

43. Ibid.

44. IslamOnline.net, January 18, 2004; *Al-Quds al-Arabi*, January 18, 2004, translation in MEMRI, no. 670, March 1, 2004, www.memri.org/bin/opener_latest.cgi?ID=SD67004.

45. *Al-Riyadh*, January 19, 2004, translation in MEMRI, no. 670, March 1, 2004, www.memri.org/bin/opener_latest.cgi?ID=SD67004.

46. *Al-Siyassa*, January 19, 2004.

47. *Al-Sharq al-Awsat*, January 26, 2004, translation in MEMRI, no. 670, March 1, 2004, www.memri.org/bin/opener_latest.cgi?ID=SD67004.

48. Zvi Bar'el, "Even the Saudi Public Discourse on Reforms Is Conducted in Secrecy," *Ha'aretz*, January 7, 2004.

49. Reuters, October 4, 1999.

50. Aluma Dankowitz, "A Saudi National Dialogue on Women's Rights and Obligations," MEMRI Report no. 183, June 23, 2004, downloaded from www.memri.org/bin/latestnews.cgi?ID=IA18304.

51. Raid Qusti, *Arab News* (Saudi Arabia), June 16, 2004.

52. Ebtisam al-Kitbi, "Women's Political Status in the GCC States," *Arab Reform Bulletin*, vol. 2, no. 7 (July 2004).

53. *Al-Sharq al-Awsat*, June 16, 2004. Cited in Dankowitz, "A Saudi National Dialogue." For more on the difficulty of measuring women's progress in Arab countries, see Sherifa Zuhur, "Women and Empowerment in the Arab World," *Arab Studies Quarterly*, vol. 25, no. 4 (Fall 2003): 17–38.

54. Elaph, March 7, 2005, www.elaph.com/ElaphWriter/2005/3/45862.htm. For the translation, see MEMRI, no. 890, April 12, 2005, www.memri.org/bin/opener_latest.cgi?ID=SD89005.

55. Elaph, February 5, 2005, www.elaph.com/elaphweb/ElaphWriter/2005/2/38710.htm?KeyWords=vZjHNMUVQ+0S+WDM66==+mqg, translation in MEMRI, ibid.

56. Middle East Transparent, March 19, 2005, www.metransparent.com/texts/mongia_saouhi_women_rights_in_tunisia.htm, translation in MEMRI, ibid.

57. *Washington Post*, January 23, 2005.

11: A THOUSAND AND ONE DIFFICULTIES

1. Quoted in Mohamed Elmasry, "Democracy or Hypocrisy," *Montreal Muslim News*, January 9, 2003.

2. Jon Alterman, "The False Promise of Arab Liberals," *Policy Review*, June 2004.

3. Tamara Cofman Wittes, "The Promise of Arab Liberalism," *Policy Review*, June 2004.

4. Sa'ad Mahyew, *Al-Khaleej*, November 25, 2003, translation in MEMRI, no. 633, December 24, 2003, www.memri.org/bin/articles.cgi?Page=archives&Area=sd&ID=SP63303.

5. Sahar Ba'asiri, *Al-Nahar*, November 11, 2003, translation in ibid.

6. Oreib al-Rantawi, *Al-Dustour*, November 25, 2003, translation in ibid.

7. Khales Jalabi, *Al-Watan*, December 3, 2003, translation in ibid.

8. *Al-Shira*, December 31, 2003.

9. *Al-Ba'th*, July 2, 2003.

10. *Al-Ahram*, January 4, 2004.

11. *Al-Hayat*, December 2, 2003.

12. *Democracy Digest*, October 7, 2004. See also *Democracy Digest*, July 23, 2004.

13. Aboubakr Jamal, "Morocco's Choice: Openness or Terror," *New York Times*, May 31, 2003.

14. Khaled Hroub, "Behind the Western Mask," *IHT*, November 19, 2004; Kamel Labidi, Beirut *Daily Star*, October 23, 2004.

15. Marwan Muasher, "Regional Development in the Middle East: A Lecture," American University of Kuwait, January 13, 2004.

16. *Washington Times*, January 13, 2004; John R. Bradley, "Path of Good Intentions," *Al-Ahram Weekly*, January 15–21, 2004.

17. Bradley, "Path of Good Intentions."

18. Ibid.

19. *Al-Sharq al-Awsat*, January 10, 2004, translation in MEMRI, no. 659, February 9, 2004, www.memri.org/bin/opener_latest.cgi?ID=SD65904.

20. Ibid.

21. *Al-Mustaqbal*, December 17, 2003.

22. *Al-Sharq al-Awsat*, December 10, 2003.

23. Associated Press, March 16, 2004.

24. Jamal, *New York Times*, May 31, 2003.

25. Fawaz Gerges, "Empty Promises of Freedom," *New York Times*, July 18, 2003.

26. Communism, like Arab nationalism, could be considered a reactionary antidemocratic force, disguised as the opposite, which delayed the modernization of the USSR and Eastern Europe.

27. *Al-Sharq al-Awsat*, December 30, 2003.

28. Transcript, Bill Moyers's interview with Shafiq Ghabra, PBS, March 28, 2003, www.pbs.org/now/printable/transcript213_full_print.html.

29. Jamal, *New York Times*, May 31, 2003.

30. Reuters, January 11, 2004; *Gulf News*, January 14, 2004.

31. *Gulf News*, January 14, 2004.

32. Edward S. Walker Jr., *The Quiet Revolution: Saudi Arabia* (Washington, D.C.: Middle East Institute, 2004).

33. Muhammad Salahuddin, cited in Lawrence Wright, "The Kingdom of Silence," *New Yorker*, January 5, 2004.

34. Ibid.

35. Ibid.

36. Ibid.

37. Michael Scott Doran, "The Saudi Paradox," *Foreign Affairs*, vol. 83, no. 1 (January/February 2004).

38. Neil MacFarquhar, "Under Pressure to Change, Saudis Debate Their Future," *New York Times*, November 23, 2003.

39. Khalid al-Dakhil, "Saudi Arabia's Reform Movement: A Historical Glimpse," *Arab Reform Bulletin*, vol. 1, no. 4 (October 2003). For the full text of the petition see www.ceip.org/files/pdf/saudipetition.pdf.

40. Report by Roger Hardy, BBC, January 27, 2004.

41. Those detained included activists Abdullah Hamid and Tawfiq Qussayer; Matrouk Faleh, a professor of politics at King Saud University; Muhammad Said Tayyib, a retired publisher; and Ali Dumaini, a poet.

42. *Arab News* (Saudi Arabia), March 10, 2004; Reuters, March 16, 2004; *Washington Post*, March 17, 2004; Mai Yamani, "Arrests Make Mockery of Saudi Reform Talk," *International Herald Tribune*, March 22, 2004.

43. *Al-Hayat*, March 12, 2004, translation in MEMRI, no. 167, March 26, 2004, www.memri.org/bin/articles.cgi?Page=archives&Area=ia&ID=IA16704167.

44. See its site at www.sis.gov.eg/eginfnew/humanrights/html/hr.htm.

45. *Mid East Times,* January 11, 2004; *Saudi Gazette,* January 4, 2004.

46. Cited in Zvi Bar'el, *Ha'aretz,* January 7, 2004.

47. *Financial Times,* January 22, 2004; Reuters, January 27, 2004.

48. Wright, "Kingdom of Silence."

49. Associated Press, "Saudi Columnist Shobokshi Fired by Papers," August 2, 2003.

50. Text of speech, January 17, 2004.

51. Interview with Abd al-Mun'im Sa'id, August 4, 2004.

52. Ibid.

53. Tarek Heggy, "Let's Assume It's a Conspiracy!" *Al-Ahram,* January 26, 2002.

54. Shafiq Ghabra, "It's Time to Tear Down the 'Arab Wall,'" *Washington Post,* November 23, 2003.

55. Ibid.

56. Ibid.

57. Ibid.

58. One could make an analogy, however, to the universal problem of liberals in past decades as having to fight authoritarian regimes while also ensuring that equally antidemocratic Communist ones did not gain power.

59. Ghabra, "It's Time to Tear Down the 'Arab Wall.'"

60. Ahmed Abdallah, *Egypt before and after September 11, 2001: Problems of Political Transformation in a Complicated International Setting,* Deutsches Orient-Institut im Verbund Deutsches Übersee-Institut, Focus no. 9, March 2003.

61. Fawaz Gerges, "Empty Promises of Freedom," *New York Times,* July 18, 2003.

62. Fouad Ajami, "Iraq and the Arabs' Future," *Foreign Affairs,* vol. 82, no. 1 (January/February 2003).

63. Agence France-Presse, February 25, 2004; Voice of America report, February 22, 2004, downloaded from www.voanews.com/article.cfm?objectID=8391080C-BCDE-40E5-86666D8BBB27A3ED; Lydia Georgi, "Riyadh, Cairo Reject US Mideast Reform Plan," Middle East Online, February 25, 2004, downloaded from 195.224.230.11/english/?id=9021.

64. Usama al-Ghazali Harb, "The Trouble with America," *Al-Siyassa al-Dawliyya,* January 2002.

65. Ibid.

66. Ibid.; Hassen Zenati, "Mubarak Leads 'Rebellion' Against Bush Mideast Initiative," Middle East Online, February 26, 2004, downloaded from 195.224.230.11/english/?id=9047.

67. Elizabeth Rubin, "The Jihadi Who Kept Asking Why," *New York Times Magazine,* March 7, 2004.

68. *Forward,* October 8, 2004.

69. Ibid.

70. Muhammad Fakih, "The Arab Line?" *Al-Ahram Weekly,* February 10–16, 2005.

71. As Ahmed Beydoun, a sociology professor at the Lebanese University, put it, "The Lebanese want their institutions to work normally, which is prevented by Syrian influence." *New York Times,* March 6, 2005.

72. *Washington Post,* February 23, 2005.

73. Al-Jazeera television, February 6, 2005. View this statement at www.memritv.org/search.asp?ACT=S9&P1=534.

74. *Forward,* October 8, 2004.

75. Text, "In Defense of the Nation," September 24, 2003.

76. Ibid. On the status of women the petition has a nicely ambiguous phrase: ensuring they can "perform their social and economic roles." This can be interpreted by the liberals as equality and by more conservative proregime elements as merely a fuller realization of their traditional situation.

77. Saad Eddin Ibrahim, "Reviving Mideastern Democracy," *Wall Street Journal*, November 26, 2003.

78. Ibid.

79. Thurayya al-Urayyid, "The Pain of Being Arab," *The Age*, June 9, 2003.

80. *Al-Hayat*, September 1, 2004, translation in MEMRI, no. 783, September 13, 2004, www.memri.org/bin/opener_latest.cgi?ID=SD78304.

81. Letter to the author.

82. *Democracy Digest*, July 23, 2004.

83. Ali Salem, "An Apology from an Arab," *Time*, September 1, 2002.

84. Fawaz Gerges, "Empty Promises of Freedom," *New York Times*, July 18, 2003.

85. Shafiq Ghabra, "My Debate with Israelis Brought Me Trouble at Home—And Then Hope," *Washington Post*, March 31, 2002.

86. Shafiq Ghabra, "Reform in the Arab World: Tensions and Challenges," *Al-Hayat*, May 16, 2004.

87. *Al-Ahram Weekly*, April 22–28, 2004.

INDEX